WHEN SINNERS LIKE ME COME HOME

WHEN SINNERS LIKE ME COME HOME

SEARCHING FOR LIFE AFTER WAR

STEELE KELLY

LIONCREST
PUBLISHING

WHEN SINNERS LIKE ME COME HOME
Searching for Life After War

ISBN   978-1-5445-0085-0 *Paperback*
       978-1-5445-0084-3 *Ebook*

"It is not the critic who counts, not the man who points out how the strong man stumbled, or where the doer of deeds could have done better. The credit belongs to the man who is actually in the arena; whose face is marred by the dust and sweat and blood; who strives valiantly; who errs and comes short again and again; who knows the great enthusiasms, the great devotions and spends himself in a worthy course; who at the best, knows in the end the triumph of high achievement, and who at the worst, if he fails, at least fails while daringly great; so that his place shall never be with those cold and timid souls who know neither victory nor defeat."

—THEODORE ROOSEVELT, FRANCE 1910

CONTENTS

———

"He who fights with monsters should beware that he himself does not become a monster. For when you gaze long enough into the abyss, the abyss also gazes into you."

—FRIEDRICH NIETZSCHE, BEYOND
GOOD AND EVIL, APHORISM 146

ACKNOWLEDGMENTS

———

I HAVEN'T FOUND A GOOD WAY TO WRITE THIS, since there are so many people who have significantly impacted my life, shown me love, and encouraged me. From my law enforcement family to my sports coaches, Army mentors, and everyone who saw my potential and dedicated their time making me who I am today, I am forever grateful to all of you, the time you spent teaching me, and all the lessons I learned along the way.

Mom and Dad, thank you for being patient and always reminding me that it's never too late to make a U-turn in life. I didn't treat you with very much love or appreciation when I got home, and I frequently lashed out with hurtful words because I was the one hurting. In those moments, you showed me unconditional love, which was what I actually needed. I can't imagine how much more difficult my world and reintegration would have been without such loving and supportive parents. I hope one day to be the husband, father, and parents that you guys have been.

To my little sister, don't ever settle for anything less than the best. You are one of the most intelligent, thoughtful, and kind people I know. Wherever you go, know that it's never somewhere I can't get to. Life is all about the chances we take. So shoot for the stars; worst case, you'll land on the moon.

Don and Jenelle, my extended family, mentors, professors, friends, and all you other salty heathens that are my military family. Your boldness and pointing out my flaws allowed me to critically evaluate myself and the relationships I've had in my life. You all shaped me into a better man. I appreciate you guys forcing me, at times, to go out, and for listening to the same stories that were repeated for months. Yet, every time you guys heard them, you acted as if it was the first time, helping me work through them.

My content editor, Kate, and her husband, this book wouldn't have been possible without you guys and the countless hours spent talking on the phone through every story's twists and turns. All of the drafts, rewrites, and forcing me to push through to completion when I was stubborn, ready to burn the book and walk away.

Aubrey, Lizzie, and Caitlin at Onnit, and the Book in a Box crew who helped with the graphic design, layout, and proofreading—this book wouldn't have been possible without you guys. With the most heartfelt appreciation and gratitude, thank you for taking a chance on me. I hope one day I will have the chance to pay it forward.

Last but not least, Peyton, wherever you are in the world.

I've debated what to say for quite some time. When you first met me, the quirky dates, loving, and happy person was the man I am. Over time, I grew into an angry person from years of denial, guilt, and remorse. I was terrified of the worst that could happen to you and the others who meant so much to me. I didn't know how to handle it at twenty-two years old. For a while, I wished I could have gone back in time to tell the struggling me that it wasn't worth holding on to so much anger or getting worked up about the little things that I would eventually miss. I desperately wanted to tell him what I know now, which would have prevented so many of your shed tears. The fact of the matter is I can't go back in time, and after the last year played out, I wouldn't go back in time even if I could. Unfortunately, it had to happen to make me a better man.

I have so much gratitude for how much we went through together, and I can't imagine going back through that dark time in my life without you.

I admire the strength and courage you had to leave, knowing I wasn't going to change, get help, or acknowledge any of my own issues while you were in the picture. You saved my life in a lot of different ways. I'll always be grateful for that and how long you stuck by my side. I feel blessed now to have felt the depth of love for another person that you filled my heart with. Had it not been for you changing my views on other countries and your ferocious sense of adventure, I would have never gone to the Himalayas to search for the parts of myself I felt that I lost in war. I would have never realized my flaws or how my actions hurt those around me. My hope is that other reintegrating relationships can learn from our struggles and heartache, which we were too young and inexperienced to handle at that point in our lives.

I hope you know that you deserve an incredible man who encourages you to shoot for the stars even when you doubt yourself. I hope you find the man that makes you want to marry him after the first date, the one who you can't imagine going a night without snuggling up to. A man who is willing to right his wrongs without pushing you away, always making sure he goes without so you don't have to. The man who can put his arms around you and make every seemingly wrong turn or dead-end road in life make sense.

You're an amazing, intelligent, and beautiful woman. Don't settle for anyone or anything less than amazing. I'll always hold a special place for you in my heart. I hope wherever you go, wherever you travel, whoever you marry, "Wherever you go, go with all of your heart," and I'll always *wanna be that song.*

"That last night at home, you think about how you could have been a better dad, a better husband, that bedtime story you should have read, or that anniversary you forgot. You don't expect your family to understand what you're doing; you just hope they understand you're doing it for them. And when you get home, you hope you can pick up right where you left off."

—VAN D. "CHIEF OTTO" *US NAVY SEAL*

PREFACE

———

"HONEY, FIND A WAY TO KEEP THE KIND, GENTLE, and loving side of your heart while you're there. Please don't let the Taliban and Al Qaeda take that away from you," my mom squeaks, tears rolling down her face.

"I love you, Mom. I promise I'll find a way. See you in twelve to eighteen months."

I pick my backpack up off the ground and sling it over my shoulder. I look at my mother, family, and friends one last time, feeling the burn of suppressed sadness building up in my throat and eyes; I turn around. I don't want them to see that I'm just as unsure, scared, and sad as they are. I don't want them to worry. I feel that, by showing any emotion or even my own worry, they'll realize the gravity of the situation. Without looking back, I walk toward the bus, pushing the feelings as far down as humanly possible—*warriors don't cry, and they don't show fear.*

Looking up at the heavens through my polarized

Oakley's, I head toward the bus. I'm secretly searching for strength, a miracle, a prayer, or any sign that will loosen the grip of my overwhelming anxiety. An unsuspecting person watching me might see a strong, calm, and collected man. They would see wrinkle-free multicam patterned camouflage clothing tapering over my 220-pound, six-foot muscular frame. Every step taken is precise and crisp, shoulders arched back with confidence, as if I had done this a million times and it is nothing more than a stroll through the Saturday market. They see a professional soldier with stature and emotional clarity, and it appears as if it is just another day of his nine-to-five routine.

What you can't see is the young—barely old enough to be considered a man—soldier hiding the truth from the outside world. A terrified boy, unsure if he will ever see his loved ones again. Looking toward the sky, I notice how exceptionally blue and bright it is. As I get closer to the bus, I feel the warm summer air softly blowing across my face. *How ironic it is, with so much grief and anxiety in the air, that it could still be such a perfect June day.* Before I board the bus, I close my eyes, taking in the fresh Oregon air just in case it would be the last time. I pray silently, asking for strength and courage. *See you in twelve to eighteen months? Yeah, if I survive.*

As fast as it filled my thoughts, the memory fades away. The reality of the desert comes sharply into focus. The 124-degree sun is slowly cooking me, with no available shade in sight. Instead of mountains, trees, and blue sky, my scenery is full of brown dirt, mud huts, and Qalat walls. Sweat rolls down my back underneath seventy-five pounds of armor, grenades, ammunition, and radios. The Afghanistan sun and heat are so intense that sweat is rolling down my forehead, past my eyebrows, stinging my eyes.

Leaving my vehicle, I'm walking toward the truck across an open area, without cover, almost 400 meters ahead of me. On the way to a known Taliban village, we approach a choke point that we must sweep with mine detectors before crossing. A choke point is a section of road or path that forces troops to cross one specific section. Most often, this is a point where there is no other way around; because it's the only path, the Taliban often wire it with explosives and mines.

I don't feel the heat when focusing on the task at hand. I look down at the ground in between scans of the upcoming village. With carefully placed steps, I look for a wire, a glisten of metal that might indicate a pressure plate, stacked rocks, or any other sign of an enemy-placed IED (Improvised Explosive Device) or landmine. I am scanning, not worrying about my own life or potential loss of limb. I'm scanning diligently, because if I trigger an IED, not only will I lose a leg or my life, I will maim or kill my brothers next to me.

The baptism through gunfire begins, and the controlled chaos takes off. Running toward the truck now

100 meters in front of me, my path riddled with enemy bullets, I take cover from the gunfire and rocket explosions impacting around me. As if I were plucked out of reality back to the air-conditioned bar where I had met my first squad leader before deployment, I hear his advice. *Before you leave the United States, accept the fact you will die. Come to acceptance and peace with this fact. If you hesitate out of fear, you will undoubtedly die.*

With the crack of bullets all around me, I am brought back to reality. My platoon is relying on me to get back to the satellite radio in my truck to call the JTAC and fighter jets from an aircraft carrier in the gulf. I take one last look at my best friend, Casey, in a *see you on the other side, fucker!* kind of way.

"Cover me!" I shout over machine gun fire. Without hesitating, I take off, sprinting from the cover of the armored truck. Bullets ricochet across the dirt at my feet as I sprint 400 meters back through the open desert, knowing that if I slowed down, I would be struck and probably killed.

The world is silent in moments like this. The only sound is the drum and slam of my heart as the adrenaline surges through my veins, accompanied by the sound of my gasps, lungs burning for air.

"Viper, this is Butcher 9-2. Troops in contact; we need immediate air support. Prepare to copy ten-digit grid for eyes on, when you're ready." I calmly send out while desperately gasping for air. "Butcher 9-2, this is Viper. Send it."

"It is the mark of an educated mind to be able to entertain a thought without accepting it."

—ARISTOTLE

INTRODUCTION

———

TODAY, IT SEEMS AS THOUGH THE MOVIE INDUSTRY is pumping out war movies with action and heroism as fast as they possibly can. Often, they're great, they're fun to watch, and the special effects are remarkable. However, in many cases, they romanticize combat, leaving out or ignoring the facts of reintegration and coming home. They leave out nightmares, fights with loved ones, spouses leaving, and they ignore the growing bar tab. The movies and stories that are beginning to come to light about reintegration tend to make it sappy, sad, and almost as if they're taking pity on us. Pity we don't want or need. They leave out the fact that many of us want to grab our boots, head back to combat, and return to the excitement of war without First World problems—while at the same time, we don't.

If you're looking for a book with nothing more than war stories—the kind with triumphant battlefield play-by-plays—this isn't the book for you. Although there are stories of firefights, courage, heroism, and death, this is a book of all the things our society does not want to discuss. It vocalizes the dark, the taboo, and the withheld side that manifests in the aftermath of combat and prolonged exposure to stress and trauma. It's the story of a soldier trudging through the deepest depths of darkness, only to recover two years after he returned home from war—alone, dying on a glacier in the Himalayas.

In society, we have a habit of being afraid of what we don't know. We become fearful of the men and women we send to combat, because as a society, we're unsure of their gruffness and the thoughts going through their head. We let our imagination run wild thinking about what they may do. We often see impregnable, unshakeable, and unafraid; cold warriors who can't be emotionally hurt or broken. It is my hope that even if you're anti-war or unsupportive of our armed services, you read this to understand that behind every uniform is a person who bleeds, cries, laughs, loves, and has emotions and feelings like every other person.

I have heard many combat veterans disclose in their darkest hours, "I feel everything has gone cold and nothing makes me even slightly happy anymore. My soul is tired, and I'm barely hanging on." Or, "I feel like I lost the person I used to be and wanted to be. I just want to go back to the happy person who loved people and could go out in crowds and restaurants without worrying about the worst. I know now that it's impossible to go back to who I used to be, and I'm afraid I won't ever feel happiness, excitement, or joy ever again. My wife left, my kids left, and I feel I have nothing left." Unfortunately, we won't ever go back to being the person we used to be before war. That doesn't mean we aren't or can't be better after working through it.

Many veterans do not discuss their personal struggles or pain because we feel that emotional turmoil is a symptom of being weak. By expressing our inner feelings, we feel we will be viewed as unable to "hack it." Or worse, we recognize the need to talk to a counselor, but fear that by doing so, the military, police department, or Veterans Affairs will seize our firearms or label us with something that will forever mark our lives and careers. Substance abuse, divorce, suicide, depression, and PTSD are problems I address head-on, because I believe them to be some of the most dangerous to the mental and emotional health of even our most hardened combat warriors.

I have received a significant amount of feedback from guys I served with overseas. For many, they are supportive of breaking the silence and explaining our struggles to those who haven't experienced it themselves. But an even more significant number feel as though I'm betraying the brotherhood and the unwritten code of silence by shedding light on many of our internal battles. I have chosen to speak up because the current veteran suicide rate is twenty-two veterans per day. Many veterans look for anything that will help lead them back to their path to peace, but they haven't the slightest idea how to find it. I certainly felt that way. Often, we convince ourselves that the feelings of insufficiency and loss are karma, or the punishment for things that we have done. The silence isn't working, and many veterans fail to find a way to pull out of their darkest hours. If keeping silent were so effective, the veteran suicide rate, divorce rate, and substance abuse rate wouldn't be so high. I am tired of watching parents lose their children, sons and daughters losing their parents, and spouses becoming widowed.

Many families of combat veterans and deployed military personnel often attempt to find books or resources on how to support their loved ones after they return. These books can be incredible resources, but most of them are written by outsiders looking into the lives of veterans. When I was looking for books to help me readjust after coming home, time and time again, the ones I found were by authors who don't have combat experience, have never served or been in life-or-death situations, and have never taken a human life. Their guidance is based on limited, secondhand experience.

My area of academic interest is in psychology with a focus in neuropsychology, psychopharmacology, and cognition. I am not a licensed mental health provider of any sort. My views and opinions do not reflect the opinions of the US Army, the Department of Defense, Veterans Affairs, Veterans Benefits, or any other institution. That said, I have a unique understanding and insight into the psychological struggles of post-war, post-combat, and reintegration struggles through my own experience and education.

I hope this book will shine some light on the mental process, thinking, and individual experiences before combat, during combat, and post-combat. I hope you can get a more in-depth look into why some of the quirks, flaws, crass and direct words, and actions pop up in the behavior of people who've experienced the high-stress environment of war.

I hope this book helps individuals who are struggling and suffering similarly to the way I was to find peace. And I hope that those people who don't understand why veterans are the way they are or why they are different post-combat will read this and have a better understanding. This story and experience is meant to help those outside of the military or the loved ones of veterans and first responders foster empathy toward individuals finding their path back to happiness and peace. It is my sincerest wish that this book finds its way to anyone who feels like they are on the verge of taking their own life—who feels their soul is broken or tired and that they will never recover. That it will reach them before it's too late, and they'll realize it isn't. I've been there. I understand it. And you are not alone. As my role model and one of my biggest heroes, my father, told me in my darkest hours, "Son, it's never too late to make a U-turn in life. You're never too far gone that you can't turn around and do one hundred miles per hour back down the road you came. You get back to the fork in the road, and you take the other turn."

I have reviewed journals kept by myself and platoon mates, as well as hours of interviews and conversations to recall the details of different events, missions, discussions, and actions to ensure the highest level of integrity and accuracy. Although I've done my best to ensure accuracy, it is important to note that eyewitness testimony is considered in court and law enforcement to be one of the most inaccurate testimonies. It's because every person remembers a story different based on their past, state of mind, and sensory input during that event. Humbly, I know my version of events in some instances may be slightly different than others'. Out of respect to my unit, brothers, and readers, I feel it is important to know that hundreds of hours were spent tracking down and conversing with almost every individual in these stories to ensure the highest level of integrity.

I consider myself extremely fortunate and blessed to have had the privilege to serve and give back to my country, which has given me so much in life. I treasure my time in the military, the lessons I learned, and all the ways it changed my life for the better. I had the pleasure of serving alongside some of the most courageous, tough, and kind men I have ever met, who even after warfare, never lost those aspects of themselves.

Through my story, I'll present my unique viewpoint,

in which I'll show how our mindset can be harmful to our emotional well-being. I will address taboo subjects that veterans, first responders, law enforcement, and others battle on a regular basis. I will critique the current way we handle enemies of the state, and I'll outline possible improvements. Most importantly, I'll explain my belief that the current level of political invasion in our armed forces, armed conflicts, and rules of engagement are compromising the lives and health of the men and women we send to war.

If you are a veteran, first responder, law enforcement officer, or family member of one of these categories, I hope you will have an open mind while reading this. I recognize the viewpoints, criticism, and communication strategies discussed in this book are not one-size-fits-all and must be taken for what they are: the words of a soldier who's doing his best to help others mitigate emotional losses he knows they'll face.

There is a common saying I have heard many times, "A wise man learns from the mistakes of others, a smart man learns from his own mistakes, and a fool never learns." Which one are you?

"For all sad words of tongue and pen,
the saddest are these,
'It might have been.'"

—JOHN GREENLEAF WHITTIER

CHAPTER 1

EMOTIONAL BREAK

———

WELL, LATE ONE NIGHT, SHE STARTED TO CRY AND *thought, "He ain't coming home." She was tired of the lies, tired of the fight, but she didn't want to see him go. She fell on her knees and said, "I haven't prayed since I was young, but Lord above I need a miracle."*

The lyrics of the song "Miracle," by Third Day, seem to overshadow through the stereo, resonating with me except for a few small differences. She didn't pray for a miracle. I didn't pray for a miracle. And she was gone. She was not the reason for my current sadness, but she was the load-breaking card stacked up on the house of cards that made the whole thing collapse. That's what happens when you build something on an unstable foundation. Years of ignoring my problems, pretending they didn't exist, came back to bite me.

It had been twenty-three months since I returned from Afghanistan. Since my return, I'd moved to three states, went back to school, transferred schools, found—and then lost—the woman of my dreams. Through the fog of destruction in everything I had touched over the last two years, I realized just how much I'd changed from the twenty-year-old kid who went off to war.

I lost the kindness and softness of my heart I had promised I would keep and, ultimately, lost myself—even down to things as mundane as hobbies. Before I joined the military, I enjoyed target practice, shooting Tannerite targets, camping, and shooting the shit with the guys. Now, even cleaning them felt like work. It felt like an auto mechanic returning home from wrenching all day to pick up a wrench and fix his neighbor's car, or a hairdresser who is only called to her friends' houses after work to cut their hair. My once-prized firearms had been in the safe at my parents' house collecting dust for three years. I no longer even wanted to pull them out to clean them.

I used to enjoy my friends whom I grew up with. I used to love spending weeks at a time staying with my parents and little sister. However, the post-war me—post-selling my soul, post-eating from the metaphorical Tree of Knowledge—was different. Returning to the home I loved, surrounding myself with familiarity, was nothing more than a reminder of who I used to be—the person I will never go back to being no matter how badly I want to. I felt as if I were having an affair, hiding a mistress from my wife. Except that the person I used to be was the wife, and the mistress was the person I became after war.

I veer right off Interstate 90 West, turning left onto 19th Avenue. Without warning, the car in front of me locks their breaks, turning right instead of left, and nearly sideswipes two vehicles. I narrowly avoid rear-ending them as I yell through the windshield, "Motherfucker!!! Are you fucking kidding me?! Learn how to drive, you stupid fuck! It's Bozeman-fucking-Montana! You drive in the snow every single winter! If you can't, then you need to fucking move!"

With each word yelled, tiny pieces of Grizzly chewing tobacco fly out of my mouth and land on the dash. Although they can't hear me, their license plates are out of state, and they're clearly lost, I still find myself irate. "You can only say *fuck it* so many fucking times in one fucking day until you start drinking," I say to my yellow lab as if she will understand my frustration. Riding in the front seat next to me, she gazes up at me with her soft, sad-looking eyes, almost as if she understands or can somehow sense the pain that is now cut so deeply into my heart. I feel it has taken over and consumed even the darkest depths of my existence.

Once again, the thought of returning to an empty house pierces my thoughts, ensnaring me back into my thought prison—the one I had spent years constructing for myself. Unfortunately, this thought prison is maximum security with twenty-three-foot concrete walls, rigged with razor wire and high-explosive ordinance—there's no escape from it.

Checking both left and right tow mirrors on my Dodge Ram 2500, I back into my parking spot.

"Maybe if you didn't park over the fucking line you fucking bitch, I would have more fucking space to get out of my truck! But no! You don't know how to drive a want-to-be SUV!" I bark at the empty car next to me.

Opening the door, the snowy air hits my face. As I turn my body around, shifting my feet, the snow crunches beneath me. I lift the dog out of the truck, grab my backpack, and walk into my apartment.

Crossing the threshold of the front door, I'm once again doused with the reminder that she's gone—and she isn't coming back. Looking around, the couches are strategically positioned at specific angles in the living room. The TV is turned to an angle complementing the arrangement of the sofas, with a lamp resting on a side table next to the couch by the door. Stacked on top of the table are hunting and rifle magazines displayed with corners rotating like a spiral staircase, with a decor candle strategically placed on top. In the kitchen, there are two flawlessly folded decorative towels hanging from the handle of the oven, and another candle, still unburnt, set in the center of the island counter. It is apparent that this twenty-four-year-old did not decorate the interior.

Rather, the décor is the result of meticulous planning and placement by a female with a knack for interior decorating. My heart skips a beat with the memory of us snuggling on the couch watching *Shark Tank*. I can feel her head on my chest with her arm dangling over me. It has been months since she left, yet the feelings and memory of her are so vivid I can smell her perfume, remembering the warmth she brought to my heart and soul, pushing me to become the best version of myself.

Tossing my keys on the counter, they impact with a metallic jingle sound as I walk through the hallway to my office. Dropping my backpack next to my desk, books and my new MacBook Pro hit the ground with a clank, no regard given for potential damage. Grasping my wallet out of my pocket, slamming it on the desk, a glisten of light off the glass and walnut frame of an Army commendation catches my eye.

"While deployed to Afghanistan in support of Operation Enduring Freedom, SPC Kelly contributed significantly to the Troop's success. His performance during combat operations was outstanding by providing accurate and precise technical decisions ensuring mission success. Throughout the deployment, SPC Kelly proved to be a vital asset. He completed every combat patrol as the Forward Observer and Radio Telephone Operator in the Herat Provence, Afghanistan. In September 2015, SPC Kelly was a vital asset to the platoon as an M240B machine gunner for the first Troop-size air assault mission to Farah, Afghanistan. This mission was essential to the safety and security of Forward Operation Base Farah, Afghanistan. His skill set was crucial in helping the platoon secure the landing zone for the rest of the Troop to land and secure the area for twenty-four hours until the mission was complete.

"SPC Kelly served as one of the four Joint Tactical Air Controllers during two direct fire engagements with the enemy. He coordinated the surveillance of four villages from fixed wing and rotary wing aircraft to the Platoon Leader. This resulted in the accurate reporting of enemy activity, giving the platoon fire superiority advantage, aiding the Troop's sixteen confirmed enemies killed in action and fourteen enemies wounded in action."

Glancing down, I think of how this award meant so much to me when I received it. Yet now, two years later, with the things I loved most gone, it doesn't signify anything more than a piece of paper on the wall.

Walking into the kitchen, I reach for the gallon of Pendleton Whiskey and pick it up. *Half-empty already? I just bought this last night. Fuck me, guess I'll get more tomorrow.*

Without regard for the standard three-finger pour, the bottle glugs, sucking air through the river of aged liquid heaven. *Half a pint glass should do.* Without warning, it hits me. The text message I had received earlier that day. I apparently didn't push down far enough.

"Hey brother, I hate to be the one to tell you this, especially over text, but Jason—Jason killed himself last night. He left a note to his wife and kids. He took a bunch of sleeping pills and a fifth. Yeah, man this is the third one for you in the last six months. I'm sorry, bro."

Downing the glass, my jaw begins to clench as my

throat tightens, clinging to the familiar, now-weak burn of whiskey. Hot tears that I struggle to hold back begin to blur the label on the bottle of Pendleton as I set the glass down on the counter. With my back sliding down against the cabinets, I sit on the floor with my knees pulled up to my heaving chest. I place my elbows on my knees and sob.

I had tried five different antidepressants, two sleep medications, a muscle relaxer, and other methods over the last nearly two years with not even an ounce of success. For the first time in my life, I begin to have an emotional breakdown. *This is it. You are never going to feel happiness again. You are one of the 10-20 percenters that antidepressants won't even work on. You fucked up, man. You sold your soul to Ares and Odin without even realizing it.* This was my harsh reality, and it was never going to change. Nothing I ever did—work out, move, change friends, or anything else, would rid the overwhelming feelings of depression and survivor's guilt that seemed to pester me even in my dreams. There was never going to be an escape.

Then, the thought occurs to me. *Well, there is a way for the pain to end. I mean you have tried every other aspect possible.* I push the idea away. Suicide isn't an option. Watching the destruction from my friends who committed suicide and the toll it takes on their families, I realize why many religions and ideologies condemn suicide—because it doesn't fix your pain. It only passes it on, a sort of nuclear fallout burdening every surviving loved one formerly in your life. I begin to sob harder. *I'm trapped with no way out.*

I stand up, wiping the tears from my face. I reach for the glass covered in condensation sweat and gulp down the nearly six shots worth of whiskey. Grabbing my phone, I scroll through the phonebook list, searching for my long-time friend in Chandler, Arizona. I was looking for some comfort, advice, or "suck it up" speech. Grabbing the bottle one more time, I pour myself another half-pint glass of whiskey and tap "Call."

"Hello?" she says.

"Hey, I'm having a hard time. I don't know how to fix it, but I want to before it's too late."

"I'm all ears," she says, distinctly concerned.

I explain what's going on, trying to hold back any sound of emotional weakness or evidence that would suggest I had been crying. I hold it back until, without thinking, I say, "I feel like I lost all the things about me that I loved and wanted to intertwine into the man that I want to be, but there's no way to find them."

"Steele, they're not lost. I know it's hard to see right now, but there's a reason you've gone through absolute hell the last two years. I don't know what it is, but I know you're the only one who can figure it out. Nobody else can. I think you need to take some time and find it. You didn't survive combat or all those crazy things in your civilian life to crumble like this. You forget how strong, courageous, and brave you are."

The conversation ends, leaving me once again to my thoughts and empty apartment. Sitting on the couch with the dog at my feet, I leisurely put my feet on her, petting her. She rolls over putting her paws in the air in a "Scratch my belly," kind of way. I begin staring off into the distance, listening to the show on TV. Once again, I'm reminded of the woman who seemed to bring rays of sunshine even to the dimmest days. I wasn't going to bed and laying next to her. I wasn't going to wake up and have her magically back in my life. Just like my depression and PTSD weren't going to magically disappear by morning.

Sluggishly standing up, swaying slightly back and forth from the liquor, I bend backward, cracking my back. Feeling the muscles around my spine begin to spasm, gradually, as if I were ninety years old with a cane, I step toward the counter. Grabbing the half-empty pill bottle, I pour out two muscle relaxers into my open hand and pop them into my mouth. Closing my eyes, I look up toward the ceiling and gulp them down. I pause for a second as if I'm going to receive instant relief. I set the muscle relaxers down and reach for the sleep medication. Pouring another pill into my hand, I start to pop it into my mouth. I hesitate, thinking of my friend who used sleep medication and whiskey to take his life the night prior. *Maybe you've consumed too much alcohol to take muscle relaxers and sleep medication? No, you've drunk way more and have been fine. What you need is to get more than three or four hours of sleep for once.* I pop the pill into my mouth, swallow it, and walk toward my bedroom.

Lowering myself into bed, I feel the icy sheets against

me. My Labrador circles around curling up next to my feet, pulling her "guard shift" watching the bedroom door. Closing my eyes, I silently begin to pray.

Hey, Big J, I know it's been a long time since you and I have talked, and even longer since we regularly talked. I don't understand why I've survived all these things, just to live through misery and hopelessness. I don't understand why you haven't just taken me by now. I need help. I can't put the bottle down. I have no idea how to pick the pieces up, let alone where to even begin. I try to find things that make me happy, but nothing does anymore. The harder I try, the less I find. I haven't been acting like the man I want to be, and I have no idea how to become him. Before life happened, I was the happy, optimistic person. Now the only things I feel are pain or nothing at all. Just broken. Please, give me a sign—any sign—of where I go from here.

Closing my eyes, I feel the pills churning and mixing with the whiskey in my stomach. Slowly but surely, my thoughts slow down, and I drift into nothing but a dream.

Feeling the wind on my face, I swing my axe, breaking the hard crust of ice that had formed on the roughly 70 percent pitch. I'm wondering why in the world I decided to climb a mountain.

"You've never climbed before, why couldn't you pick a beginner mountain like Mount Hood or Sisters first? But no, you're Steele Kelly. You had to start in the fucking Himalayas," I say, struggling to catch my breath in the thin air at 20,000 feet.

"One more step, push yourself." Reaching up, I slide my ascender along the fixed rope, struggling to take another step. Everything fades to black.

On my knees, the early morning sun beating down on me, I reach over and grab my ice axe. I begin swinging it at the ice near my feet on the summit of the mountain. I continue swinging and digging a hole. My breath clouds the air with each fast, shallow exhale. I reach up to the zipper hidden by my Carhartt face mask and beanie. The teeth of the zipper hiss as I unzip my jacket to my waist. Pulling my right glove off, I reveal my bare hand, steaming from the physical exertion of the climb in the frigid mountain air. Carefully placing the glove in my jacket, I reach into the chest pocket with my right hand and pull the shiny, platinum diamond ring out of my jacket. Holding the ring at eye level and gazing at it, the sun hits the diamond, illuminating the precise edges of the princess cut, its clarity unmatched.

With one smooth motion, I slowly move my arm toward the hole. With hesitation, I open my hand, allowing the ring to tumble into the hole. I hesitate again, holding the picture from my wallet. *She looked so beautiful in that picture. We looked so happy. What a shame it had to come to an end. I knew it would; I just didn't think it would happen for another eighty years. I miss her and wish it had ended differently.* Closing my eyes, I let go of the picture. It falls like a feather into its shallow grave. The world abruptly fades to black.

Suddenly, wet slobber and a warm tongue slide across my face. I open my eyes, seeing my eighty-pound dog on my chest. "Yeah, yeah, I know, Lucy Goose. It's time to go to chemistry and you want your breakfast."

I begin to realize it was all just a dream. Even though it felt so real, complete with the wind on my face, it was nothing more than a figment of my imagination. I slide out of bed, bending over toward my toes, swaying side to side, cracking my back to the left and right. Standing up slowly, I walk toward the closet. Grabbing a pair of jeans and a shirt, I look to the right. There it sat. Reaching up slowly, I feel the felt of the ring box against my fingers. I open the case and see the shimmering diamond and platinum ring.

Would have looked a lot better on her finger.

* * *

SITTING IN CHEMISTRY CLASS, THE MUFFLED VOICE of the instructor fades into silence as I slip deep into thought. *What if that was your sign? I mean, you did ask God what to do next. In your dream, you were in the Himalayas. Nepal. Maybe you need to climb a mountain and leave the ring there. Maybe the dream was telling you to find the lost pieces of your soul.*

Quietly pulling my laptop out of my backpack, I cruise the internet searching for mountains to climb in Nepal. I froze.

No fucking way.

There it stood at just shy of 21,000 feet—the mountain from my dream. *Imja Tse? Never heard of it, but Google images don't lie. That's it. That's where you're supposed to go.*

Without any hesitation, I pull my credit card out and book a flight to Kathmandu, Nepal.

Well, you have a little more than three weeks to learn everything you can about mountaineering. 'Cause your ass has never climbed before. You're going to climb just shy of 21,000 feet, almost twice the altitude of Mt. Hood, you crazy fuck.

I have no idea why I felt the need to do this. I can't explain it, but for some reason, I knew I had to get away. I knew I had to leave everything I was comfortable with in order to fix what was broken and find the part of myself that was lost. I knew, with the severity of how lost I felt, I was headed for a place that I couldn't come back from. With confidence and determination, I knew I was either going to find what I was looking for, or I would die trying.

"The best people possess a feeling for beauty,
the courage to take risks, the capacity for sacrifice.
Ironically, their virtues make them vulnerable:
they are often wounded, sometimes destroyed."

—ERNEST HEMINGWAY

CHAPTER 2

GROWING UP

———

FOR MANY OF US WHO STRUGGLE AFTER COMBAT, the problems aren't merely war-related or directly from the war. Frequently, war exacerbates the problems we didn't know were there prior to war. Without us knowing, the problems under the surface magnify our issues earned in warfare. Everybody has a different story; every saint has a past, and every sinner has a future. However, to provide context and background to understand how underlying issues can manifest, I feel it is essential to talk about the past.

There's a common joke in the secondary education system when you study psychology. It goes, "No matter how great your childhood was, how amazing your family was, every single one of us in our minds came from a dysfunctional family or town." I, however, had a difficult childhood in a different way. It was not from gang violence; it was not from poverty; it was not from alcoholism, abuse, or neglectful parents. Instead, my family and I suffered a significant amount of grief through death. Between the ages of five and twenty-four, I had attended over twenty-five funerals. These were not funerals I was forced to attend for people I hardly even knew. They were for family members and friends whom I loved deeply and felt the ripples of loss through my life for years to come.

First, I want to acknowledge that I grieve differently than many of my peers. I have experienced the grieving cycle so many times and with so many loved ones that I am desensitized when it comes to death and loss. I grieve for a day or two when I hear of the loss. Then, I attend the funeral, go to the bar, and wake up the next morning over it. I don't mean "over it." I mean genuinely, fully grieved, and over the experience. I recognize that this is not common, and every length of time or process is individual-dependent. Due to my spiritual leanings, I believe that I will see my loved ones who have passed again one day. For me, this makes their loss that much easier. I accept the fact they're gone in this life, but I am comforted by the assurance that I will see them again.

I have always had a sense of intuition, and I frequently have gut feelings about a person or situation that usually turns out to be right. I have had gut feelings where I know something is off or will be off, and if somebody is good or bad. When I was fourteen, I learned I was the type of person who runs into danger without fear while on a family trip to Bend, Oregon.

For those of you who are not familiar with the drive over Santiam Pass, it is incredibly windy, with many sections that have blind corners and drop-off cliffs on the side of the road. It can be a dangerous drive any time of the year, with little forgiveness if somebody crosses the line into oncoming traffic. We were headed home after a long weekend in the sun. We were tired, and Oregon's weather decided to change, raining sideways the entire drive back. My mother and sister were a mile or two ahead, in a car filled with my sister and her teammates. Fortunately, my dad and I were spared from the young girl drama that surely was discussed for three hours, because we took a separate car.

About an hour into the drive, we turn down a steep blind corner near Detroit Lake and see brake lights, cars stopping, and fire. Squinting through the torrential rain hitting the windshield, I see a truck on its side, teetering, ready to roll upside down at any moment. Coming to a stop, I throw my seatbelt off and sprint 300 yards toward the truck.

When I get closer, I see another man going to the side of the truck. Seeing flames out of the bottom of the engine compartment, I realize the gas lines could ignite at any moment, shooting back to the fuel tank. I can't see through the windows as they've now fogged over. Suddenly, like a horror movie, a hand slaps against the window, clearing the fog with five perfect fingers and a palm print sliding down.

"We've got people inside! They're alive!" I shout to the two gentlemen next to me and my father.

The man next to me (whose name I never got) begins kicking the back window as hard as he can until it shatters, jumping through to unlock the passenger door. Meanwhile, my dad and I climb as fast as we can up the side of the truck. We heave the door open and look down into the cab like a hatch on a submarine. Unbuckling the woman passenger in her mid-fifties or sixties, we pull her out, setting her on the support arm for the door. Sliding down off the bed as if I were one of the Duke boys in *Dukes of Hazzard*, I run around to the other side, and the lady is lowered down to me.

The flames rapidly grow more massive and more intense. Bystanders without access to a fire extinguisher or water hose begin throwing dirt on the fire, attempting to extinguish or slow the fire down in any way they possibly can. Jumping back up onto the truck, the driver has blood trickling down his face from a deep laceration. His eyes look entirely disoriented, and he appears confused as he attempts to regain consciousness. He, too, is in his late fifties or mid-sixties and seems extremely weak and confused. Pulling him up the same way we did with his wife, we set him on the door support.

Before I hop down, I see the man who had crawled through the window, and I can't help but notice the panic in his eyes. His foot is caught, the seatbelt is looped around his boot trapping it between the broken window and the ground. He begins to panic uncontrollably, realizing the flames are rapidly growing bigger and consuming more of the truck. While fearing the gas tank would blow at any minute, it is a vicious cycle—the more he panics, the more stuck his foot becomes. Realizing I have to tend to the driver hanging off the door before helping the other rescuer, I hop off the truck and pull the driver to the ground. I support his weight by placing his arm over my neck and shoulder using his arm as leverage, carrying him to the front of another car, forcing him to lie on the ground. Dismissing his attempts to stand, I forcefully continue pushing him onto the road.

"Sir, you've been in an accident. Your wife is okay. She's right here next to us. You have a cut on your head, you're definitely concussed, and I'm worried you fractured your neck. You need to stay on the ground until the paramedics get here," I say in a soothing, yet commanding tone.

While I was struggling to keep the man on the ground, an off-duty paramedic sprints over to my side. I tell him what I think is wrong with the man, as he simultaneously moves above the man to position him into the C-spine neck support hold. We keep him on the ground for the next forty-five minutes until the first responders arrive.

This was my first lesson in the adage, "Sometimes you're the teacher, and other times you're the student." You never know which one you are, or even both until you look back in hindsight. The man who had been trapped by the seatbelt freed himself and came over to say goodbye before heading out. He told my father and I that he had come upon an accident the week prior, nobody helped, and by the time he decided to help, the fire had spread and all the occupants had burned alive. He said he wasn't going to let that ever happen again, and he felt this might have been the chance to redeem the actions he hadn't taken. I still think about that from time to time. Quite honestly, that incident may be one of the significant pivotal moments in my life that instilled one of my sacred core values of never passing a cry for help, no matter the danger.

It turned out, the driver had several cervical spine fractures, and the doctors told him that one of the vertebrae had fractured entirely into pieces. Had he continued to move, there would have been a high probability that he would be paralyzed from the neck down.

This defining moment, as well as being surrounded by death, though certainly not something I would wish on anyone else, did help me narrow down potential career options. I knew I wanted to help people, to be beneficial to society, and to feel proud of my job. After this incident, when I was a teen, I enrolled as a cadet, training for a career in law enforcement. Under the guidance of the sheriff's office, I'd gone on almost every type of call you can imagine. Officer-down calls, officer-involved shootings, countless calls in which CPS had to take children to a new guardian because their parent overdosed on some opioid or was killed by an angry lover. Coupled with my history of familial loss, I was relatively unshockable. Two calls still stand out from the rest that contributed to how I treat people and situations. These were calls where I learned that there are people in the world who would do everything they can to harm or kill you. If you hesitate in moments like these, or are reluctant to visit violence, you will not survive.

On one occasion, I was riding with Officer Powers, and the dispatcher asked over the radio, "2255, are you guys free to respond to a welfare check?"

"This is 2255. Send it to us," I respond.

"It's a little confusing here, and I'm not quite sure what is going on. The caller who reported it said he is the manager at the local hotel. A man in his mid-forties has been staying there for a week. The caller has only seen a little boy about the age of five go in with the man, but he hasn't seen the boy in a couple of days. The caller also said the man hasn't been back or paid his bill, and when the caller entered the unit, there were little girl clothes and toys all over the room. It all seems very, very weird." From her tone, it is clear she is worried about a possible kidnapping, or worse.

"We'll head that way, maybe send another car or two our way in case it turns into something bigger or the individual comes back," I respond, clicking the radio mic into place.

As we head toward the hotel, our small talk is interrupted by dispatch once again.

"2255, actually I need you to divert to a medical assist

for an AED (Automated External Defibrillator) for a woman in her forties, unresponsive, no pulse."

"En route," I respond, as Powers switches the lights and sirens on, pulling a U-turn in the busy road.

Arriving on the scene, we enter the house about the same time as the firefighters and paramedics. It is in an area that is lower income and frequently responded to for fights and drug overdoses. I walk into the living room, seeing a man later identified as the woman's brother. He is in his forties and appears as if he's still shaking off "the nod" from heroin or some other type of opiate. He is extremely out of it and in a cloudy type of alertness.

He points down the hallway to our right, fumbling his words in confusion, "She's down the hall on the left."

The house looked as if it needed a deep cleaning and some organization. We turn a sharp right down the hallway from the entryway, hooking an almost immediate left into the bedroom. There is a disheveled bed on the left side of the room, a suitcase, and clothes strewn everywhere taking up the remaining available space on the floor. With one foot in the closet and one foot under the bed, I see a morbidly obese woman who is in need of an AED. Getting a better view, I see her right arm still propped up by the bed, the left arm extended outward on the floor, palm facing up, and her head facing to the left. It is apparent the woman is deceased.

Standing next to her is a five-year-old boy, poking her in the stomach with a wooden toy sword. He's angrily yelling, "WAKE UP!" as if she were playing a game and intentionally ignoring the boy.

Holy shit, is he poking his mother's corpse with a stick?

Immediately, we shuttle the boy out of the room and into the living room. We sit him on the couch next to his uncle. Meanwhile, the firefighters enter the room and begin to place all kinds of wires and sensors onto the woman. We return to the doorway, blocking entrance from the hallway, to prevent further traumatization for the young boy. Roughly five minutes later, a firefighter exits the room and asks to speak to us outside, away from the boy.

"Yeah, she's dead," the firefighter says, keeping his voice low so the boy can't overhear. "There's a whole bunch of prescription bottles in the closet. I don't know if it's an overdose or a concoction of alcohol, pills, and a medical condition."

Grabbing the mic clamped to his uniform, Powers says in a low voice, "Dispatch, 2255. Can you page detectives for a death investigation? As well as the chaplain for a five-year-old boy who is here."

Over the next several hours, more and more information is revealed on the situation. In a weird kind of circle, the officers who responded to the original welfare check ran into the man when they showed up at the hotel. It turned out our deceased woman was his girlfriend, and the boy was her son. They had an altercation when the boy got the stomach flu and began vomiting in the hotel room. The man grabbed the five-year-old boy by the head and neck, dragging him by his hair to the bathroom. Forcefully placing the boy's head into the toilet bowl, he submerged his head beneath the water, yelling at the boy, "You fucking puke in here." He and the deceased got into an altercation, and she took off to her brother and sister-in-law's house, where she eventually died.

In an even more tragic turn of events, the chaplain, while searching for a next of kin responsible enough to care for the boy, discovered an unfortunate, yet common law enforcement scenario.

"Powers, Kelly, can I talk to you two outside for a second?" she whispers in a melancholy tone.

Stepping outside and closing the door quietly behind her, she says, "So, I just got off the phone with the grandma. It turns out she has all of her kids' kids because all of her kids are hooked on drugs and neglectful. They have been removed from their homes by Child Protective Services and have been placed with the grandma. She said it would be a while because she has a play downtown to attend."

"Um, did you tell her that her daughter is dead and we can't remove the body until the child is gone?" Powers says, as if he's trying to comprehend the concept, discovering your child was dead, then seemingly not caring.

"Yeah, I did. Will you try giving her a call? Maybe you can be more convincing."

Powers calls the grandma, and she reiterates her plans to attend a play downtown. She's not going to change her plans for anyone. She had almost eight grandchildren she was responsible for, and she most definitely did not want another one burdening her.

* * *

THESE EVENTS TOOK PLACE AT 4:00 P.M. THE grandma didn't arrive until nearly eight and a half hours later at 12:30 a.m. During that time, the chaplain remained outstanding with her kindness and compassion for the boy. It turned out that he had an anger management problem, getting him kicked out of several kindergarten classes for his angry outbursts and aggression. In the time we spent there waiting for his grandma, the boy had several dozen outbursts, attempting to run to his mom's room where she lay dead. We were forced to stand in the hallway blocking the entrance for the remainder of the time. The more time that passed, the more frequent the anger outbursts became; he wanted to see his mother. However, with how volatile the situation was, knowing a loved one would not be there for an unknown length of time, the chaplain, Powers, a supervisor, a detective, and I decided that it would be best to allow the grandmother to tell him when the corpse was not in the house.

The events of that night stuck with me as a lesson of the most kindness, compassion, and patience from the chaplain that I have ever seen. The later it got, the more tired and agitated the boy became. She rubbed the boy's back in a motherly fashion until he fell asleep around 10:00 p.m. When the grandmother arrived, cigarette still in her mouth, she was angry that her daughter burdened her and was not the least bit upset by her death.

Throwing the cigarette onto the ground, she hollered, "Alright, where is the little fucker? I'm ready to fucking go! Just another little shit I have to fucking take care of."

Walking in quietly, the chaplain asked if I would pick the sleeping boy up off the couch and carry him to the car. As if I had been a father who had carried all of my kids up the stairs to bed, I quietly picked the boy up. My heart sank as he put both arms around my neck, laying his head on my shoulder, immediately falling back to sleep. Gently, I set him in the back seat of the van, reclined the chair back and fastened the seatbelt over his tiny body. As I slid the van door shut, I began to feel an overwhelming sadness for the boy.

I couldn't stop thinking about how angry and miserable his grandmother was. The fact she showed no sadness and only feelings of burden was unimaginable. In addition, he would be in a house with eight other kids who most likely did not have positive role models to encourage them, show them affection, or give them hugs. *What kind of trajectory is this kid on? He is only five, and he has an anger problem of this magnitude. What will happen when he is sixteen?* It wasn't that I thought he was doomed for trouble. It was that without a father, mother, or a positive role model, such as a sports coach or mentor who could be patient and work with him, the cycle was looking as if it wouldn't be broken. He didn't seem like a dangerous or violent kid. He wasn't a kid who was evil. He was just a young boy, desperate to be loved by anyone.

After the medical examiner removed the body, we got back in our patrol car and headed to the police station. Breaking the silence and contemplative states we were both in, I asked Powers, "This is how the cycle of violence and troubled kids continues, isn't it? His grandmother is almost worse than a foster care system, isn't she?"

"Yeah, man, it's sad. She already has her hands full. Probably on a shoestring budget and barely handling the ones she has now. It isn't that they're bad kids. They just haven't been shown a different way. The chaplain staying with him and you carrying him to the car might be the only caring actions that he experiences in his childhood," he said somberly.

The drive back to the station was filled with silence.

The next morning, I had a pretty long conversation about what happened with my mom, who is a social worker. To this day, I still think about her response and reaction to the story.

"Honey, what you aren't seeing is that man who submerged the kid in the toilet water was once that little boy who was desperate to be loved by a positive role model. That's how the whole scheme of things works. That's how the whole cycle is repeated. In a weird series of events, you saw the beginning of the cycle with the child and the end of the cycle with the man."

"I know, Mom. I just don't know how you can ever overcome it without being a permanent fixture in their life," I solemnly responded.

"You do it by attempting to have positive interactions with every person you meet. Try to be loving and kind to each and every one of them, no matter how mean they seem. Your one act of kindness could change the entire outcome of events. For all you know, you and the chaplain may have a lasting impact on this boy, and it may be a strong enough memory that he turns his life around in the future," my mom said.

* * *

SIX MONTHS LATER, PARKED WITH THE LIGHTS OFF, it's 2:30 a.m. We're watching an empty side street of Gladstone, Oregon, trying not to fall asleep, when I see a vehicle pass. There wasn't anything blatantly wrong or out of the normal, but my gut was telling me something was off. As it passed by, almost two hundred yards down the road, I say, "Dude, stop that fucking car!" excitedly folding down the computer screen.

"Kelly, our shift is over in twenty minutes. It's only a brake light out. They're probably headed home from a Christmas party. Turn it down a couple notches," Jack says—joking, but still serious.

"Nah, man, I got the vibe," I say, emphasizing *vibe* in a superstitious kind of way.

"Yeah, that's what I mean, your *vibe* is going to keep us here until 8:00 a.m!"

I give him "the look," and he can tell I'm saying, "Yeah, but we're not off work yet!"

Throwing the transmission into drive, he presses the gas pedal down, accelerating rapidly out of the parking lot while turning his headlights on. Picking up speed, we close the distance between the cars. Noticing the windows beginning to fog up, both the passenger and driver begin nervously checking their mirrors.

Knowing that I was right and that we would most likely not be off until 8:00 a.m., he says, "Fine, Steele, call it out."

"Four David Eleven, traffic," I say through the mic.

"Four David Eleven, go ahead."

After giving the location and license plate number, Jack turns the lights on. Exiting the vehicle, our exhale is visible in the crisp December air. Red, white, and blue lights bounce off the surrounding trees, buildings, and car. As I step closer to the vehicle, I can now see everything inside the vehicle illuminated by both the flashing lights on the patrol car and our flashlights beaming off the thick fog. As we reach the trunk, Jack on the driver side, me on the passenger side, we look through the 1980s hatchback window. Brand new electronics, wrapping paper, and packaging fill the trunk space. As I approach the forty-something-year-old passenger, a life of narcotics, alcohol, and abuse are visible in every wrinkle of his face. With his hands holding a backpack, I see a large butcher knife protruding out from the top of his pack with the handle next to his right hand.

"Put your hands on the dash, dude," I command.

He hesitates.

"Do as I say! If you reach for the knife, I'm going to fucking shoot you. Do you understand me?"

Immediately, his hands shoot to the dash of the vehicle, but without warning, I hear the sound of metal sliding on plastic. Taking a step back toward the patrol car, I look over to see Jack with his gun drawn.

"Put your hands on the steering wheel, right fucking now!" he says to the driver.

I had spent hundreds of hours in a patrol car with Jack. In doing so, I knew many of his actions, his demeanor, and often what he would do next before he even did it. Jack was calm, cool, and collected as a deputy. He was certainly not an individual to draw his gun in a preemptive action without a substantial reason.

The teenaged-looking boy complies, though he keeps looking down toward the center console and belt line. Holstering his firearm, Jack instructs the boy not to move.

"What's your name? Don't lie to me," he says calmly to the teenage driver.

Without breaking eye contact, I write his name down. Jack remains at the car while I walk back to our patrol car, typing the name and date of birth to search the database. "Not found." *If he had a license, it would show. Must be a fake name.*

When I tell Jack nothing has come back, he tries to reason with the kid. "Look man, it's Christmas, you only had a brake light out. Just give me your real name so we both can head home."

"That is my name," he lies.

"Look, I hate being lied to. We both know it isn't your name. At this point, if you don't want to give it to me, I'm going to take you to the jail to run your fingerprints until we determine who you are."

"Okay, here's my name."

Once again, I walk back, running the name he gave me. "Not found" displays yet again. Knowing this guy is playing a game that is often the result of having a warrant for their arrest, I pick up the mic in the center console. "Dispatch, Four David Eleven, send a cover car our way, please."

This time, walking more cautiously to Jack, I say, "Bad name, again."

Looking down at the teenager, Jack says empathetically, "Here's the deal. I have a three-strike rule. Currently, you just used strike three. But it's Christmas, and I would rather you spend time with your family than waiting for your fingerprints to run. This is your last chance to give me your real name so we can take care of whatever is going on."

The teenager attempts to slowly and subtly reach for his waist and center console. Jack, seeing this, places his hand on the grip of his firearm. "Hey, put your fucking hands on the steering wheel!"

Without breaking eye contact, reaching up to the radio mic on my collar, I say, "This is Four David Eleven, we need our cover to step it up."

As if the kid has a death wish, he begins reaching toward the center console again. By this point, both Jack and I know that something is in the center console. By leaving him in the driver seat, both our lives and the passenger's life could be decided by whatever was in there. Now seeing our cover car pulling up, Jack glances at me quickly. I step closer to Jack's left side as he opens the driver's door.

"Without reaching for anything, I want you to get out of the car."

As the teen steps out of the driver seat, Jack simultaneously grasps the teenager's left wrist in his left hand, placing his right hand on the teen's shoulder.

With one motion, the world goes silent, the teenager turning towards Jack and I, swiftly reaching once again for his waist with his right hand. Within a half-second, I see the silver metallic flash from a .38 special revolver now halfway out of the waistband and aiming toward us.

"GUN!" I lunge forward, smashing all three of us into the side of the car.

The cover officer draws his gun and runs straight toward the passenger, commanding him not to move while the three of us are still pressed into the door and side of the car, grappling for the gun. Within a few seconds, I'm able to get my right hand on the firearm, pulling it away from him by pushing his face into the roof of the car with my left hand. Jack simultaneously puts the guy's hands into cuffs. Backing away, I open the fully loaded revolver, emptying the rounds into my hand.

"Good work. You just saved both yours and Jack's lives," I hear the cover deputy say to me.

* * *

IT TURNED OUT, THE PACKAGES IN THE VEHICLE were stolen from a burglary they had just committed, and they were headed to sell the newly packaged electronics. Ultimately, he refused to give us his name, but the jail confirmed his identity and the fact that he was sixteen years old. He had a history of poor decisions, burglary, and firearm charges. I couldn't help but think later on of the five-year-old boy. "So this is the cycle when they turn into teenagers. This is what happens when they are raised in a toxic environment without positive role models, parents, or coaches—exposed to gangs, violence, and drugs."

I had no idea that the hours spent teaching, mentoring, and training from police officers at the Tigard Police Department, and eventually deputies at the Clackamas County Sheriff's Office, would have such a positive and lasting impact on my life. I genuinely believe that, had these amazing men and women in uniform not taken the time to teach and train me, I would have died at several different points in my life. I learned a lot about life and being a good person, and I was able to see firsthand the effect of treating people with respect versus treating them poorly.

Although it's hard at times, I still try to "Be the type of person that, no matter where you go or where you are, you always add value to the lives of others around you." Naturally, I still bobble that. I still lose my temper at times, allow my lousy day to spill over, or sometimes I simply don't want to talk. However, I make an effort every day to live by that motto.

I still think about the five-year-old kid who went into his grandmother's custody, wondering how he turned out. He would be about fifteen or sixteen years old now. I think of all the football, lacrosse, and baseball coaches that I had growing up who took the time to give words of wisdom, teach discipline, and provide encouragement to kids who might not have gotten it elsewhere. Many of the people out there who are coaches, teachers, and mentors have no idea what life they could literally be changing. They have no idea that they may be the only person in a kid's life who can stop a destructive cycle. I hope this was the case for the boy—that he was able to think back to the night and see a different side of kindness and compassion. That possibly he enrolled in sports or other after-school activities and is now looking at going to college or pursuing a trade. That he decided he wanted something different for his life and future family. I choose to believe he did, instead of looking at him as just another criminal on the streets who is destined to succumb to drugs and violence, entering and exiting the prison system. I choose to think of him this way, because any of us could be in those shoes had we not been so fortunate.

Call it luck, call it destiny, call it whatever you want to call it. I was exposed to some very graphic, violent, and morbid incidents at a relatively young developmental age. It wasn't until my adulthood that I realized just how much that affects individuals. I have remained close with several officers and deputies that I spent hundreds of hours in a patrol car with. I have seen marriages from law enforcement families crumble from alcohol, depression, PTSD, stress, infidelity, and many other things. I feel very fortunate that now, almost seven years later, I can see what happened and how the careers of these individuals have grown, ended, or remained the same. I feel blessed to have been able to look behind the curtain—behind every badge, gun, and uniform—and realize there is a person. A person who struggles, who loves, who cares, who gets angry, who has a soft spot somewhere, and is just like everybody else.

Now that I am an adult and have taken a step away from my life and evaluated different events from a rigorous third-party perspective, I realize how many things I experienced and saw that many kids and even adults don't otherwise experience. I believe these things ultimately shaped who I am today, pushing me toward taking the difficult path. Instead of learning lessons over thirty or forty years, I learned them painfully in four or five.

Today, I have little quirks that seem strange to others as a result of the losses and my close-call experiences. Anytime I leave the house or my family's place, I always make sure to give them a hug and tell them I love them. I make the best attempt to never storm off angry without telling them I still love them. I have come to the morbid realization that all of us will die without knowing when that will be. I have lost enough people to realize I don't want my last exchange to be a negative one. No matter how intense, heated, or upsetting the situation is, if your last words are said with anger or show hatred, you will always wish you had said something different, regretting the final exchange. This is one of the many reasons that I believe life is way too short to go to bed angry with your significant other. Very rarely is any fight ever worth it, and going to bed angry means waking up angry, which means the fight continues longer.

Also, I frequently fly by the seat of my pants when it comes to my everyday life. I live in a manner that is extremely spontaneous. If I get a random idea that seems like a good time (within my moral and ethical compass), such as climbing a mountain in the Himalayas when I've never climbed before, I go for it. I have come to accept that I don't know how or when I will go out of this world. I would much rather live every day as if it were my last, even if people think my spontaneity is crazy or rambunctious, or that I have a screw loose that causes me to be impulsive. However, they are not living my life, and I am not living theirs. Quite honestly, it is none of their business if I wake up tomorrow and decide randomly to purchase a squirrel suit and start base jumping.

Live every day as if it's your last. Love too hard, fall too easy, take care of your body, and treat others with kindness and respect, for you may be the one saving a life unbeknownst. "Never water yourself down just because somebody can't handle you at one-hundred proof."

"Then I heard the voice of the Lord saying,
"Whom shall I send? Who will go for us?"
And I said, 'Here am I. Send me.'"

—ISAIAH 6:8, NIV

CHAPTER 3

THE SANDBOX

———

ALMOST FOUR YEARS AFTER THAT CHRISTMAS EVE in the patrol car.

"We've arrived into Afghani airspace. Forty-five minutes until landing," the flight captain says into the cabin of the C-17 as the green lights simultaneously transition to red.

Feeling the sudden thrust of the C-17 sending us into a nosedive, we drop out of the air and land onto the small runaway of the airstrip. The "Combat Landing" is a method used in combat zones where you maintain altitude until the last minute before plunging down to the runway so you won't be in as much danger of being shot out of the air—a slow decrease of altitude makes for an easy target.

As we touch down, I can feel the cabin of the plane heating up within the first five minutes of landing. "On your feet!" a voice orders inside the cabin.

Sitting with my back to the port of the plane, I stand

up out of the jumper seat, now facing toward the tail of the aircraft. Mechanical gears tic as the back ramp drops and the fiery sunset of Afghanistan shines through the doors. I can feel the 125-degree air flood the fuselage of the plane as the smell of burning trash, rubber, and sewage of our new home wafts into my nose. Suddenly, it dawns on me. *This is your new home for the next year. You can't call in sick on Monday when a weekend is too hard. You won't be stopping by the family's house for Sunday dinner. You're here, and there's nowhere to go but work, seven days a week.*

After getting settled in, two days later, it's time for "left seat/right seat ride," an effective strategy where half of the new unit patrols with half the unit they are replacing. The guys you are replacing are salty and effective from prolonged combat exposure, and they help the new guys "pop their cherry" if they come under fire.

It would be my first mission outside the wire, and of course, it happened on a night that had very little ambient lighting from the stars and moon. When there's low lighting, it makes your night vision less effective, because it magnifies ambient lighting. We waited until dusk to make our approach, walking in to a known Taliban village that the previous unit had several direct fire engagements with in the weeks prior.

Many guys remember their first dismounted mission outside the wire, even if it's uneventful. Before leaving the base, I had placed fresh batteries into my infrared laser, NVGs (Night Vision Goggles), turning them on, focusing, and ensuring their proper function. We entered the village around 2100 hours (9:00 p.m.), just as the village mosque begins a sudden, prayer-song type of chant. It was unusual timing, quite coincidental, that we happened to be entering the village with thirty men at the exact time it began. It was more of a signaling to the enemy that we were there, to prepare for us.

I entered the village in the back of the formation, and my senses were heightened. Every corner in the dark and every sound or movement was magnified. I scan, worried a fighter will charge me from every doorway in the alley. Through the green night vision, I can see the flash of eyes as villagers narrowly open their doors to look for us. My heart's racing faster, and every possible scenario runs through my head. Halfway through the village, it begins: my NVGs are falling out of focus with every step. Reaching up to turn the focus knob, it won't get back into focus, and I'm walking blind. *Fuck, my nods just broke. Worst fucking time possible. I even checked them and trained for the last three months with them.* Everything in my other eye is black, and there aren't any street lights.

Without seeing my platoon ahead, handing each other off a ten-foot drop-off, I take one step off the edge, falling head-first so abruptly that when my weapon impacted the ground, it sparked as if I discharged my rifle, fading to nothing but black.

Between spots, I can't figure out what's going on. *How long have I been out? Does my platoon even realize they left me behind? Can the Taliban see me? Am I going to be the next POW like Bergdahl or beheaded on the Jihadi news?!*

Scurrying as fast as I can out of the drainage canal, I climb out, running, falling, and fumbling into the darkness, unable to see out of my broken NVGs. The rest is fuzzy, and I don't remember the walk back to the trucks or returning to base. However, the next morning I was told by my buddy, Casey, that he saw and halted the formation until I caught up. He could tell I was only semi-conscious and on auto-pilot trying to find the platoon.

I went back to work the following morning, and within three weeks, we got into our first firefight. After, the heightened sense of awareness on any patrol was gone. It was merely a stroll through the park. We were growing salty ourselves, desensitized to the dangers of the unknown.

* * *

A FEW WEEKS LATER, WE'RE HEADING DOWN SOUTH for a mission. It's in an extremely dangerous village, where several American soldiers had been killed throughout the war in Afghanistan. The village is near the location where the late and honorable Command Sergeant Major Martin Barreras of the 2-5 Infantry Regiment was shot and killed in action. I'd sat in on the coordination for air support planning with the other FO (Forward Observer) and JTACs (Joint Tactical Air Controllers). I didn't like the mission plan from the beginning.

Sitting in the mission briefing with my platoon, I still can't shake the disquiet I'd felt. *We're dismounting with ten soldiers into an extremely hostile village from the east right at sunrise. We have an 800-meter open area to cross without any cover. AND the sun will be silhouetting us? We have night capabilities—why not hit the village at night? The enemy can't see us, and there will be low ambient moonlight.*

A sergeant interrupts my reflection, "Guys, does anybody have any thoughts, concerns, or ideas about the mission plan?"

Looking around, I know nobody is going to say what many of us were thinking, out of fear of ridicule. *However, they asked, and I've got a better idea.*

"Hey, Sergeant, this may be a dumb question or suggestion. Maybe we should hit the village around 3:00 a.m. when everybody is in the middle of REM and deep sleep. We have night capabilities, they don't. We can get in, blow the objective, perform our snatch and grab, and by the time the enemy wakes up to the blast, we'll have accomplished the primary and secondary objectives. When they come out to check, we'll already be lost in the darkness with our prisoners. Maybe crossing the open area in the cover of darkness won't be so risky? If it goes bad, we can back off as a tertiary plan and call an airstrike on the objective with minimal civilian casualties, and aerial support will cover our move back to the trucks," I suggest, with complete respect.

"Kelly, are you fucking scared?" the sergeant condescends.

"Negative, Sergeant, I am just looking to minimize American casualties. By hitting the objective where American soldiers have recently been killed, at dawn, we'll be sitting ducks. Not to mention, if I were them, I would place remote-controlled IEDs and mines in the open area, detonating when I saw troops."

"Kelly, shut the fuck up and do your job. I'm tired of hearing your stupid fucking ideas."

"Roger that, Sergeant," I say, swallowing my anger.

The next morning, we rolled out the gates at 0100 hours (1:00 a.m.) with nearly twenty gun trucks, headed four hours south to the Zerkoh Valley. I couldn't shake the feeling that it was going to go wrong.

It was 0530 when it happened. The explosion echoed through the valley.

Switching over to the *fires frequency*, I begin coordinating with the other FO and JTAC, getting eyes on the village from above. Our aerial support isn't due for another fifty-three minutes, and we are blind in the sky. As our platoon begins pulling guys out of the blown-up vehicle, pulling sensitive equipment and preparing for extract, I see smoke signals from different areas of the village, women and children exiting the village, and men running back and forth. I'm relaying back and forth on the *fires frequency* with the FO assigned to the first platoon who was flanking from the north. Suddenly, sniper rifles begin taking accurate shots at us. DSHK .57 Caliber, PKM, and RPK machine guns began shooting at our team, sweeping the vehicle.

"Butcher 9-1, Butcher 9-2, taking heavy machine gun-fire! We have seven guys pinned down. What's the ETA of Viper team? Requesting air support, over."

"Butcher 9-2, Butcher 9-1, you'll hear them in two mikes, over."

"Butcher 9-1, 9-2, has ground commander cleared hot for ordnance? Over."

"Roger, Viper 3-1 will be entering from the south, dropping ordnance, and exiting to the north banking to the east, for Viper 3-2's follow up strike. How, copy?"

"Confirm, prepare to copy friendlies at grid—" I say, reading them our coordinates.

"Butcher 9-2, 9-1, you boys hold onto your drawers. Ordinance strike will be danger close 150 meters, over."

Interrupting my transmission, it's the sound of two supersonic fighter jets that'd covered the 500 miles of ground from Bagram to our local in the twelve minutes since the explosion.

I watch the first jet bank down from the south, dropping altitude to nearly thirty feet off the ground, firing 200 rounds of 20mm ammunition on the village line, thrusting to the northeast. His wingman follows right behind him with another 200 rounds.

Pinning the enemy's head down, my platoon engages the enemy fighters with .50 caliber M2 machine guns, and my truck engages with a 40mm MK-19 auto-grenade launcher firing rounds at the enemy. This gunfire allows our pinned-down squad to make a break for the cover of my truck. Suddenly, I hear pounding on the left side of our truck. *Fuck, did one of my guys get hit?* I throw my map to the ground, unplugging from my radio, unlatching the lock, opening the door.

Shouting over the continuous machine gunfire, "Hey, you guys okay?"

"Shut up, Kelly. I'm not walking in case there's a secondary. Driver, open your door, too, so that I can hold on," the sergeant from the briefing says.

What the fuck is wrong with you? We have six lower-enlisted walking behind the truck. Walk with them. Lead by example.

Getting the team to their truck, we attempt to get the stable injured to a Casevac from QRF (Quick Reaction Force) back at base. When it begins, I hear a thud. Watching ahead, the enemy starts launching and even-bracketing (one over, one under, closing distance to the center) our platoon with mortar fire. After four rounds, we realize they're zeroing in on us, and we have to risk moving closer and pushing to the south around the obstacles and blast site fearing secondary explosives.

Realizing the enemy is getting extremely close with mortars, I reach for the mic, "Butcher 9-1, this 9-2, over."

"Butcher 9-2, 9-1. Send it."

"Enemy has fixed our location, taking accurate mortar and—" I release the transmission button.

Holy fuck, this is it. How do they have this much firepower? I'd never been in a firefight with insurgents who were so well-equipped, having weapons as accurate and powerful as these.

As I see the blast from 300 meters away, it's a 107mm rocket, increasing speed, headed directly toward the engine block of my armored vehicle.

This is it.

Suddenly, the rocket is in imminent distance, with force headed directly toward my truck. "Jew Bear! Get down!" I shout over my headset, pulling with both hands the harness of my gunner into the armor of our vehicle.

Without realizing my truck commander has a hot mic on our platoon frequency (still transmitting over the platoon frequency), "Holy shit, there's a rocket headed straight for us! Thirty feet, it's bouncing toward us! Twenty feet! Prepare for impact, guys!"

Abruptly, the rocket stops, without detonation, ten feet from my truck.

The four of us nervously laugh in the face of death, as I shout over the truck intercom, "Holy shit, sir, let's fucking move before that bitch explodes!"

Interrupting our quick gasp for air, Jew Bear jumps right back up into the turret firing grenades from our MK-19 when I hear my call sign over the radio, "Butcher 9-2, 9-1, are you guys alright?"

"Butcher 9-1, 9-2, close call. I say again, we are taking accurate mortar fire with bracketing, and taking critical rocket fire. Requesting a follow-up strike, prepare to copy grid, over."

"Butcher 9-2, negative. Viper is headed to refuel and resupply. They expended all ammunition. Commander urges you guys to maneuver 400 meters to the south. It will require the enemy to re-position indirect fire equipment, buying you guys time until they are back on station, 9-2 out."

As if the situation weren't dangerous enough, I hear the explosions from our grenade launcher stop with a loud, unmistakable metallic clank, indicating a jam.

"Jam!" I hear Jew Bear yell through the headset.

Veterans familiar with the MK-19 understand how slow and potentially lengthy it can be to clear the jam of a MK-19 when there is a failure to extract a spent shell casing. Often, you must get out of the cover of your armor defilade to get a rod into the breach and ram the casing out, fully exposed to incoming gunfire.

Looking out my window, hearing enemy bullets ricochet off our truck, I knew he needed suppressive, covering fire. Moving my M4 rifle off my lap onto the floor near the gunner platform of the truck, I reach over my right shoulder between the seat and door, pulling out our M249 SAW automatic weapon.

Knowing I had to make a split-second decision to protect my brother, I yell through my headset, "I'll cover you, Jew Bear!"

Without hesitation, I kick my door open, step out with one foot on the side rail and one foot inside. Meanwhile, several enemy fighters about 150 meters away stand up, shooting over the wall at us, then kneeling back down.

Ripping the bolt back, slamming the cocking handle forward, I switch it to "fire." Shouldering my weapon, I aim down the iron sights and begin shooting three- to five-round bursts at the fighters. The enemy continues shooting back at me, with rounds impacting on the dirt and planking off my open armored door, all around me.

In moments like this, you don't feel fear, hate, or anger—you only feel recoil. You aren't thinking about your wife, family, or friends back home. You're thinking about your brother's life, a life for which you're willing to give your own.

I continue with five- to ten-round bursts, suppressing enemy fire. Hearing the sudden and repeated thuds of our MK-19 firing grenades at a cyclic rate of 325 rounds per minute, I know the jam is clear, and I return to the safety of our armored truck.

That day, the barrage of firepower lasted from 0530 in the morning until nearly 1830 (6:30 p.m.) at night. We returned to base, failing to accomplish the primary or even secondary mission objectives. In a mission debriefing, it was suspected a new interpreter had tipped off Taliban forces who had been waiting for our arrival. Later on, unofficial intelligence estimated forty to fifty Taliban fighters from the valley had been waiting for the ten of us to dismount, entering the village with a fish-in-a-barrel situation in an alleyway.

The lowest of us enlisted re-supplied the trucks with ammunition, replacing our magazines of spent ammunition, hand grenades, and truck ammunition as soon as mission debrief was conducted.

Interrupting the music and evening chores, a fellow soldier came over to me and asked, "Kelly, want to go grab a smoke real quick?"

"Bro, I don't smoke, you know that."

"I know. I need a smoke, and I want to talk to you. Have a dip, I don't care."

"Give me five. I have a few more cans of MK-19 ammo to tie down in my truck."

Heading over to a corner area away from the usual "smoking area" behind some barricades, he confides in me.

"Look, I need to talk to somebody I trust, and I know you won't say anything, Mr. Psych degree."

"Hit me with it, brother."

"One of our sergeants, he's such a fucking asshole. I literally can't take his ignorance and constant berating of me."

"Bro, you're in a scout and infantry unit. We talk shit to each other out of love. You sure you're not just rattled from today, and you took it the wrong way?" I ask, assuming he's tired and being sensitive.

"You don't understand. For the last month, every mission, for the entire mission, he berates me."

He continued, explaining that it was not playful shit talk. It was pretty personal, brutal, and unethical, similar to schoolyard bullies.

"I get it, bro. You won't get moved squads though. He's

fucking ignorant, not a great person, and you'll be better off in life than him. Don't let it get to you," I say, trying to comfort him.

"Look, man. The final straw was briefing last night. You called exactly what was going to happen today. What you said made total sense about moving the mission timeline. I think he wants to die in combat. He doesn't care about any of our lives, and he's going to get one of us killed," he says, shaking with frustration as his voice speeds up.

"Look, is he an ass? Absolutely. But suicidal or a death wish? I'm not sure I see it."

"Are you fucking kidding me? Look at today! My sergeant is an asshole and our platoon sergeant is a coward who knows our vehicles are meant for blasts when the doors are closed. He had your truck open the doors to stand on the rails. He knew that as your truck moved while we walked behind for cover, there was a risk of hitting a secondary explosive. If you did, we would all lose our limbs or die. He was too scared to walk behind the truck, and in doing so, if you guys hit a secondary, not only would it have killed all of us behind, it would have killed all of you in the truck!" he says, frantically lighting a third cigarette.

"Look, there's nothing I can do about any of that. I can't let my mind leave the mission. In the platoon, my role is air support and rifleman. If my mind wanders to things I can't control, I'm putting you guys in harm's way. If you're that worried or upset, I encourage you to utilize the commander's open door policy. He's a good man and leader."

Although I agreed with him and with what he said, I knew there was nothing that could be done. It was a world of alienation for speaking out against your brothers. Unless a crime has been committed, the veil of silence is understood, and any problems internal to the platoon are handled "like men," behind the tents. This individual had surrounded himself with other sergeants who did not embrace any ounce of the NCO creed—to take care of your soldiers, placing them before yourself.

The following day, we loaded up for another mission at 0500 hours. I forgot to grab an extra fragmentation grenade for the mission, so I only had one frag and one red smoke for medevac. Walking to one of the other trucks to ask my buddy that I had talked to the night before for an extra grenade, I sling my rifle behind my thigh pistol holster, opening the back door where my buddy is sitting. His sergeant was obliviously climbing in when I saw it—my buddy, with the most hateful and disgusted look on his face.

Standing two feet below where he sat, looking up, my right hand still on the door handle, I do a double take to see what is going on. With his rifle under his arms, he has a frag grenade in his right hand, on the body of the grenade holding the spoon. In his left hand, his finger is through the hole holding the pin, which is still safely located inside the spoon handle. Realizing what is about to happen, I decide not to stop it. I understand his hateful disdain. I recognize that, in his mind—the mind of a respectable, selfless individual—he wanted to make a stand to do what he felt was right. He felt an act of self-sacrifice would save the rest of the platoon from a "suicidal egomaniac." Without guilt, I nonchalantly close the door with my right hand. Backing away as if I didn't see anything, walking ten feet away from the truck, I pull a can of tobacco out, take a dip, and wait for the boom. Hesitating for a moment, I climb into my truck. *Didn't think you would.*

This story is one that has happened countless times in warfare and was very frequent during the Vietnam War. In combat arms, the NCOs (Non-Commissioned Officers) and officers can make or break a group of warriors. It has been observed since the beginning of warfare and even talked about by Sun Tzu in *The Art of War*. A good leader leads by example. He knows when to make fun and when to poke fun at his men, as it is a gruff career that makes for gallows humor and banter. However, as a leader, it is essential to know when you are pushing too far and when you are subjecting your soldiers to unnecessary harm.

Having good leadership is crucial for younger warriors because they look up to, even idolize, their leaders. They perpetuate the mentality, ethos, and values of the leaders. Often, these soldiers are formed from their early service days to be a particular kind of leader. If they experience a leader who broke down morale, refused input, and failed to lead by example, they often become the same kind of leader. This eventually carries over to their civilian lives, and they emulate what they've seen.

The stories I've shared all took place over a four-to-six-week period. I believe it's important to see how fast de-sensitization, detachment, and dissociation happens. By examining this, you can better understand why we don't want to discuss what we've done with our loved ones, and why we often worry whether they would still love us if they knew the decisions and judgment calls we routinely made. You can see how an individual can switch from high-strung on the first mission to walking in the park, unafraid, and quite literally laughing in the face of death. Many veterans face much more extreme firefights than the few I've discussed. You can begin to see a glimpse of how some cases of four-hundred-plus days of combat can take a toll on even the most hardened person. You can start to see, by the way I closed the door on my brother, how cold and hardened we become in situations that would terrify or be unfathomable to the general population.

In First World countries, our lives are relatively safe, civil, and we don't have the same hardships and violence that many Third World countries do. We take young men, drop them into combat zones with a few hundred others, hand them explosives and high-powered weaponry, and instruct them to go find the bad guys without dying. Then, a year later, we give them a plane ticket to go back home, expecting them to remain unchanged. Don't get me wrong,

I believe many of these men have protective and genetic traits that help them survive and run toward danger in hostile situations. And our military does an exceptional job training and preparing our combat troops for combat. However, even with all the training in the world, there is no way to simulate the actual feelings of rockets, explosives, gunfire, or shooting another person.

During my training for Afghanistan, we were taught if one of our men becomes a casualty, unless you are the medic, you are to ignore his cries for help, quite literally stepping over him until enemy forces have been neutralized. It is taught that if you are the one injured in combat and your unit is taking active engagement from enemy fighters, you are to place your tourniquets and perform your own life-saving care if you want to survive.

When you add all of these factors together, and you take a young eighteen- to twenty-eight year-old man from combat and send him home to see his family several days later, why are we surprised that he doesn't feel like himself or is struggling to figure out which person he is? Why is it a surprise that he coped by dissociating and becoming a different person at war compared to who he was remembered as back home?

To survive, we are forced to make split-second decisions. We often perform levels of violence the average American could never comprehend, which are frequently contradictory to the values on which we were raised. After a while, we find ourselves routinely taking action and making decisions without concern. Decisions that were at one point a significant moral dilemma. After a while, we no longer feel we even resemble the person we used to be. It becomes an internal struggle between how we feel society expects us to feel and behave, versus the lack of remorse many of us feel for actions we view as righteous, even required to protect the ones we love most. Ironically, for those like me, we feel like a bad person for not feeling like a bad person.

"Learning to love your enemies does not bring you peace.
Learning to love the enemy within every
single one of us brings peace.
Do not confuse the two,
peace is not the absence of conflict from within,
it is the acceptance of the conflict within."

—STEELE J. KELLY

CHAPTER 4

FORGIVING
OURSELVES

WE HAD BEEN IN THE COUNTRY FOR NEARLY SEVEN
weeks. Supplies were dwindling, and the once FOB
(Forward Operating Base) was quickly becoming a COP
(Combat Outpost). Troops were pulling out of the region
in support of former President Obama's downsize strategy,
we had lost our dining facility, and the Taliban probes
were increasing.

"Kelly, wake up. It's your time for truck guard. I'll bring
you breakfast in a couple of hours, brother. What do you
want for chow?" I hear, waking up out of a deep sleep.

I had been awake roughly twenty-seven hours prior to
falling asleep. Although I had seven hours of sleep, I still
feel exhausted, as sleep is becoming increasingly more
difficult to find. Operation tempo was increasing, yet
manpower remained the same. It was not uncommon for

the platoons to rotate with guys going thirty-plus hours without sleep.

Rolling over, I check my watch: *0237, twenty-three minutes early.*

"Thanks, brother. You couldn't let me get fifteen more minutes of sleep, fucker?"

"Nah, rise and shine, muh fucka! You know what they say—the early bird gets the worm!" Cat Daddy says.

"Yeah, but the birds don't wake up until at least 0430!" I say, rolling out of bed.

"Tell you what, bring me eggs, bacon, and American whiskey by 0530, and we'll call it good. 'Cause you know I'm 'Murican. I like my freedom with a plate of bacon, whiskey, and lead!" I say in the most macho and arrogant voice I can muster.

"Well, I can do eggs and bacon, but you're gonna have to wait at least 330 more days for that whiskey. You know General Order One. No titties, porn, or booze."

"Yeah, yeah, I'll settle for OJ instead. Don't be late! I expect it twenty-three minutes early, as well!" I order, in an attempt to demand but laughing by the end.

Carrying my weapon out, I can't help but notice it actually feels like fall. The air is crisp and refreshing, yet not so cold you need a jacket. The air smells fresh with a hint of campfire, reminding me of growing up in Oregon during the fall. The day seemed like any other day. I had no idea this would be the day that would change so many aspects of myself and the way I treated suspected Taliban—that it would be the day that would harden my empathetic side.

I had finished my morning truck guard. This was the twenty-four-hour QRF shift my platoon was on. We rotated every twenty-four hours on QRF with first platoon, resulting in twenty-four on, twenty-four off shifts. However, off-days usually resulted in several missions in the morning, afternoon, and evening. By this point, our dining facility was nearly gone, and we had started rationing MREs (Meal-Ready-to-Eat) for the approximated next sixty days. When a platoon is on QRF, they are essentially the "911" for the other platoon on mission. It required one man monitoring the radios in the TOC (Tactical Operations Center) who would alert and wake up the sleeping platoon, and another man sitting next to the armed and ready-to-roll trucks. If troops outside the wire came in contact, the man on truck guard was to start the vehicles and get his gear on as the platoon ran from the tents to the trucks. We were expected to roll out of the gates within five to ten minutes of an alert.

Sitting on my TOC rotation, flipping through the most recent edition of *Sports Illustrated*, reading about the sexual exploits and controversies of several athletes, chaos suddenly roars. The radio explodes, "Saber Main, this is Butcher 1-1; troops in contact!" I can hear the sound of automatic weapons, grenade launchers, and small arms firing in the background.

What in the fuck? They were only doing Snap Tactical

Control Points looking for drugs, guns, and explosives. I didn't hear a boom. No fucking way they engaged Taliban within five kilometers of the base.

"Saber main, I say again, troops in contact, one American possibly KIA, requesting immediate medevac and QRF, OVER!"

Without any order or command, I dart out of the TOC. Sprinting past the current truck guard, I yell as loud as I can, "START THE TRUCKS—WE GOTTA GO NOW!"

Running out of the motor pool, I sprint another 200 yards, busting through the tents.

"QRF! QRF! FIRST PLATOON IS IN CONTACT, ONE AMERICAN POSSIBLE KIA!" By the time I finish the sentence, I'm already halfway to the tent next door.

"QRF, LET'S GO! TROOPS IN CONTACT, ONE POSSIBLE KIA!"

I didn't have to stop to check if they were grabbing their gear. Without hesitation, soldiers storm out of their beds, hot on my heels. We are sprinting for the trucks, knowing our brothers' lives depend on us.

Throwing my plate carrier on, snapping the buckles together around my rib cage, I pull my Kevlar helmet on, fastening it under my neck while throwing my headset on, plugging each cord into both of my radios. Looking down, I turn each portable radio to the right channels, one for our platoon, and one for my air support requests. Sliding across the seat, I turn the truck radio up onto our troop/company radio frequency.

Hearing first platoon, "Dust Off, this is Saber Main, nine-line medevac request, over."

"Saber Main—send it."

Interrupting the request, my thoughts start racing. *Who is it? I hope it isn't Griffin. I hope it isn't Pratt. I hope it isn't one of my brothers in first platoon. Fuck!*

Reaching into the comforting left-hand shoulder pocket under my ISAF patch, I pull out a fresh can of chew. Rubbing my fingers together, I get the leaf residue off my fingers, snap the lid closed, and place the can back in my left shoulder pocket.

"Vikings, this is 2-1. We're going to do a handoff with first platoon. We will meet them at the ECP (Entry Control Point) taking them to the helipad. After, we will do a handoff of the injured and then go back to the village for a BDA (Battle Damage Assessment) and look for further Taliban forces to apprehend or engage. Focus, gentlemen. Push this out of your head. We're all depending on each other out there. It's Michaels. We don't know the status yet," my truck commander says over the radio.

Seeing first platoon roll through the gates, we take off in front toward the airstrip, passing each other to close off intersections, attempting to get our fellow brother to the helicopter as fast as possible. Looking out my window, I see a Blackhawk helicopter with a red cross painted on the side coming in fast overhead, decreasing altitude sideways. Still almost thirty feet in the air, the doors whip open as they prepare to land on the airstrip.

Watching from a distance, they pull my close friend—
my brother—out of the armored M-ATV strapped to a
backboard, sliding him onto the helicopter. I close my
eyes, spitting brown chew spit into my spitter, and I begin
to say a quick prayer. *Hey, Big J. I know it's been a while.
Please, please don't let him die. He's one of the best men I
know. And please, let us find the motherfucker who did this,
so we can send him to you for his mother fucking judgment.
A-fucking-men.*

Opening my eyes, I look out the window as the wire
and gates disappear from sight. Looking down at my M4,
I pull the bolt back, racking a bullet into the chamber. Sliding my finger to the safety, I give an extra push to ensure
it is on safe. Sliding my hand up the receiver until I feel
the metallic flap, I push the dust cover on the port ejector
closed and give the magazine an extra tap.

"Vikings, we'll stage the trucks near Checkpoint Bravo
2-3. We will begin from the south where first platoon
engaged Taliban forces. We will follow any blood trail
and kick in doors as necessary. Due to the hostile actions,
before crossing open areas, alleys, or doorways, we will
have guys on each side providing long cover. We will clear
as we go," the platoon leader says.

One after the other, all platoon truck commanders
acknowledge the transmission. As we get closer to the
infiltration point, the platoon leader keys up on the radio
one last time. "Gentlemen, remember the rules of engagement. They're strict. Don't fire unless you are fired on

first or you see a weapon in their hand aiming at one of us. Don't let your emotions land any of you in Leavenworth."

Jumping out of the truck, I'm ready for anything. Falling into the wedge formation, we find the truck. It's riddled with hundreds of bullet holes and shrapnel. Opening the door, searching for intelligence, we look down at the center console and steering column. There are several pints of blood caked into dust and mud pooled near the pedals. Arterial blood spray spatters in straight lines across the driver side door and the steering wheel. Observing the angle of blood spray on the door and location of the entrance hole of the bullet, it is apparent the Taliban member received a 7.62 bullet through the femoral artery. Leading away from the truck door is a trail of shoes, clothing, and roughly three pints of blood.

"Well, his body is fucking gone! The other Taliban came and scooped him up right before we got here! There's no fucking way he's alive. There is way too much blood loss and no hospitals!" I hear the alpha section squad leader say.

Walking past, I look down at the ground at the amount of blood pooled in the dirt. *Yup, the fucker's in hell. That's a lot of blood.*

Following the blood trail, we walk into an alley. Alpha squad leader gives the hand signal for a staggered column (one line on each side of the alley, leaving a gap staggered between each man). Approaching the first alleyway, the first men on both the left and right side point their weapons down the left and the right alleyways as each of us run across.

That night, we stayed out for hours. Unfortunately, enough time had passed that the blood trail dried up, and we were recalled to base.

A couple of days later, we were called out on another QRF mission. Tensions were still high; frustration, exhaustion, and sleep deprivation had begun to take their toll. First platoon had caught a military-aged man, digging an IED (Improvised Explosive Device) and placing a pressure plate and charge. They, quite literally, caught him red-handed. Because we were headed to a village south of them and they were due back to base to begin their QRF shift, we met up with them, took their detainee into custody, and relieved them of their responsibility.

Our platoon had waited around for several hours, bored, annoyed, and ready to return to base for some much needed sleep. In the distance of the dimly lit desert, a trail of dust, Humvees, and machine guns bounce on the horizon, gradually closing the distance. Upon arriving, the ANA (Afghan National Army) commander, who appears barely old enough to shave, exits his Humvee and walks toward us with our interpreter and the detained Taliban member.

Through the help of our interpreter, we show the ANA commander the implanted explosive, the tools used, and where he was discovered. He walks back to the man, snatches up his cell phone and starts looking through it.

Scrolling through the media gallery, the commander stops in his tracks. Hitting play, he watches as several Taliban sympathizer videos show Afghan National forces being beheaded, United States military convoys getting blown up, and suicide vest bombing attacks in crowded markets. Visibly pissed off, he asks the detainee a few questions in Pashto and concludes the conversation. Seeming to acknowledge his fate, the man looks solemn. I turn around, following the guys back to my truck. Before rounding the corner, I spin around standing next to Casey, ready to tell him one quick "fuck one, kill one, marry one" joke.

Taking one last look at the detainee now in control by ANA forces, I wonder what will happen to him. I see him bent over at the waist at the tailgate of their Humvee with his hands restrained behind his back in zip ties. With one last draw off his cigarette, the ANA commander throws it to the ground, signals us to leave, and we drive off.

The following morning, it was discovered that a man matching the description of the detainee was found on the side of the main highway, dead. That afternoon, we got to the ANA checkpoint, and I asked one of the soldiers, "Hey man, where's the Taliban prisoner?"

"What Taliban prisoner?"

"The one I handed to you yesterday."

"I don't know what you're talking about. I don't remember."

* * *

A FEW DAYS LATER, WE RETURN TO THE VILLAGE where we had followed the blood trail in to look for Taliban activity. It's approximately 0500 in the morning, and we're still fueled by hate, Red Bull, and nicotine. Before entering the village, we observe a sixteen- or seventeen-year-old kid, military age, acting extremely nervous and looking around for avenues that could make for a quick escape. Our platoon quickly closes the distance and pulls him aside to talk.

Knowing I am out of view from aerial surveillance, I respectfully request, "Sir, why don't you walk out of earshot and walk up to first squad? I want to try a new tactic."

The men of each squad pull security in separate directions. I know that nobody besides Ahmed (our interpreter), and I are looking at our suspected terrorist. I begin aggressive tactical interview questions.

"Ahmed, I want you to tell him that nobody is watching us, that I don't give a fuck about what happens to him, and that nobody else here does either."

Continuing, "Ahmed, you fucking tell him that I know he's either Taliban or knows where they are. My friend was hurt by them, and I bet the ANA would love to have a chat with him."

"Kelly, he says he doesn't know," Ahmed says, in a convincing tone.

"Ahmed, what do you think? Do you think he knows where they are or has information? Is he fucking with us right now, or is he honest?"

"I don't know. It could go either way. I can't tell."

"Look, Ahmed, I'm gonna call his bluff. See if he'll talk. Go with it."

Grabbing the kid, I spin him around, slamming him up against the wall and simultaneously kick his legs apart with my boot. Pulling his arms behind his back, I press the right side of his face against the rocky wall.

"Ahmed, I want you to tell him that I'm all done fucking around. I'm tired of these fuckers shooting at us every goddamn day, and we're all pretty fucking sick and tired of riding around waiting to get blown up. If he gives me some information, I'll let him go. If he wants to continue to lie, then I have no fucking problem giving him to the ANA. We all know what the ANA does to his kind."

"Kelly, he's a kid. I don't know if he's lying," Ahmed says with a clearly empathetic tone.

"Ahmed, you fucking tell him what I just said. In the exact goddamn fucking tone I just said. Do you fucking understand me?" I say as if I'm giving an order to a subordinate, rather than an Afghani civilian who is risking his life to help us.

In Pashto, I can hear the same tone I had. I know that Ahmed is interpreting accurately because the kid begins to shake. He literally starts to tremble uncontrollably with fear of what the ANA might do to him. He knows his fate may very well be decided in the next several minutes— what he doesn't know is that I'm bluffing.

"Ahmed, tell him he's a fucking liar, that I'm calling

the ANA, and we're dropping him off at checkpoint Bravo where they can handle him. He's not my fucking problem, and I'm out of patience."

By this point, Ahmed can't figure out if I'm still bluffing or if I'm serious. However, he complies without hesitation, trusting my judgment. After the second word, I take my right hand that was pressing his face against the rough edges of rock on the wall and reach to the back lacing of my plate carrier. Pulling out a thick plastic zip tie, I zip his hands tightly together. Ahmed stops mid-sentence.

"Ahmed, what did I fucking tell you? Tell. Him. Exactly. As. I. Fucking. Told. You." I say, enunciating every word.

With hesitation, Ahmed continues, and this time tells the kid precisely as I instructed. I know he has followed directions because the kid begins shaking harder than a leaf on a maple tree in a fall windstorm. He is petrified and knows what the ANA will do to him if he is a suspected Taliban.

"Ahmed, tell him I'm feeling extra generous this fine morning. Tell him I'll give him one last chance before we load him up. Is there anything he wants to tell me?" I command.

I can hear a brief exchange, and Ahmed looks up to me, "Kelly, he says he doesn't know anything."

"Do you believe him, Ahmed?"

"Yeah, I do," he responds with confidence.

"Alright, brother," I say, now pulling my switchblade out of my pocket.

Pushing the button, the blade snaps swiftly out of the handle. Placing the sharp edge between his restrained hands, I push down on the plastic, severing the restraints, and put my knife back into my pocket. Using the man's face on the wall as leverage, I push off, taking a step back into a fighting stance. I did this so that if he decided to come at me, I could quickly grab the fixed blade knife off my belt, incapacitating the potential combatant.

"Ahmed, tell him to get the fuck out of here. Taliban or not, if he continues acting like Taliban, he's going to get swooped up like Taliban."

* * *

THIS IS ONE OF THE STORIES I AM NOT VERY PROUD of. The reason I am not proud of it isn't because of interrogation tactics, bluffing, or even being physically aggressive with him. I'm not proud of it because it was a moment that I realized what I was capable of—when I lost much of the humanity I once had. I had hardened to the point where I didn't care if he was guilty or not, dead or alive. I felt he was getting in the way of me doing my job, and he needed to get out of it, or I would make him by any means necessary. I knew I had just crossed a line from which there is no coming back. Once you realize what you are capable of, it contributes to your fear of what your loved ones would think about you if they knew.

It had only been eight weeks into deployment, and

most signs of the person I had been in America were gone. De-characterization was rapidly growing.

In time, I realized that by treating every person as if they were Taliban before it's confirmed or there's concrete evidence to suspect them of being so, after enough encounters of being treated that way, eventually they may become one. It would be the same as accusing your significant other over and over of being a cheater or cheating. Not in every case, but in some cases, they become one, figuring, *Well, if I'm presumed to be one, I might as well be one. At least they'll have a reason to call me one.*

Several sociologists, psychologists, and researchers have researched this phenomenon. By demonizing people and judging people based on the actions of a few, we begin to categorize them. Eventually, this leads to racism, bigotry, and hate groups. Nothing good ever comes out of it, and all that eventually happens is you see the worst in every group. You become a hateful or negative person, pushing positive people, positive experience, and a positive life out of reach.

"Darkness cannot drive out darkness;
only light can do that.
Hate cannot drive out hate;
only love can do that."

—MARTIN LUTHER KING, JR.

CHAPTER 5

FINDING HUMANITY

IT HAD BEEN A LONG DAY. OUR FIREFIGHT HAD
lasted over six hours, and I was attempting to daydream
a beach, waves, a light summer breeze, a beautiful woman,
and a beer in my hand. *Hell, I'd take a Keystone Light, a
plastic swimming pool, and a lawn chair about now.*

"Casey, how good does the beach, beer, and bikinis
sound about now?" I say between bites of food.

"Dude, I'd give my left nut—maybe not my right! That
one I need. You know, for kids and shit." He laughs.

Then two Special Forces soldiers we had talked to off
and on throughout the deployment walk over to our table,
interrupting the daydream. I had talked to them about my
desire and training plan to go to selection, asked them for
advice about how to prepare physically for it, and what
they recommended to prepare mentally.

"You guys mind if we sit here?" one of the bearded
men asks.

"Nah, pop a squat, man. You're both welcome amongst us salty heathens," I say sarcastically, knowing they're much more experienced.

After a couple bites of food and awkward silence, one of the bearded men breaks the ice.

"So, we saw you guys got in a pretty good TIC (Troops in Contact/firefight) today. You guys have been doing some good work."

"Yeah, man, it's been that way lately. It might be nice to occasionally get out of the truck and take a piss before they start shooting though!" Casey laughs at his joke.

We chat back and forth until the conversation drifts to the "Us vs. Them" topic.

"Kelly, you're the one who wants to go to Special Forces, right?" the other bearded man asks, after glancing at my name tape.

"Yup! I'm re-enlisting in a few months, hoping to go to selection when we get back home!"

"After a while and enough engagements with the enemy, you begin to get a little salty and seasoned. You have to keep a couple things in mind when pursuing this or any career that has violence as part of the job. Do you know what makes us different than our enemy, no matter who they are or what country they come from?"

"Hmmm, I can think of lots of things. But, now I'm curious."

"It's our humanity and respect toward our enemies. No matter how long or how many times you engage the enemy in combat, you must always keep in mind that every single one of those we kill is loved by someone, somewhere. No matter how awful, evil, or monstrous of a human being they are, by killing that person for the greater good, you are causing somebody pain by the loss of their father, son, brother, and so on. If you forget this fact, disregarding them as human beings with a different ideology, then you become no better than our enemy."

This philosophy has stuck with me. I have mulled this idea a million times over in my head. The way we handle our enemies over long periods of time may not be the most efficient manner. Through our recent history, we've had to deal with many of our conflicts several times. Several examples would be Desert Storm, Iraqi freedom, and now Operation Inherent Resolve. We seem to perpetuate this cycle of conflict by roping more and more generations into the burdens of war. Our politicians are intimately intertwined in our military lives, conflicts, frequent changes of ROE (Rules of Engagement), and they have indirectly contributed to the loss of many American military lives and injuries. As a soldier who deployed, it often felt that cops in America have had more leeway in the use of lethal force than we did.

There are several cases of members of our armed forces sentenced to prison for decisions that are potentially the right call in the heat of the moment and life-or-death situations. Although tragic for both sides, the actions are Monday-morning-quarterbacked by high ranking officials or politicians in an air-conditioned office in the safety of America. The men who execute on these split-second decisions may spend a life in prison for what could have possibly saved an entire squad or platoon of service members. One case, in particular, US vs. Lorance (2012) was highly controversial, with multiple sides giving drastically different versions of the story.

A young lieutenant whose platoon had come under fire several times over the week, resulting in the death of four American soldiers and wounding others, gave a command to fire several rounds at an oncoming motorcycle that had disobeyed ANA and US troop commands. Both men, who ended up being civilians despite their disobedience of the ANA and US orders, were killed. After a lengthy trial, Lieutenant Lorance was found guilty of murder and was sentenced to twenty years in prison. The case is currently under appeal, and it's a high-stress and complicated case for all sides involved.

Since the beginning of time, civilians have been caught in the crossfire of war. I do not know all of the facts other than what is published on the White House petition website, the *Army Times*, and other media outlets. However, understanding the flip side of the coin, had the men turned out to be wired with explosives upon BDA, it would have been considered a "good call." If the men had continued to ignore commands to stop and had been wired with explosives, they could have detonated their explosive vests amongst the platoon formation, killing several soldiers and wounding others. In that case, Lorance would have had to live with the decision of not acting and would have been held responsible for not protecting his men. Wives would have been widowed, sons would have been gone, and it would have become another sad story on CNN that the American people barely acknowledge.

Decisions for troops on the ground in combat are arduous at times. It becomes even more difficult when several comrades are killed days prior in neighboring villages, and the reality of your own mortality sets in. When the ROE becomes so strict and frequently changing, combat troops often become afraid to do their job. They become reluctant to pull the trigger, even in extremely violent encounters. Why? They are fearful of being placed on trial for the use of lethal force and sentenced to life in prison by individuals who have the luxury of reviewing the engagement with their morning coffee from the comfort of their desk.

War should not be a decision made lightly. The decision to go to war or conflict should be a very burdensome one, weighing the loss of life on both sides. However, sometimes violence must be visited against the oppressor or evil regime, as seen with Hitler, Al Qaeda, the Taliban, and ISIS. In which case—when violence is the only viable option—it is often argued that when you face an enemy after deciding to wage war, you must begin by being the most violent, ruthless, and feared individuals on the battlefield. Although morbid and contrary to popular belief, by starting out this way, in the long run, fewer civilian lives, enemy lives, and ally lives are lost. By establishing superior firepower and the willingness to do the unspeakable, the cat-and-mouse game with the enemy as seen so frequently in Iraq, Afghanistan, Syria, Somalia, and other places, ceases to exist. After we gain control of the wicked, we can shift our focus to winning the war.

Following this idea about ruthlessness, Sun Tzu understood that to win the war and not strictly one battle, one must fully understand their enemy—their motives, ideology, tactics, and beliefs. You must truly understand them. He explains ruthlessness and goes on to say, "When you surround an army, leave an outlet free. Do not press a desperate foe too hard. To subdue an enemy without fighting is the greatest of skills."

I believe we are currently handling the post-invasion era of the conflict poorly, unsustainably, and in a way that will only continue conflict in the region for generations to come. I still believe, after winning the battle, that violence is necessary to free the locals from the suffering of oppression during this peace-keeping process. However, we are building gas stations and handing out money, supplies, etc., to people who often don't even have their most basic needs met. Many of them are uneducated, illiterate, and simply want to live as farmers or shopkeepers. They couldn't care less about a gas station or some fancy building that will most likely get blown up by a suicide bomber.

Unfortunately, many of them are forced to pick sides

because they know that America is going to leave just as the Soviets, Alexander the Great, and Genghis Kahn did— leaving them vulnerable to retribution if they side with us. They know that when their protective older brother leaves, the bully from down the road (the Taliban) will come back, and there will be nobody left protecting them. Often, this is why they side with the Taliban and refuse to pass information on to NATO forces.

On one mission in particular, we were on a foot patrol in a village that had one of the largest marijuana grows I have ever seen. It was probably close to one square mile. Next to this marijuana field were freshly plowed and tended fields of opium. Often, the Taliban, Al Qaeda, and other terror groups are funded by these cash crops. This is why the "fighting seasons" correspond to the multi-harvests throughout the year. During these fighting seasons, the bombs are more prominent, the explosions are bigger, and the amount of firepower drastically increases. Most often, if you have a village in your Area of Operation (AO) that has these crops, it's one to keep your eye on to watch for terrorist activity.

When we arrived at the village, there were large ditches dug at every entrance and exit of the town. The trenches were nearly six feet deep and four-to-five feet in width. While patrolling, we were approached by a local villager who was a farmer, and his wife. His wife's arm had been mutilated and cut off from the mid-humerus bone above the elbow. Through our interpreter, we asked why the ditches we crossed were placed there, as we had never seen the likes of them before. The man seemed happy to talk to us and provide information. This was apparent in his mannerisms, facial expressions, and the way he engaged in open dialogue. The man told us that the ditches were dug in an attempt to deter the Taliban from driving into the village at night. By placing the trenches, it made the Taliban go in at night by foot, giving the villagers more time to prepare for their arrival.

The man and our interpreter, Ahmed, pulled his wife's sleeve back, showing the area of amputation. He explained how the Taliban was unhappy with the crop growth, telling him and other villages to work harder. To incentivize him and the other villagers, they cut his wife's arm off with a machete.

Immediately, I could see how the drug trade and the war on drugs in America affects people and their families on the global level. Not only does it fund weaponry and explosives against our troops and terrorist attacks around the world, but it escalates the level of brutality that is taken on the villages and farmers who are essentially slaves to the trade. After seeing the global effect, it created the feeling of a personal attack toward me if friends, family, or acquaintances back home bought drugs and partook in the behavior. It felt like a personal attack because the money used to purchase drugs and use drugs illegally in America climbs up the dealer pyramid and eventually lines the pockets of evil, oppressive, and terror organizations. Those were the same organizations that actively harmed and killed my brothers, local villagers, and other innocent victims.

Having friends in agriculture, I have a basic understanding of crop rotation. I understand that you cannot plant the same crop year after year without a break or rotation and expect a high yield. We asked the man if they plant the crop in the same place every year or if they planted other things. The man responded, "No, we plant the same thing. That's what they want."

While over there, I had several conversations about day-to-day life with our interpreter. He was very well educated, had a college degree, and was looking forward to getting married after our deployment ended. He explained to me how many of the villagers in rural regions of Afghanistan cannot read or write. Most cannot afford to send their kids to school because they need them in the shops and fields, and to help the family. He explained that many go to religious services and are only told by one person what the Quran says, what it means, and the interpretation—that many of their ideals weren't even within the Muslim religion. However, due to their illiteracy, they had no understanding that they were being indoctrinated by corrupt leaders with specific agendas. In fact, many of the religious leaders are illiterate themselves, and the ideology behind terrorism is passed down from generation to generation.

I sat on the information for quite a long time, thinking over our conversations and searching for a possible solution. One day after church, I realized the connection and what I was trying to figure out. I realized how many of the villagers' houses I had been in and searched, and yet I had never even seen a copy of the Quran. *They're so radical and extreme, but most didn't even have a copy of their most sacred texts about their religion? It seems a little odd.* I had the epiphany that the solution to dismantle an evil ideology was there the entire time, right in front of us.

In the Old Testament of the Bible, there is a section discussing crop rotation (Exodus 23: 10). Because Islam and Christianity are both Abrahamic religions, I was sure that the Quran shared a few aspects of the Old Testament. After doing research, I learned that, just like in the Bible, there are several sections in the Quran discussing crop rotation. One passage, in particular, (Surah Yusof: verses 43–49) explains a seven-year crop rotation.

It dawned on me that if these individuals had access to the Quran, if they understood it, they would know the importance of the rotation of livestock and crops. This is one simplistic example of the many other contradictions amongst these radical groups. Due to their lack of education and literacy, they are unable to read and interpret these things for themselves.

This manipulation of the populous isn't unique to Islam. There are countless religions that have used personal hateful ideology to further political agendas. The nature of radical and extremist Islamic oppression, indoctrination, and manipulation is underground and guerrilla warfare style. They take children from villages to training camps, indoctrinating and manipulating them using the Quran and other Islamic texts as tools of their agenda. There are many videos showing children, young men, and others who have been transformed into "holy fighter" terrorists, yet they can only recite select verses for "the jihad" and have no understanding of the meaning and context to which the verse was written, or the implications of what they have regurgitated.

There is no difference between them and radicals of other religions who selectively take verses out of any other religious text, manipulating them to whichever interpretation they choose, to further their own agendas. Self-proclaimed Christian movements, such as the Orthodox Christian-influenced Iron Guard in Romania and the distorted Protestant beliefs held by the Ku Klux Klan in the United States, equally use such distorted interpretations of scripture to rationalize violent lynching, arson, murder, and rapes on religious teachings. No matter what group, ideology, religion, or belief, there will always be a percentage of people who manifest their own sick and twisted ideals, using indoctrination to accomplish an agenda.

Religion, politics, and personal ideologies are not one-size-fits-all. Any attempt to make it that way can, and will, lead to hate, violence, corruption, condemnation, and the oppression of others. This can be seen in the Inquisition, Holocaust, the communist movement, and even during our current political movements. Until we understand that grouping people leads to hate, we will continue to experience violence, hate, and division. Instead of being kind to others, regardless of their religion, color, sex, or orientation because it's the morally right thing to do, we will continue to play the "us vs. them" game, which is contradictory to the cause, whatever that may be. It creates a larger wedge and even more unwillingness to support or change.

Social media in America, especially regarding politics, has produced a society where everybody is entitled to speak their opinion, mind, and beliefs regardless of whether the information is factual or not. It has led to a culture where having an opposing opinion or viewpoint is immediately categorized as evil, bigoted, racist, or simply wrong. We have learned to speak up, but we have not learned to listen. We pass judgment before a thought is completed, closing our minds to growth, change, and the ability to better understand our own values and beliefs through understanding others'. By passing judgment so quickly, we miss out on the opportunity to realize we have more in common with those who have different political beliefs than we ever thought possible.

I believe the only way to end the wars in the Middle East—to "win" the war on terror—is to understand that we are at a different point in our historical timeline than they are. We need roads, laws, order, infrastructure, gas stations, parks, etc. However, for them, they often don't have running water or even electricity, and their homes are constructed from mud. Once we acknowledge that they have not developed their country to the same level as we have, we can look at other strategies. We must understand their needs and what is causing the problem.

One of the first causes for extremist ideology is the lack of literacy and education. Instead of building useless buildings, we should start by helping fund and set up schools. The schools should be taught by educated natives of that country who can teach the future generations core curriculum similar to other First World countries—reading, writing, mathematics, the history of their country and the world (Mujahideen and the Taliban included, including their indoctrination tactics), and implementing a kindergarten through twelfth grade schooling system.

Eventually, through education and literacy, combined with combat operations keeping the enemy away, they will understand how fundamentally corrupt these terror groups are. They will have the knowledge needed to reject indoctrination, making educated decisions to choose their own religious, political, or spiritual beliefs. The civilizations that have fallen to uprisings have always feared knowledge and education. They fear this because education sparks ideas and ideas spark revolution.

The second problem is their knowledge of agriculture and lack of infrastructure. By teaching agriculture basics, their crops will yield higher harvests, and they will have higher efficiency and amenities. This will result in lower amounts of time spent working, which will free up time to focus on their future aspirations in academia, innovation, and the pursuit of happiness.

Currently, with archaic agriculture methods, the children of many farmers aren't allowed to attend school. There are several reasons, including financial ones, but one of the major reasons is because the children are needed to help on the farms. If the farmers send their children to school instead of having them work in the farm, they may not produce enough crops to feed their family for the year.

If we were able to cooperatively assist these farmers in bringing First World agriculture technology to their ancient methods, or even teaching the basics of rotation, irrigation, and fertilization, it would have unmeasurable results that could change the face of the country.

This type of efficiency and innovation will permit less labor and larger amounts of free time, allowing them to send their kids to get education and spend time learning about the religion and world they truly know or understand little about.

Ideally, the combination of innovation and education will spark an intellectual revolution among the youth that will quash oppressive regimes and will bring forth the basic human rights that many of us take for granted.

By bringing First World amenities and education to the most rural regions of a Third World country, such as modern housing with heat, air-conditioning, electricity, and internet; it will raise their standard and comfort of living. It's similar to a teenager in America who gets their cell phone taken away. Once they appreciate the standard of living, they won't want to return to their prehistoric ways.

Although seemingly complicated, this strategy could be relatively simple and much more cost-effective than the money we've thrown into the war from 2001 to the present day. This could be accomplished by protecting a 500-square-mile area with fencing, ground sensors, drones, and combat troops providing security, which is similar to the way we protect the Edwards Air Force Base in Nevada, commonly referred to by civilians as "Area 51." The locals would not be imprisoned and could leave and return, provided they undergo entry and exit screening security protocols. We would build an agriculture college with modern farm technology, livestock, and equipment, while providing K–12 education for the children. During this cooperative movement with different crops and livestock, the amount of food required to sustain the community would remain in the community, while the excess would be sold to other rural villages in the country. The money would be spent building the infrastructure and housing, and for further expansion of these communities.

In a sense, the industrial revolution could be brought to them. Thus, it could bring enlightenment, a thirst for knowledge, and growth to the rural villages that are essentially stuck in the stone-age. As the saying goes, "Give a man a fish, and he'll eat for the day. Teach a man to fish, and he'll eat for a lifetime."

However, there isn't a short campaign to win this game. It will require us to occupy the country for a generation of children to reach the age of power, be elected into office, and become those who make policy or economic decisions. It will require us to take the fight to the extremists so they can't take the fight and indoctrination to those we're trying to educate. It will require us protecting the herd of impressionable minds, similar to the way we protect the impressionable minds and herd of our homeland.

At this point, I imagine many of you are calling me all sorts of names, calling me naive, overly optimistic, and many other colorful things. However, outside of benefits, education, or other answers, when you ask a service member or veteran why they volunteered to join, volunteered to go to war, or chose combat arms, you will often hear, "I did it so my kids (or future kids) won't have to. I did it so my loved ones and people back home don't have to. I did it because I love my country and I don't want bad things to happen to the people in it." Or, "All it takes for evil to triumph is for good men to do nothing."

These are the reasons I chose to do it, and the reasons why I would go back tomorrow without a second of hesitation. Until the day I die, I would happily give my life in the worst ways imaginable to keep terrorism, radicalism, oppression, and evil away from the people and country

I love most. I, like many veterans, am willing to do this, so the rest of our country will never have to experience the horrors of war, famine, and violence for themselves. Unfortunately, terror attacks continue to happen, troops continue to be deployed, rotating through combat, and we send troops back to the same countries we were in during the '80s and '90s. We continue to employ the same strategy over and over, expecting a different result. We continue to throw money, resources, and lives at the problem expecting, "This time will be different!" Ironically, one definition of insanity is doing the same thing repeatedly, expecting a different outcome. As Albert Einstein said, "We can't solve problems by using the same kind of thinking we used when we created them."

At the rate we're going, if changes aren't made, our kids are going to end up in the same war zones we were in. They will end up zipping their friends into body bags, placing tourniquets on the blown-off limbs of their buddies, absorbing the same horrors of war and issues we did. The camouflage and uniform may be different then, but the fight will be the same. Our sacrifice, time spent away from home, reoccurring nightmares, frustrations, divorce, and broken hearts will have all been for nothing.

Although I openly support the Global War on Terrorism (GWOT), I believe there is a time and place for violence. Even though I would not hesitate to pull my boots and uniform out of the closet to go back, I want something different for our future as a country.

Similar to General George Patton, I believe violence must be had to win a battle in being the most ruthless, feared, and yet still honorable and respected warriors on the battlefield. I am not explaining ruthlessness in the sense of dishonorable acts as defined in *The Law Relating to War Crimes and Crimes Against Humanity* and the *Geneva Conventions*. I am explaining ruthlessness as the willingness to seek and destroy our enemies without a cat-and-mouse game.

To win the war, I believe in looking for and practicing kindness, compassion, and understanding, and searching for common ground with the locals who are non-extremists or of the enemy regime. I believe in acting as a warrior in a garden, winning hearts and minds for the cause. I believe in winning the war because the civilians of our enemy respect, support, and believe in living without oppression and violence. Because they believe, we can help lead them to peace for a happier and more prosperous life.

As Sun Tzu said, we must learn to "subdue the enemy without fighting." I believe, to subdue the enemy in the case of the GWOT, that it must be a combination of violence to subdue and gain control of enemy strongholds, but we must use what they fear most against them. That is education and free thinking—for the locals to have the freedom to pursue happiness, even if that isn't Islam. When you're watching ISIS, the Taliban, AL Qaeda, the Muslim brotherhood—or many of the other terror organizations beheading locals, burning pilots alive in cages, beheading journalists, detonating suicide bombs in crowded markets, and cutting your wife's arm off for not growing enough opium—it isn't hard to see how this fear breeds control and how the extremists maintain rule over the country. The only way to win this war after the battles have been fought is through psychological and educational campaigns that show the benefits of ousting extremism for personal freedom. This vastly outweighs oppression, violence, and tolerance of radical fighters.

Most importantly, I want something different for my future wife and kids. I don't want my family and future veterans to live a life filled with war and terrorism like my generation had to. I want to see money that's currently spent on aid to foreign countries who hate us and fund terror organizations against us, instead spent on research, innovation, and growth. I don't want my future son to make the same mistakes I did with Peyton and many others because they're wrestling demons earned in combat.

Similar to Confucius, who said, "Wisdom, compassion, and courage are the three universally recognized moral qualities of men," I believe no matter how much we disagree, dislike, or are at war with a nation, the majority of humans who are simply trying to carry out our daily lives are inherently good, even when we make mistakes. If we don't have anything in common with somebody, it means we aren't looking hard enough. And if we have nothing else in common, we will always have the same desires of providing for our families and raising our children to be better off than we are. We want to be happy, laughing and loving our kids and spouse. At the end of the day, we all want the same thing. I believe this is one of the fundamental ideas that has been forgotten in our society in general.

In an appearance on the *Joe Rogan Experience* podcast, Megan Phelps, former member of the Westboro Baptist Church, explained how and why she left the church. Through a several-hour conversation, she discussed her use of social media to spread the word of the church. During her use of social media, she regularly received hateful messages and comments. One day, she had an interaction with a Rabbi. At first, the Rabbi replied back somewhat hostile; however, he changed his tactics to questioning and eventually sent messages of love and kindness. Over an extended period of time, Mrs. Phelps explained that the messages began sticking, and she started questioning different ideologies and concepts, until one day, she decided to leave. None of the hate-fueled interactions pushed her to make a change or self-reflect. However, the interactions of love and kindness meeting the hate are what truly made the difference in the outcome of events and her future. Ultimately, it is love and kindness that transformed her destiny, not hate fighting hate.

In the words of the late, and great Dr. Martin Luther King Jr. in his famed speech, *I Have a Dream*:

"With this faith, we will be able to hew out of the mountain of despair a stone of hope. With this faith, we will be able to transform the jangling discords of our nation into a beautiful symphony of brotherhood. With this faith, we will be able to work together, to pray together, to struggle together, to go to jail together, to stand up for freedom together, knowing that we will be free one day...When we allow freedom to ring—when we let it ring from every city and every hamlet, from every state and every city, we will be able to speed up that day when all of God's children, black men and white men, Jews and Gentiles, Protestants and Catholics, will be able to join hands and sing in the words of the old Negro spiritual, 'Free at last, Free at last, Great God a-mighty, We are free at last.'"

"No man steps in the same river twice,
for it's not the same river,
and he's not the same man."

—HERACLITUS

CHAPTER 6

HOMECOMING

———

"FALL OUT!" COMMANDS OUR COMPANY COM-
mander, attempting to hide the excitement building in
his voice.

Suddenly, without control, loved ones and family
members charge the fairgrounds with little regard for
small infants they may squish. Excitement fills the air, and
many soldiers have mixed emotions. On one hand, we are
excited and chomping at the bit to see, embrace, and be
with our loved ones. On the other hand, we can't help but
wonder if they'll still like the person we've become. *Are
they going to see me as a monster or Hollywood's representa-
tion of returned warriors? Do they still love me? Am I going
to be the next divorce?* Before I realize it, I'm hugging my
parents, immediately forgetting all the worries.

On the three-hour car ride back to my hometown, I
can't help but feel the tension and awkwardness in the car.
It's as if my parents are trying to figure out if their little boy

is under the uniform of the man they hardly recognize. In return, I'm wondering what they think of me. *Do they think I am different? Are they scared of me? Is it possible for things to return to what they used to be?* I attempt to break the silence with small talk while trying as hard as I can to avoid the long awkward pauses. Finally, as small talk conversation runs out, we arrive at my favorite restaurant. You know the one—the one you go to for comfort food, for celebration, or for any other excuse you can find to go. The one you tell your buddies about at least once a week on deployment or training. The one you've waited fifteen months to gorge yourself on as if you hadn't eaten in weeks.

"Enchiladas! Nothing changed! I'm still getting what I always get without trying anything else!" I excitedly exclaim. "Oh, and a margarita! Patron! The biggest one you have!" I say, giddy laughter punctuating my order.

Scarfing my food quickly, as I've done for the past year and a quarter, I clean the plate of food and down the margarita in nearly one gulp. After dinner, we head home.

When I walk through the door of my parents' house, my Labrador and parents' Labrador seem to avoid me. My dog, who was a fifteen-week-old puppy when I left, is now a fully-grown, adult dog. Together, they sniff my uniform, still smelling the scents of Kabul. They scurry away, hiding behind the corner of the kitchen island. Uneasy and a little unsure of whether they remember me after being gone so long, I sit down on the floor, coaxing my parents' dog Jett over to me. After several minutes of coaxing, they finally remember me and drown me with slobber-laced affection.

Interrupting the exchange between me and the dogs, my mom says, "Honey, your dog Lucy laid by the front door on the entryway rug where you set your bags before you left. For about six months, she did this every single day, all day, from the time she woke up until it was time for bed—waiting for you to come home."

Feeling bad, I brush it off. By this time, it is almost nine o'clock in the evening. Both parents have to work in the morning, so they start making their way toward their room for bed.

"Honey, I'm so glad you're back and safe," my mom softly says, holding back tears with long-repressed fear in her voice.

"Me too, Mom. See you in the morning. I love you guys," I say, still in my completely detached and monotone voice.

Unzipping my uniform top, ripping the Velcro wrists apart and folding gently, I place it softly over the dinner table chair. I meander toward the living room, sitting down on the middle cushion of the leather couch. Through the windows across from the couch, gazing intently into the darkened, dimly-lit window by the reflection of a single lamp, I can see a man whose face now has lines from stress and sun. He has eyes that have seen so much of this world. The light in his eyes has faded from cheery optimism to a dark emptiness of a hardened man.

What now? I wonder, looking at the reflection of the

man I hardly recognize. *I never planned on making it out of Afghanistan alive. Worse, the 180 guys I've been with are now all in their own little worlds, and I'm on my own, all alone. Where do I go from here?* Interrupting my peace and contemplation, panic and anxiety fill me. *Oh shit, where are my nods (night vision)? Where's my rifle?* As fast as the panic began, it disappears. *Oh, that's right, you turned it in.* I exhale.

That night, both dogs jump onto my bed and lay down against my legs. As the fog of sleep falls over me, the final thought surfaces: *what next?* The question crosses my mind as I drift away into dreamland.

The next morning, I wake up, slowly stepping out of bed, fumbling towards the bedroom door and opening it clumsily. The sound of a herd of elephants fills the hallway as I make my way toward the kitchen. To my surprise, my dad is standing in the kitchen. Looking at the clock, I realize it's 9:00 a.m.

"What are you doing home? Don't you have to work?" I say, half wondering how to function without a cup of coffee.

"Figured I would take the day off to spend it with you. Go shower and get dressed. We're going for coffee and a trip around town," he says with an upbeat, ready-to-tackle-the-day kind of enthusiasm.

Standing in line at the local Starbucks, I can't help but watch all the people who seem to have no clue or understanding how lucky they are to live in America. A middle-aged soccer mom—whipping her Louis Vuitton purse across every person in line, pushing every customer out of the way as if she were the most important person in the room—reaches the front of the line.

"Are you fucking kidding me? This is the third time in a month. What don't you understand about sugar-free, no foam? There is at least an eighth of an inch of foam! Why am I not surprised that this Starbucks, in particular, chooses to ruin my day every time I come here?" she spews at the barista.

Looking at my dad in a disapproving way, I whisper, "This is what I'm talking about. She isn't wearing seventy pounds of armor, in 130-degree heat, or riding around waiting to hit a roadside bomb. The general population has no grasp of how lucky they are to simply have running water. The people there didn't even have that. If a coffee ruined her day, I would hate to see what real world trials and tribulations would do to her." I make sure to be just loud enough that I'm hoping she will hear.

* * *

OVER THE NEXT FEW DAYS, I CONTINUED TO SLOWLY reintegrate, forcing myself out and about leisurely. My parents, sister, and friends shuttled me around since I was still not ready to drive myself. I frequently caught myself scanning for dead dogs rigged with explosives, trash bags with artillery shells aimed toward the road, and fishing hooks dangling from fishing line on overpasses waiting to snag our gunners. When I was on the freeway riding in the car, I felt as if the cars near us were traveling around a NASCAR track. There was too much stimulation and too many thoughts racing around in my head to jump behind the wheel.

As fate would have it, the day I finally was ready to get behind the wheel, on the freeway, I experienced my first "life is different" lesson. With the windows down, listening to the radio, I had cautiously merged onto Interstate 5 northbound, double checking every mirror like a first-time driver. Merging behind an eighteen-wheeler, I looked down, turning my turn signal off. Glancing back up at the road, without warning, *BOOM!* The left rear tire of the truck blew, sending rubber into the air, over my truck, and around the road. Adrenaline pumped my veins with ice, and I was back *there*.

"Hey, pussies, I don't care how cold it is up there, my ass is back here! Turn the A/C back on. I can feel sweat dripping down my ass, and it's only 5:00 a.m.!" I attempt to say without laughing.

Feeling the 55,000-pound armored M-ATV crawl through the desert at five mph, I look out my six-inch window, scanning for signs of a roadside bomb, impending gunfire, or rocket-propelled grenades. Seeing nothing but open desert, I turn the volume up on the speaker. With crisp, knock-off speaker quality, "Theory of a Deadman" and Alice Cooper blast out to the song *Savages*.

Run, run, run for your life. Lock your door and stay inside. Save yourself, if you can, 'cause your god has a heavy hand. Red blood sky overhead. My dark side is coming so you better play dead. Deep down, we're all enraged—don't wake the beast inside its cage!"

"Hey, Jew Bear! So, no shit—there I was!" I say through my headset.

"Kelly, I don't want to hear about the one-time donkey show or the hookers you picked up at the bar," he sarcastically snaps back through the headset.

"Yeah, yeah! Look, that was one time in college and it doesn't count!" I joke back. "So, as I was saying—fuck one, kill one, marry one!"

"Hush, I like this part of the song!" B, our driver, shouts across the mic.

Pausing for a few seconds, I interrupt the song again.

"Hey, sir, Viper 3-2 should check in and give play time in about—"

With a blast, dust fills the air. Everything goes silent, including the music, and life decelerates into slow motion. I rock forward with the four-point harness stopping me and throwing me backward into the seat. The 55,000-pound truck that was just fifteen feet in front of me is gone. All I see is brown as the shockwave of the explosive ripples through our bodies. *Where is the truck? It was just there! How is it gone?*

"Butcher 2-2, are you okay?" truck three barks out.

Silence.

"Butcher 2-2."

Snatching on the transmission button, my truck commander grabs the mic, shouting, "HEY! RADIO SILENCE—THIRTY SECONDS—YOU KNOW THIS!"

Everything remains silent. Pins and needles of anxiety creep down my spine.

I can feel the adrenaline pumping through my veins with every second that passes. *They're dead, all of them. There's no fucking way they survived. That's the biggest explosion I've seen yet, and it happened in half a second. It was just fucking there.*

What seemed like three hours later, "Butcher 2-1, this is Butcher 2-2, we're okay."

Realizing it was just a truck tire, I snap back from Afghanistan. I take a few deep breaths, wiping the beads of sweat off my forehead. Realizing my shirt is now soaked in sweat, I laugh at myself. *Well, they were right. Things do change.*

* * *

THIS WAS MY FIRST OF MANY REALIZATIONS THAT life was different—that these experiences were permanent changes. There would be no going back to the pre-deployment Steele. The experiences had shaped me into a different person. I would never be able to go back to the person I was before. I would never be able to turn off reactions to events that may trigger an experience or a memory. It was also when I first realized that I might have Post-Traumatic Stress Disorder (PTSD).

There are a few things I would like to clear up that contribute to many of the post-critical incident stereotypes. As a result of misinformation, Hollywood dramatization, and the media, many people misunderstand PTSD. Often, the media makes PTSD appear as a monster under the surface—a beast that, if awoken, will violently destruct, harm, or kill anybody in sight. Like angering the Hulk. This may be the case for some who suffer from the disorder, but it isn't the majority. For the majority, PTSD is displayed in controlling or hostile/combative tones they often don't recognize. Frequently, it stems from fear—fear that the atrocities you have seen in the world will happen to the people you love most.

Much of the time, PTSD for individuals like me is a subtle fear under the surface. Unfortunately, due to the stigma within these careers, seeing a counselor is viewed as a weakness—it is seen as the inability for the individual to "hack" combat. Also, the VA and other agencies have made efforts toward the immediate seizure of firearms, suspension from work, and other ramifications toward individuals who attempt to seek counseling services or medication. It is seen and felt by many of us as a preemptive strike, even prejudice, against those of us who try to get help. So, why would you get help if they're going to look at you as a violent monster before you even open your mouth? Or, if you do open your mouth, they'll immediately think you are going to kill everybody and have no remorse.

One of the common complaints from individuals who initially sought help was their counselor, social worker, or psychologist attempted to relate and "understand." It's hard for us to accept that they "understand" when many of them have never even held a rifle—let alone been shot at, seen their best friend killed, witnessed limbs blown off, or attempted to place a tourniquet as blood spurts with each pulse like many veterans have faced.

We're immediately told, "I understand what you're going through," when that can't possibly be true.

Although many of the providers in these fields have good intentions, most simply don't know how to provide treatment other than textbook solutions. In a personal example of this, I was searching for a counselor after moving back to Portland, Oregon. During the first couple weeks, I began talking about things that bothered me. I recalled an incident that happened in combat, and the provider, a young woman recently out of college, started gasping and saying, "Oh, my God! Oh, my God! I can't believe that happened!" At the end of the appointment, I felt like I had traumatized the poor woman and that going back would be cruel and unusual punishment.

My frequent problem was lack of sleep. I slept a maximum of three hours a night in a series of fifteen-to-thirty-minute naps. Sleep deprivation can cause depression, emotional instability, anger outbursts, memory issues, and many other things. Many mental health providers prescribe SSRIs and SNRIs right out of the gate for anxiety and depression. However, they overlook treating sleep deprivation before jumping to more severe diagnoses. One drug that has been a form of miracle drug for Vietnam Veterans and early Iraq Veterans is an old blood-pressure medication called Prazosin.

The drug was discovered in 1963 by a German organic chemist, Dr. Hans-Jürgen Hess, PhD, who was researching a pharmacological answer for a peripheral anti-hypertensive agent. Because of Prazosin's chemical composition, it has minimal effects on the blood lipid profiles. Unfortunately, it only worked in mild to moderate hypertension patients.

The drug came to the United States in 1976 and didn't become commonly prescribed for PTSD until the 2000s and remains unknown to many providers for its use in minimizing nightmares related to trauma. There still isn't a firm scientific correlation as to why the drug is so effective for sleep and nightmare prevention. However, it is hypothesized that the drug lowers the patient's blood pressure just enough to relax the patient's sympathetic nervous system (fight or flight), preventing the blood pressure and adrenaline spikes associated with nightmares. For myself and many other veterans, I know this has turned three hours of sleep per night into the standard eight to ten hours, with nightmares minimized, drastically improving our quality of life.

I believe providers must be trained differently on how to conduct behavioral and cognitive therapy with veterans, before labeling the patient with a diagnosis that carries a stigma or prescribing a concoction of daily pill regimens. They must not pretend to understand, pass judgment, or downplay any of the situations that the veteran is disturbed by. As seen in this story, often it is the seemingly minor things that bother us when compared to the major events that occurred. In addition, it is vital for the veteran and their spouse to have couples counseling with a non-biased provider so they can learn to communicate or explain why specific behaviors, words, actions, or unspoken physical gestures become irritating or triggering to us. It is a team effort and must be treated as such. It is not the sole responsibility of the veteran to adapt and overcome. Although there are many individual aspects to our reintegration, it is crucial that we work with our loved ones to foster a support system and foundation to cultivate a happy and functional life after war.

THE PARADOX OF OUR TIME

We have taller buildings but shorter tempers;
wider freeways but narrower viewpoints.
We spend more but have less; we buy more but enjoy it less.
We have bigger houses and smaller families;
more conveniences, yet less time.
We have more degrees but less sense; more knowledge
but less judgment; more experts, yet more
problems; more medicine, yet less wellness...
We drink too much; smoke too much; spend too
recklessly, laugh too little; drive too fast; get too angry
too quickly; stay up too late; get up too tired; read too
seldom; watch TV too much; and pray too seldom.
We have multiplied our possessions,
but reduced our values...
We talk too much; love too seldom and lie too often.
We've learned how to make a living, but not a life;
we've added years to life, not life to years.
We've been all the way to the moon and back,
but have trouble crossing the street
to meet the new neighbor.
We've conquered outer space, but not inner space;
we've done larger things, but not better things;
we've cleaned up the air, but polluted the soul;
we've split the atom, but not our prejudice;
we write more, but learn less;
plan more, but accomplish less...
we learned to rush, but not to wait...

We build more computers to hold more
information, to produce more copies than
ever, but have less communication...
These are the times of fast foods and slow
digestion; tall men, but short character; steep
in profits, but shallow relationships.
These are the times of world peace, but
domestic warfare; more leisure and less fun...
more kinds of food, but less nutrition.
These are the days of two incomes, but more divorces;
these are times of fancier houses, but broken homes.
These are the days of quick trips, disposable
diapers, cartridge living, throw-away morality, one-
night stands, overweight bodies and pills that do
everything from cheer, to prevent, quiet or kill.
It is a time when there is much in the show
window and nothing in the stock room.

—DR. BOB MOOREHEAD

CHAPTER 7

OUR AMERICAN SOCIETY

———

IT HAD BEEN A FEW WEEKS SINCE I GOT HOME FROM
Afghanistan. I was getting out more, going places, and
trying to find my new place in society. Even so, it felt
incredibly awkward to have conversations about the
Middle East with friends and family. I did my best to
skirt every question or conversation brought up about
the Middle East. I understood and valued their curiosity,
and I knew they cared about me and my experiences—they
were asking about the war to show their love and support.

Unfortunately, I was so young and had seen so many
guys glorify their war days that I didn't know where the
line between respectable war dialogue and breaking the
ethos of silence stood.

The ethos, thin line, or code of silence among combat
veterans is the unspoken understanding that upon return-

ing home, you go back to your life without burdening anyone or discussing the things you did or experienced in war. You return home and move on with your life as if nothing happened, because those around us who haven't experienced violence firsthand or made decisions that resulted in the death of another human can't understand. Often, through their inability to understand or comprehend, we find those who haven't had similar experiences are scared of us or judge us and the decisions we made. An example of this is all the Americans who called Vietnam Veterans baby killers when they returned home. Nowadays it often isn't as blatant, but due to our training and experience reading situations and people, we don't miss the sideways looks or disapproving body language gestures.

For many of us, we have seen the person at the bar who is "stealing valor" or claiming things they were never part of, stories that never happened, and bragging about awards they never earned. We often feel that, by talking about our service and some of our craziest, most unbelievable stories, it is just another form of us devaluing our service. We embrace the idea that the truly experienced or dangerous man is the one who doesn't feel the need to share a single story—the man you would never expect to be so courageous, brave, and violent because of his humble and kind stature.

Depending on the deployment mission and region, connection to current events in America is limited. For the first few months of our deployment, before moving to

Kabul and eventually the ISAF Headquarters downtown, our mission tempo was extremely high, and before leaving our first FOB, internet access and television disappeared. For my entire deployment, I called home three times to speak to my family for less than a ten-minute conversation. I couldn't tell them what I was doing or what was going on. All you can do as the person deployed is listen to what is going on back home with your family, friends, significant others, and everything you're missing. For me, to remain mission- and battle-focused, I had to turn the switch to fail off. Calling home opened a can of worms, making me homesick, and I preferred to shut it off completely. I rarely got on social media, and I only checked or returned emails once, possibly twice a week.

Because I intentionally isolated myself on deployment, when I returned, I had no idea what had been going on in America. I didn't even know the Ferguson riots had happened. It became a weird dichotomy in gatherings or the parties I went to when I got home. I wanted to talk, socialize, and hide any signs I had changed. I didn't want them to see I had changed, because then I would have to admit to myself that I had changed. I feared that I would never return to the person I used to be—the person I wanted to be again.

About four weeks after getting home, I was invited by my friend Erin to a family and friend gathering. I hadn't met Erin's family or friends yet, and they were eager to meet me after hearing so much about me. When I showed up, it was late into the BBQ, and most of them were pretty well buzzed. Sitting down, Erin's friends wanted to grill me and find out just who I was, something I'm routinely guilty of doing to my younger sister's friends. Because of my experiences, I found their "interrogation" skills to be comical, but I played along.

They continued asking my opinion on the most recent celebrity, athlete, and other First World gossip, followed by repeatedly asking what I planned on doing now and in the future. In all honesty, I didn't know how to answer it. I was just drifting through life. It wasn't that I was lazy; it was the simple fact that I never planned on making it home alive, so I didn't have the answer.

A few days later, Erin told me that her parents and everybody liked me, but her mom thought I talked about Afghanistan a lot and didn't have anything else to contribute. At the time, I was shocked and didn't know how to respond. The only thing I said about Afghanistan was short answers—like, "Oh, I don't know anything about Ferguson. I was overseas," or, "Oh, I don't know, I've been gone so long I'm trying to figure it out." I didn't once bring up a war story.

A few months later, after spending more time around Erin's house and family, I was trying to reintegrate and find things to talk about or have in common. However, most of the time I remained silent, with little to say because the only thing I could think about was going back to Afghanistan.

I was caught off-guard when Erin's mother said to me shortly after Christmas, "You know, I've known you six months. You don't talk much in group conversations, and when you do, it's small tidbits about not knowing what to talk about or anything outside of Middle Eastern politics. I don't understand why you haven't moved past the war by now. It's been six months, and it's time to move on with your life."

Although crass, not well polished, and a seemingly rude comment, it wasn't intended to make me feel bad about myself. She made the comment because she, like the majority of Americans, truly *do not understand* the process of reintegration or have the ability to comprehend what post-combat exile is like.

There's a new rule of thumb being taught in secondary education for combat veterans. It's estimated that for every week spent in a combat zone, it will take three to six weeks home to return to a relatively normal state of awareness. If you add up a typical nine- to twelve-month deployment, not including train-up time, it will take two to five years home before their heightened awareness and edge wears off. And that figure doesn't take into account the number of combat or trauma incidents experienced by more intense deployments or compounding tours.

There are many issues we face coming home, and a lot of them have to do with issues or changes within ourselves. In a combat environment, it is survival of the fittest. The only thing we are concerned with is staying alive. To stay alive while deployed, the only things that matter are: When is my next meal? Where is the ammo re-supply? When can I sleep? And where in the *fuck* is my care package?

After being in an environment like this, the trivial "issues" of the civilian population from day to day become petty, annoying, and sound like nothing more than the whining of entitled people who can't understand what real hardship is. This is where the divide begins and ends. We, as veterans, can't understand your bad day, and you can't comprehend ours. What is trivial to us is a big deal to you, and we have a hard time understanding that both bad days and hardships are equal; it's all relative.

After the first few months at home, one of the many frustrating things is seeing how our society is superficial, divided, and takes their freedom for granted. We watch as the VA fails us—infecting hundreds of veterans with HIV; bodies quite literally liquefying in the VA morgue; thousands of veterans dying waiting for necessary surgeries; and others killing themselves on the front steps of the VA because they feel they aren't being helped or even heard.

On top of that, the Veterans Benefits Office works dirtier than a claims adjuster. When we file for retirement benefits, scoring a combined disability percentage over 200 percent, one would expect we would receive 100 percent of our retirement pay. Instead, their convoluted, difficult-to-understand matrix means we only receive a fraction of our retirement pay. We watch as the Reserve and National Guard soldiers deploy two or more times with over twenty-four months in combat, yet the government and VA only gives them 70 percent of their GI Bill for education. The general public glances over all of this, refusing to take notice, then cries out for the benefits of illegal immigrants.

As a soldier who was excited for our interpreter Ahmed, and ANA soldier Sgt. Adele, to become citizens, I feel I can say the following: For many of us, the immigration issues and lack of border security are security issues, knowing how many wolves and terrorists get through and mingle with the rest of our herd of sheep in America. We deployed to keep them away and to keep our loved ones safe, so the lack of screening grinds our gears. To further perpetuate our hardline stance, we watch as the Dream Act, education benefits, and free healthcare are handed out to illegal immigrants, when our veterans who sacrificed for this amazing country are treated so poorly.

We, as an American Society, veterans included, are more connected than ever communication-wise, yet, we are the most disconnected from the things that are important. We are told by society to consume, to move on to the next best thing, and we are never satisfied. You can see it in ads telling us what new consumer goods we "deserve." You see it on billboards and commercials that use sex and the objectification of women and men to sell.

These consumer marketing tactics have led to a form of societal conditioning that has trained us to always look for better, anticipate what is around the corner, and to never be satisfied with what we have. As a result, we lose the sun while counting the stars. Over time, we watch as the country is consumed with negative media and plagued with fiction, opinion, or lies sold to us as facts.

We often have the opportunity to connect positively with so many others around us with deep, meaningful relationships, but we often ignore or reject them. We live in a society where the media and politicians stand on platforms of fear and distrust. Selling us subliminal messages on the evening news not to trust our gut feelings, neighbors, friends, and the rest of our society because we are told repeatedly the world is out to scam, manipulate, control, or change us. We live in a world where we value and trust a friend or squad leader's opinion who may set us up with toxic or seemingly wrong situations time and time again in betrayal. Yet, we justify keeping them in our life by the amount of time they've spent with us and not by the quality they add to our life. We wonder why we as a society are left feeling lonely, unfulfilled, and somewhat ashamed or disgusted. We value quantity these days rather than the quality.

We chase our ego and superficial desires, disregarding what our heart and soul wants, out of fear of ending up with what we don't want. Because of our consumerist and expendable society, we push away partners and friends who are a work in progress. We ignore the astonishing traits—the connection, love, and fear of losing them—

because there might be a better option around the corner. Our society has perfected the "grass is always greener" mentality.

This is one of the many reasons you hear so many soldiers express our desire to go back to war and the time when life was much simpler and more straightforward. The time you were with friends who would give their life for yours, and you for them. The *real* meaning of friends. We want to leave behind the superficial and shallow aspects and how many "followers" you have on social media.

Unfortunately, many of us realize the option of going back for deployment after deployment isn't possible, and that's when many of the problems sink in. This is why so many of us alienate ourselves from civilian friendships and only surround ourselves with other service members and first responders who understand.

This isn't all the veteran's issues, or strictly society's issues to reintegrate. Half the problem is creating a society that we want to reintegrate into—the America we bled for, died for, and sacrificed for. It is time to go back to a foundation of love, forgiveness, and family. It is more important than ever to close chapters on previous sections of life with exes, old friends, high school flings, hookups, etc. Those avenues make it too easy for temptation to creep in when our lives, marriages, and relationships aren't working out.

We've preached hate, violence, negativity, security,

and paranoia since 9/11. As a result, we have grown to be a country more divided, scared, depressed, and unfulfilled than ever before. We live in a world where the media and internet show us the hate and horrors of mankind in split seconds. Through the evening news, it appears we live in the most violent, racist, and hateful time in American history. However, violent crime statistics tracked by the FBI don't lie, history doesn't lie, and numbers can be skewed to meet any individual's agenda. As Sebastian Junger explained in his book *Tribe*, our brains were not designed to track over seven billion people on the planet. We have evolved and developed to track roughly 140 people—the typical size of our "tribes" in evolution. We were not made to sit in the isolation of our living rooms watching the news.

In the future, I would love to see a news channel strictly designed for "what's good in the 'hood," instead of showing "if it bleeds it leads"—only acts of kindness, love, and positive things in the community are shown. Instead of dehumanizing our cops, military, doctors, or anyone else for that matter, we should work on humanization and bridging the divide instead of creating one. Instead of focusing on the oppression of one group, we focus on the human race and find a solution for the underprivileged, creating opportunities regardless of the color of somebody's skin, whether that's a trailer park or a ghetto.

The division and lack of appreciation for the American freedoms and way of life calls into question the sacrifice veterans provide. Most of us enter combat situations because we believe in the American Dream and the core values our country espouses. Yet, when we come home and see how unappreciative the average citizen is of their daily comforts and the privileges they take for granted, we often grow bitter. We remember the Afghan soldiers, interpreters, and many foreigners who embrace and believe in the American dream more than our own society does at times. Watching the hate for the American values, colors, and—although it is freedom of speech—the desecration of the American flag often makes our sacrifice feel it was for nothing, or has at least gone unnoticed. With all of those things in consideration, it isn't a fair question to ask why it's hard to reintegrate to society. Re-joining a group who doesn't believe that what you fought for is valuable only makes us want to pull further away.

"The truth is, everyone is going to hurt you.
You just got to find the ones worth suffering for."
—BOB MARLEY

CHAPTER 8

DATING DIFFERENTLY

AFTER A FEW DAYS AT HOME, I DECIDED TO GO TO dinner with an old high school flame. I had been gone so long and still cared about her, even loved her. I thought there wouldn't be any harm in visiting to see if things could be rekindled. Unfortunately, this was the moment I learned the difference between being "in love" with somebody and loving somebody.

When I first got there, things seemed like they had changed. She was friendly, excited to see me, and eager to catch up. We decided to go to dinner and hang out. Because I had only been back home about a week and a half, I was still people-watching every time I went out. While sitting in a corner booth, facing the door—scanning every individual who walked in the front door for indications of a suicide vest, explosive, or shooter—I was frequently distracted from the conversation. I continued to tune in with the occasional, "Yeah, I know. Mhmm.

Yeah, how about that?" However, a table of about fifteen people had gotten up from their chairs, heading toward the exit.

The patrons left pounds of food on the table, not bothering to take home leftovers. I couldn't help but remember an instance overseas.

Laughing, I hear my buddy Casey, "Hey, Stella, you gonna give these little goons some soccer balls before you go in or what?"

Pulling the soccer ball out of my pack, I begin to inflate it, then remove the valve and kick it across the field, sending all the kids running. Shyly, a little boy around four years old comes around the front of my truck. Judging from the thick layer of dirt on his face, feet, and hands, I guess he hasn't been cleaned or bathed in at least a month.

"What's up, little man?" I smile at him.

Looking at me with the eyes a puppy gives his owner for food, he holds his fingers in a cone fashion and gesticulates it towards his mouth, begging shamelessly. I realize that he's probably much older than four, but his physical development has been stunted by lack of nutrients. He looks famished, and I really can't tell the last time he ate. But by this point, there were supply issues. Our unit had not had a real meal in over a month and a half. We had been eating freeze-dried MREs (Meal Ready to Eat) and had only been rationed to a small number of them. We were feeling the effects of minimal food.

Without hesitation, I open the door to my armored

vehicle and pulled out my ration for the day. I hide it in front of me where the other kids can't see. I do this because, in the past, I have seen the older kids beat up the smaller children who received candy or food from soldiers.

Walking over to him, I sling my rifle and gesture for him to come close. I take one last look around for other kids and put it down his shirt, concealing the 2,000-calorie meal, telling him to run home in Pashto. I turn around, pulling up my rifle, and head toward the outpost for a leader engagement.

Piercing my daydream, I hear crisp and slightly irritated words. "Steele, are you listening to me? Did you hear what I just said?"

"Oh. No, sorry."

"What were you thinking about?" she says softly, with an affectionate voice.

"Oh, nothing, just staring off into space," I lie.

"No, really. I want to know."

"Honestly, I was just thinking about all the kids and people I saw over there who hadn't had a meal in days, even weeks. I was looking over at that table thinking about how much food we waste here in America," I admitted, genuinely concerned about the wastefulness of my peers.

"Wow," she says, her frustration evident.

"What?"

"That's so fucking depressing. Look, I don't know what happened over there. I don't care to know what happened over there. Keep it to yourself," with disgust dripping in her voice.

It was at this point that I realized things were not salvageable and we had grown apart. She had grown one way, and I had gone another. As a combat veteran, I didn't need somebody who could take every single syllable of war or gore. But I certainly couldn't be with somebody who didn't care or want to know why the man standing in front of her wasn't the man she first dated.

I returned home to Portland, realizing dating was going to be different than it used to be, and that the women I would be attracted to going forward were much different than girls I had dated in the past. I can only imagine how difficult this must be for individuals who return home from war and other life-changing experiences when they are married and have kids. I can only imagine how much more difficult the transition back to reality and civilian life must be once you no longer have the ability to pack up and leave without sacrificing your family.

If you are the significant other in the situation who "doesn't want to know," the more you act unaccepting, the more you are pushing the one you love away. When you tell them what my date said to me that day in the restaurant, they hear, "You have become a monster. I don't want to know the awful things you've done."

Now, this may be your intention, in which case you have some serious self-reflection to do. However, I choose to believe that it is said lovingly. It is said in a, "I love the person I met and know, and I don't care what it is you did, because I love the person I know you to be regardless of what happened." However, this isn't what the combat veteran hears. We are overwhelmed with criticism, negativity, and fear from social media, the news, and Hollywood. We take it as you seeing us as a monster—that you're terrified of the things we've done and the things we have the capacity to do.

I'm not a marriage counselor, and I'm not a clinician. However, I have been through the experience. In addition to the dinner incident, around a year after being home, there was a major family disagreement. My mother, a licensed social worker and one of the most loving and caring women I know, made a mistake in a heated discussion, saying through tears and a saddened voice, "I just don't know where my kind little boy went."

"Where the fuck do you think he went, Mom? Do you want me to break it down, Barney-style for you, as to why he isn't here anymore?" I fired back with anger and hate, storming out of the house.

I wasn't angry at her. I was hurt because I missed the person that she was missing too, and more than anything, I was afraid she wouldn't and didn't love the man I had become. I wanted to be the person who loved everything and everyone without hesitation. The person who could sit at a restaurant without worrying about a deranged individual storming in and shooting or blowing the place up. I just couldn't find him.

If you are in this situation yourself, where your loved one has changed or you don't want to know what they've done, I would encourage you to be delicate. Instead of saying, "I don't want to know what you've done," etc., I would try to say, "Look, I know you've changed a lot, and I can't blame you. I can't imagine or pretend like I understand what you've seen and are going through. However, I know that I love you. I love the person you are at your core, and nothing can change or take those things away. I want to support you. I just don't have the training or specialty to do so. I can support you in other ways and reassure you that I'm not going anywhere. But talking through things would be much better for a third-party whose job is to help you work through these things. If you still decide you want me to hear to better understand, I would be more than happy to go with you. I just don't want to set us up for failure."

If you are the parent, mentor, or other family member, and you find yourself wondering where the younger version of your combat veteran went, I would encourage you to avoid saying, "I don't know where so-and-so went." It comes across as a guilt trip and is painful to hear. We already know we're different, and you reminding us feels like rubbing salt on an open wound. I would encourage you to bring up the discussion away from an emotional or heated conversation, alcohol, and other individuals.

It may be more constructive to say, "I know things have changed. I love you and know you well enough to recognize that you might be having a hard time. I want to help you find happiness again. To find the laughter, smile, and tenacity that you used to have. How can we find it together?" Obviously, this is not a one-size-fits-all. However, I would find a way to communicate that you do not think less of them. They are important, they are not alone, and in a way, that still gives them hope of once again finding happiness.

Regardless of how it is brought up, it will be very challenging for us to accept or realize it in the moment. However, after we have time to think, it will leave the door open in the future when we hit an inevitable low point, knowing you will be there and hope is not lost.

*"You can't go back and change the beginning,
but you can start where you are and change the ending."*

—C.S. LEWIS

CHAPTER 9

VETERANS FORGOT HOW TO LOVE

OVER THE LAST FEW YEARS, I HAD TO BE INTOXI-
cated to be open about my feelings. I felt if I showed
emotions, internal struggles, or empathy, I would be
viewed as weak. I had bought into the idea that strong
men don't have weaknesses. Later, I learned that by staying quiet about our struggles, shortcomings, failures, or
wisdom, we are not able to serve and teach those around
us. Some of the most fundamental building blocks in my
life have been from men and women strong enough to
voice all of those things. I learned that sometimes, one
conversation is all it takes to provide the hope to carry on.

Putting aside all judgments or concern of how they
would be viewed, men and women who chose emotional
vulnerability showed me how to embrace my own. I made
a promise to myself to discontinue the toxic bottling of

emotions, to break the veil of silence, and to become the kind of man who can overcome adversity and help others struggling through leading by example.

While learning more about empathy and love, I came across Plato's love ladder, the idea that each rung of the ladder represents different, more complex forms of love. According to Plato, as we climb the ladder, we are exposed to deeper and more profound love, and the more shallow love of the bottom rungs become less satisfying. A similar satisfaction-rung system applies to combat veterans, first responders, and other individuals who have been in hostile, violent, and extremely stressful situations. Instead of rungs related to love, they are related to excitement, stress, and adrenaline.

Often, you see these individuals partaking in "risky" categorized behavior, such as driving fast, skydiving, climbing mountains, racing motorcycles, etc. It is my belief (and a hypothesis that I would like to test in a clinical setting one day) that once you have experienced the stressors of combat where your body has released dopamine, norepinephrine, adrenaline, and serotonin, it changes your threshold of stimulation for excitatory responses. I believe it changes our brain chemistry and builds a tolerance similar to the way addictive drugs or alcohol does. While deployed—dodging roadside bombs, rockets, gunfire, and the enemy—over time, it dampens our scale of excitement range and neuronal firing. For example, before combat, skydiving may have been a complete ten out of ten—the top rung on a ladder that you base other exciting activities off of. After, it may only rank a two out of ten because you've experienced much more excitatory stimulation on the brink of death.

For a person who has led a life without the stressors or hardships of violence, their excitement scale seems mundane to a combat veteran. Unfortunately, after the harsh near-death excitement from violence, it becomes nearly impossible to reach activities that stimulate our reward circuit to those levels. I believe this is why we often feel like we will never be excited or feel excitement again. Not even the most extreme things in our civilian society or sports come close to the previous experience that shaped our ladder of excitement.

Through combat, we are inundated with adrenaline and stressors. To survive, we learn to turn the vulnerable side of ourselves off, matching the hate and violence given with our violence and hate magnified. We learn how to compartmentalize and disregard the feelings and suffering of others, including the people we love, to push through the objective, accomplishing the mission. In war, there is never the time or ability to be sad at the misfortunes, fate, or pain of others.

In doing so, our ability to express empathy dwindles, because if we feel bad for every person we see, shoot, or who tries to blow us up, we could be killed.

There are so many veterans I have met who bounce around with a new sexual conquest every weekend. They never allow anybody to get too close, and the second their conquest gets too close, they cut them off and move on to the next. It perpetuates a cycle of loneliness, heartache, and unfulfillment. Many men I know who do this say they don't feel bad, or they say they don't care about her feelings, yet deep down, many of them do. Once you get them drunk, they explain how awful they feel for breaking her heart when she became attached. Instead of making changes, many pour another glass and move on to the next, ignoring the root causes of their suffering.

I think that's why so many of us hold women, especially, at arm's length. We've turned off the ability to be vulnerable, and we don't know how to turn it back on. We keep everybody at a distance so we can drive on, always placing the mission first. Over time, this defensive mechanism is forged through fire, hate, pain, and suffering, because it is the easiest and only way we know how to survive. When the inevitable day comes—whether you're eighty and lying in a hospital bed holding your wife's hand or you're holding the hand of your buddy as you tell him your final words, begging him to tell your wife you will always love her and to find happiness with another man—the words won't cut into the wounds so profoundly.

What I have embraced is that I am a hopeless romantic. A combat veteran and hopeless romantic who forgot how to be loved and how to love others. I continuously wage war between the two sides of myself—the side that urges softness and love, and my brain, which has been reprogrammed through combat to minimize heartache by remaining detached.

I was a control freak over my heart and my level of vulnerability in an attempt to protect myself. All of my instincts, training, and experience told me to expect and plan for the worst and to never hope for the best. Because when you hope for the best, you're going to be hurt and disappointed when it inevitably goes off course. As all combat vets know, nothing ever goes according to plan. In the end, it wasn't others who missed out—it was me.

I forgot how we are supposed to treat and love our person—the one you love and who loves you more than anything in the world. I learned to disassociate myself from those who were important to me to avoid the feelings of the inevitable. I did this with my eventual girlfriend, my friends, my family, and anybody else I cared about. I had become so efficient at it that, by the time I returned home from war, I would not have cried at the funeral of my own parents. Sadly, I had perfected detachment.

This method worked for a while. It kept all of my demons locked in a cage. Over time, though, they began rattling the cage, fracturing my concrete foundation. I became irritable, short-tempered, hot-headed, and emotionally weak. I began pushing people away while telling them I loved them, my actions belying my words.

Instead of handling the problems as they occurred, I stowed them away in the bottle, putting more and more duct tape over the lid to prevent their escape. When they finally did, it was a pain like I had never experienced, and it was the realization of several steps and decisions I had made to get myself into the situation I was in.

Many of us act this way in our relationships after combat. We embrace a push-pull mentality, wanting our person to prove their love for us repeatedly, despite our poor behavior. Quite honestly, it's an unreasonable request. It isn't healthy, it isn't beneficial, and it only hurts both parties involved. One person will feel the person won't prove their love, while the other will feel like they won't ever be able to prove their love or be good enough. Ultimately, it ends in heartache and pain for both people, with more bridges burned far past the phrase "beyond repair."

That being said, the first step in any problem is recognizing there is a problem. Another thing society has said and done that pushes us to reject seeking help is the idea that insecurity is unattractive, repulsive, and weak. I firmly disagree with this. I think the social constructs we have built that dictate how we should and shouldn't feel, which insecurities are acceptable and which ones are not, is crudely grotesque. What should be repulsive, weak, and unattractive is a person who fails to admit they have any insecurities, any shortcomings, or anything wrong with themselves. The denial and damage created by attempting to fulfill societal expectations should be considered disgusting.

Why is it acceptable for somebody to be self-conscious

about their body, yet if they are self-conscious about their ability to open themselves up to being hurt by others, they somehow lack or are insecure with no self-confidence? The only difference is that one is a physical insecurity and the other is emotional. If I had been honest with myself and had verbalized my weaknesses to my loved ones, things would have been a lot less painful for everyone when I returned home. It is healthy to admit to our emotional shortcomings. We *should* be looked at as bold and courageous for admitting something that we otherwise hide from the world.

We are all going to say and do hurtful things that hurt our significant other, both intentionally and unintentionally, and vice versa. It is the implementation of compassion and forgiveness that enables us to overcome adversity together. If a relationship was always smooth sailing, without conflict, without disagreement, and without frustration, how would we ever know the strength of our vessel? How would we know that our relationship will survive when things get tough?

If we come home irritable and angry at the world, have zero patience, and are closed off emotionally, odds are, our significant others are going to walk the other way. Compare that to coming home to your significant other saying, "Wow, babe, today was one of those days. Extremely irritating. I need a beer and a few minutes of you sitting on the couch snuggling up to me watching our show." This interaction still communicates that you aren't in the mood for controversial subjects and that your patience is low, yet you are inviting your loved one to show you affection while asking them for love and support.

When you communicate your frustrations with your partner, it won't leave them wondering if they were the ones that did something wrong. If they have compassion for you and you for them, the odds are that they're going to be thankful that you communicated you had a rough day. They will be more than happy to spend some quality time snuggling on the couch, unwinding, and watching your show together before bed.

In scenario one, there is a high probability you will go to bed angry, and your significant other won't want to snuggle or even touch you. In the second, odds are that your significant other will roll over, snuggling up to you, and the two of you will wake up the next morning on a fresh page. In this scenario, you are taking a negative experience or day, turning it into relationship growth, and furthering your communication skills. It isn't easy to do, but it is an emotional muscle that must be trained and exercised. Eventually, your communication skills will improve, and you and your partner will be able to turn each of these interactions into an instrumental building block of trust, love, and patience. Every action is either a step forward or a step backward in our relationships, and we have the choice to strengthen or break another straw every day.

Another thing I learned about learning how to love

again after war is picking my battles. Too often, I picked a fight with loved ones or chose to get irritated over things that, looking back, were entirely trivial and weren't worth the nights spent lying in bed, back to back, without saying, "I love you." Looking back, only one or two of the countless fights were worth getting upset over, and even with the ones that were worth getting upset over, I didn't learn how to communicate effectively, which made the problem exponentially worse.

I realized that all the times I was upset or told my loved ones to leave me alone, I actually didn't want them to leave me alone. But how could they have known? I never communicated effectively or explained my needs. The biggest thing I've realized about myself is that the only way I am able to simmer down when my pot is boiling over from anger at my significant other is by exchanging love or affection. However, my ex would have never known any of it because I didn't communicate those needs. Ways that defused a situation for me were ways that increased her frustration. We never learned how to communicate ways to turn a negative interaction into a positive stepping stone in our relationship.

It is important to appreciate what we have that is real. It is important to let people go in life who no longer push us to work on our lives, relationships, and personal struggles. It is time to let go of those who silently hold us back because they never want us to leave their life or excel farther in life than they will. It is important to focus on those who matter. I encourage you to go talk to your neighbor, say hello to that homeless man, look at your significant other and concentrate on the good they bring to your life, and stop noticing only the bad. Stop pointing out their struggles and shortcomings and start focusing on your own. Start being thankful for what you do have instead of focusing on what you don't.

Every single day, write down the good things that happened and the things you love about your spouse or significant other, and focus on giving them three sincere compliments or indications of love. This is love, not war. A relationship should not be similar to a job evaluation where you struggle to find one or two "sustains" followed by an overwhelming list of "improvements." Stop focusing on everything wrong and work on building each other up. We have enough reminders of what we do wrong, so don't create more.

"I didn't want to kiss you goodbye,
that was the trouble;
I wanted to kiss you goodnight.
And there's a lot of difference."

—ERNEST HEMINGWAY

CHAPTER 10

SILVER LININGS

—

"EVERYONE COMES WITH BAGGAGE. FIND SOMEONE who loves you enough to help you unpack."

It had been three days since the date from hell, and about three weeks since I returned from Afghanistan. Despite this, I woke up with an extra pep in my step. I can't explain why, but I felt an overwhelming happiness and excitement to start my day. I had a doctor appointment for a post-deployment checkup, which had been a pain to make, due to location logistics. I had made the appointment in one city, decided the traffic would be too miserable, and changed it to a different town at the last second.

Somewhat out of character, I jumped in my truck, singing along to the radio, admiring how beautiful of a June day it was. Keeping with my daily routine since my return from deployment, I stopped by the coffee shop, starting this extra glorious day with two extra shots of espresso in my coffee.

Typically, the morning rat race of traffic would drive me out of my mind. However, for some reason, I was exceptionally happy. I sang along to the radio, taking sips of coffee during verses I didn't know. As fate would have it, when I checked in at the front desk, the doctor I was scheduled to see had a nurse who called in sick. So, of course, he was running behind. Because of my great morning, I didn't mind waiting and maintained my enthusiasm for a new day. Over the next hour, I saw patient after patient who showed up after me called back, yet I was still waiting.

Deep in the distraction of my phone, I'm caught off guard when I hear her.

"Mr. Kelly," says a voice that I can only imagine is the sound of the angel who calls our name at heaven's pearly gates.

Looking up, I see the most breathtakingly beautiful woman I have ever seen in my life. Her eyes, striking a chord of beauty and vibrancy that only an ocean sunset could imitate, glistened as the morning rays of sun shined through the windows, illuminating her face. Her smile, bright and shining with brilliance from the sun, somehow takes the wind out of my lungs. Lovestruck, I don't even feel myself walking, I feel as if I'm floating through the office toward her. As I get closer, I begin to notice how her beautiful blonde hair has every strand perfectly placed and pulled back in a ponytail, allowing the full features of her face and smile to be seen. While dazed, I damn near trip over myself walking to the height and weight station.

"Follow me," she said.

"You can sit in the chair; we have some things to go over," she says in the most professional tone.

I can't help but think about her. Unfortunately, for whatever reason, I can't help but realize that she is probably married. *She's married, dude. How many cops, doctors, and nurses do you know who don't wear their ring while they're working? Lots.* I nearly miss her questions while I'm still thinking about how big of a shame it is that she's married.

"Alright, the doctor will be in with you in a few minutes," she says in that same heavenly tone she called my name in.

Closing the door, I can't stop thinking about her. *Damn, why is she married? What a lucky guy. He must be a pretty awesome guy to come home every night to a woman like that. See, that's what you need to find—an all-American woman who is beautiful, smart, and friendly.* Promptly, the door opens. Peering around the corner, hoping it's her, I see a middle-aged man walk in.

"Mr. Kelly, I'm the doc. How are you?" he says enthusiastically.

"Man, I'm awesome. Another day in paradise!" *Especially since I met your nurse today.*

"You married?"

"Nope, thank God!" I say, hoping he'll tell her I'm single, in an unprofessional wingman kind of way.

"Ohhh, that's alright! You will be soon!" he says in a foreboding tone.

Yeah, hopefully to your nurse.

Throughout the checkup, I can't pay attention to a single thing. I can't stop thinking about that nurse, hoping I'll see her again and can ask her out to coffee or dinner.

"Alright, Mr. Kelly, we're going to do some blood work and check for parasites, so you'll have to do blood, then bring a sample to the lab every morning for the next week," he informs me, concluding the visit.

"Alright!" This was the best news I'd heard since I got home. I now had seven more chances to run into her.

"Wow, my patients normally aren't excited to have to come back every morning for a week."

"Oh. Yeah, I'm just happy to be back in the US!" It was just a half-truth.

Of course, still in the moment, I walk toward the elevator bypassing the lab. Pulling out my phone to send a text message about the nurse to my buddy, I'm interrupted by the "ding" of the shining silver elevator doors sliding open. I take my first step into the elevator when I hear her beautiful voice again.

"Mr. Kelly, you forgot to do your labs!"

Here's your chance, dude! However, turning around and following her, all my words are gone. I can't think of a single word to say. I'm tripping over all my words like a teenager going through puberty. Walking into the lab, the lab technician says to the nurse, "Do you want to draw his blood or should I?"

"Oh, no! No, you can!" she says in a rushed, trying-to-leave-the-room kind of way.

I begin small talk with the lab tech, a little let down that the nurse left the room so fast.

"So, do you have a girlfriend?"

"Oh, no, I'm single," I say, hoping the nurse will overhear.

"Really? Deployment do that?"

"Eh, something like that."

"You know who else is single?"

I begin to think of ways I can turn the lab technician down politely. She is friendly but much, much, older than me. And I am still thinking about the nurse.

"I don't know," I say reluctantly, worried she was going to ask me out.

"Nurse Peyton. Nurse Peyton is single." She's clearly attempting to play matchmaker.

"Really? I thought she was married!" I say, using every effort to hide the excitement in my voice.

"Nope, she's very single. You should leave your number for her."

"Hmm. Well, you see, this is my first visit, and the last thing I need is a sexual harassment complaint." I laugh, sincerely hoping she'll ask again.

"Nope, you should leave it. You won't get one."

I grab a piece of paper and a pen, scribbling my name and number on the corner, tearing it off. Walking out of the building, I'm damn-near skipping to my truck, high on life, hoping and praying I get a text or phone call from her. But then reality sets in. *Dude, tons of guys probably leave their number hoping for the same thing as you.*

Sitting at lunch with my best friend, I begin telling him about the nurse.

"Look, Romeo, your beer has sat there for thirty minutes. You going to take a break for a sip between your love confession for Juliet or am I going to have to drink it for you?"

As if the timing were orchestrated, my phone goes off with a text message from Peyton. Nearly jumping out of the booth, I look at my buddy as if I had won the lottery.

"Dude, dude, dude, she just texted me! What do I say?"

"Steele, you have the gift of gab. This isn't the first girl you've asked out. You've been to fucking war, bro. What's your deal?"

Over the next several hours, we text back and forth. By the end of the afternoon, she asks me to go on a date with her downtown. I want to see her extremely badly, but I was still struggling with crowds and wasn't sure if I was ready to go to a crowded nightclub, especially with a woman I wanted to date. I didn't want to go and then be unable to stay. But I decide I want to see her more than I'm worried about crowds, so I agree.

Walking through the front door as if I were floating in the clouds, I enter the kitchen smiling.

"Well, somebody had a good day! What happened? How was your appointment?" my mom says.

"I met my future wife today!" I say with conviction and confidence.

"Woah! That's a shock! You've never wanted to get married or have kids! I'm a little worried you're serious—and you just met this woman?" my mom responds, caught off guard, immediately realizing this woman was different.

"She was my nurse, and I'm going to marry her one day! I just hope I didn't meet her too soon after deployment. I don't want to break this girl's heart or lose her before we have a real chance," I say, with both middle-school-kid excitement and worldly concern.

* * *

ON THE NIGHT OF OUR FIRST DATE, I REALIZED I was in love with her. I couldn't explain why, but I just knew down to my core. I had dated several women, and I knew this one was different. Ironically, I found out the day she came home from work that she had a similar conversation, telling her family that she met her future husband. On the second date, I took her to the beach for dinner and a bonfire with wine to watch the sunset.

Sitting by the fire, admiring the first sunset I had watched since Afghanistan, I can't help but wonder how I hit the lottery with her sitting next to me. *How in the world is she doing this to me? I never get spun up like this or so head over heels for anyone. I didn't even get heart palpitations before missions like the way sitting next to her does.*

Uncorking a bottle of wine, doing my best to hide any sign of admiration, I try to smoothly, without shaking, pour each of us a glass of wine in the highest-class red Solo cups.

Sitting there as the fire dwindles, watching as each flame bounces off her beautiful eyes, I can't stop my mind and heart from racing. *Holy shit, I think I'm in love. I think she's the one. Put your hand on hers—wait, don't—act normal. Act. Normal. She's probably not into you anyway.*

As I move closer, leaning in toward her, I place my left hand gently next to hers, our shoulders touching softly. Suddenly, a man in his late twenties darts over, jumping in the sand, sitting down across from us. As if it were second nature, I compute an immediate threat evaluation, sizing the man up. I can't help but notice the cuts on his knuckles from repeated fist fights, dirty clothes, and the overwhelming smell of cheap liquor on his breath. Following his hands to his torso, a well-worn fixed blade knife is wedged into the sheath on his waistband. In split seconds, I begin unraveling, strategically in my mind, all the possibilities that are about to happen. It's as if it flipped a switch, flashing me back seven months prior to November of 2014.

It was the end of fall, but the temperature outside made it feel like the middle of winter. By this point, we were living on MREs, Rockstar energy drinks, and nicotine. We were securing a FOB built for a division of soldiers—a division usually consists of 15,000 combat troops, and

8,000 support troops. We were doing this with approximately 200 combat soldiers and seventy-five support troops. As the outpost drew down, there was an unusually large volume of aircraft traffic removing sensitive equipment from the FOB. Because of this, it became incredibly apparent to the locals monitoring base activity for the Taliban that we were leaving.

Probes from the enemy were increasing at nighttime. They took pop shots at our troops on tower guard and our aircraft attempting to land on the airstrip. To make matters worse, the Mongolians who were manning the nearly 140 towers around the base were sent back to Mongolia a month before we were set to exfiltrate the base.

Because we were running a skeleton crew, we were unable to man all of the towers. As a result, we manned every fourth tower in the areas of high risk, abandoning the others.

At night, aerial surveillance picked up groups of Taliban jumping the wire, attempting to scout our task force's sleeping quarters. There were several extremely credible threats from intelligence sources that they were actively planning an attempt to overrun our base with hundreds of Taliban fighters from the Zerkoh Valley, only fifteen kilometers to the south.

Because the ROE was so frequently changing, and the closest QRF with the combat capabilities to support us was four to six hours away, we sent a request to Central Command. Our command explained that with the number of combat troops we had, the size of the base, and with the credibility of the threat, we were in imminent risk of getting overrun by Taliban forces. We requested the ROE to be reviewed, giving us permission to use lethal force on any individual who jumped the wire. Our command justified the request, knowing if the Taliban successfully breached the wire with the number of fighters estimated, we wouldn't survive long enough for a QRF to reach us.

I was told that this request went all the way up the chain to Washington, D.C. and the Pentagon, under former President Obama's administration. We received a response a few days later. It was denied. We were instructed to allow the breach of suspected scouts and ordered not to take any action until we were being actively engaged from our tents inside the compound.

It was infuriating. We felt they cared more about Taliban lives than ours. It's one thing to understand when you enlist in combat arms that you're an expendable combat troop, and it's a completely different thing to be told that you're expendable while they sit in a heated office with a comfortable office chair. As a result of their decision, we were forced to fortify our tents with sandbags and razor wire, placing an armed truck on both the north and south side of our tents. They were armed with a gunner and two roving guards equipped with night vision and thermal optics from sundown to sunrise, protecting our sleeping task force.

"Kelly, wake up, bro."

Rolling over, looking at my watch, it displayed 1400 hours (2:00 p.m.). Through a groggy voice, I say, "What's up, Casey?"

"LT asked me to assemble a squad. The TOC picked up some scouts on aerial surveillance. We're pretty sure they're planning to jump the wire tonight, scouting for the attack while we're asleep."

"Uh? Why not send first platoon? They're on QRF right now. Wait, why just a squad? Shouldn't we take the entire platoon?"

"First platoon is already on mission, Bravo squad is already checking out a possible breach in the wire on the flight line, and Charlie Troop found an IED. They're escorting EOD (Explosive Ordinance Disposal) out. Sooo, that leaves the nine of us. Grab your kit. It will be our problem if they slit our fucking throats while we're sleeping tonight."

Rolling out of the gates, we're unusually low-equipped. We only have two armored gun trucks and five dismounted soldiers to kick out and clear the compound.

Following Casey in the wedge formation, covering the three-hundred-meter distance from where our trucks kicked us out, a rock catches my eye.

"Hey, Casey, you see that rock that looks about twenty-five years old and painted red?"

"Nah, Stella, you're high. There's nothing but dirt out here," Casey says, punctuating with a laugh.

Walking a little further, I say in a loud whisper, "Casey! Stop!"

Freezing in his tracks, he asks, "What do you see, Kelly?"

"Dude, ten meters to the west—a line of those red painted rocks. Remember when we got here, we were briefed on the landmine fields the Soviets left in the '90s? Command said most of it had been cleared by EOD, but there were still areas that hadn't been cleared. I think we found one of the uncleared minefields, bro. We're walking in the fucking middle of it."

Walking in my tracks, boot print for boot print behind me, our lieutenant evaluates the situation and says, "I think Kelly is right, but we have to check the compound. Continue mission, push twenty meters to the east, away from the painted rocks."

Echoing to the two soldiers behind him calmly: "Gents, watch your fucking step—we may or may not be walking through one of the Soviet minefields."

We begin walking carefully, jaded to the dangers of an unclear minefield. After twenty minutes of walking, we get to the abandoned compound. Most of the locals' houses were made out of mud and rock, but this one is different. Looking at the building, it's made of concrete, with an enormous thirty-year-old painting on the outside. On the weathered painting, a MIG Fighter Jet and the unmistakable Soviet Union hammer and sickle below is still clearly visible through the years of sand, wind, and snow erosion.

From thirty meters out, we halt the formation. "Well,

guys, I think it's safe to say this is a former Soviet compound. My only question is, why is it two kilometers from the airfield and the base they used? It doesn't make sense," I rhetorically ask the guys.

"Kelly, Johnson (Casey), GPS coordinates say this is the compound. Last visual showed two men in all black clothing, in and out of this building with AK-47s. The three of us will stay out here and pull security. You two clear the inside. If you're able to make contact without lethal force, disarm and secure them with zip ties and call for our interpreter Ahmed. Our goal is to get information from these guys, so keep it in mind. Lethal force is a last resort."

We approach the building from the south, sweeping the corners and potential fighting positions with the barrels of our rifles. As we get closer, the two soldiers and lieutenant peel off to their positions, pulling security. Silently, Casey gives me the hand signal to get in front of him. Swiftly, I take the lead as we approach the door of the compound. Stopping two feet from the door, we stack up inches from the wall, facing to the north.

Turning slightly, with my right hand on the grip of my M4 rifle, I gesture with my left hand to my flashlight. Both of us turn our flashlights on, returning to our two-man stack at the door. Pointing my weapon at the opening of the "fatal funnel," Casey places his rifle over my right shoulder, providing long range cover. I can feel Casey's knees pressed against the back of my legs as we prepare to make entry. With a second-nature tap of his left hand supporting the barrel of his rifle on my right shoulder, I know he's ready.

Shouldering my rifle, I crouch down into an athletic stance. With one last preparation, I flip my weapon from safe to fire, resting my finger above the trigger guard. Grasping the angled foregrip of my rifle tightly, I lean back into Casey, initiating entry. He rocks forward, still pressed against my back, using our momentum to breach the door.

Hooking an immediate left, button-hooking around the corner, Casey crosses through the door to the right side of the room in one fluid motion. We clear every corner, moving toward the center of the room, stepping heel to toe as to not make a sound. The room layout feels like the reception room of a doctor's office. Except it doesn't have any windows, and the flashlights attached to our rifles are the only light in the room, illuminating every dust particle in the air with a cone-shaped beam.

Seeing another door in the southwest corner of the room, silently, Casey gives me the hand signal that he will go first. Stealthily, he approaches the right side of the door, standing against the wall, as I approach the left side directly across from him. Giving me the head-nod, Casey moves across the doorway to the left, skirting the wall. I simultaneously cross over to the right, brushing against his back as we storm into the last room.

As we enter the room, clearing from the corners to the center, chills shoot up my spine with a harrowing feeling of darkness. The kind of feeling you get when you know something awful took place where you're standing. Looking into the large, operating-sized room, our lights bounce off every four-inch glossy white tile that covers the room from floor to ceiling. In the center of the room, two examination-style tables, seven feet in length by three feet in width, are permanently built into the floor. They're spaced perfectly, three feet apart from each other, also covered in the continuous glossy white tile.

On top of each table are remnants of worn steel hooks and leather straps used to secure a human's head, arms, and legs. The top of each table is subtly sloped to the center, pooling into a two-inch, tiled drainage canal. Each table's drainage canal flows down symmetrically to the floor space between them, meeting a large stainless steel drain in the center. The originally white grout lines on and around the prisoner tables are stained a dark brown color. Following the stains and glossy white tile nearly five feet up the wall, dark brown splatter marks fill the bright white grout lines between the clean and shiny tile, in patterns congruent with an arterial bleed.

Using the flashlight on my rifle, I follow the stained grout lines on the wall until I reach a stainless-steel sink in the far corner of the room. The sink looks as if it were pulled straight out of a doctor's office. Caught in the moment, I'm struggling to comprehend what I'm looking at. It's as if my brain can't believe what my eyes are seeing.

"Bro, is this what I think it is?" I say apprehensively to Casey.

"This is the creepiest shit I've ever seen, dude," Casey says quietly, as if he didn't want to disturb "the darkness."

"This is a fucking torture chamber, bro. I've heard the stories from Ahmed. Apparently, after some high-ranking Soviets were killed down in the Zerkoh Valley, the Soviets would regularly kidnap suspected Mujahideen and their families in the middle of the night. They strapped the Mujahideen down in a torture chamber and tortured him for information. Then, they brought one of his immediate family members in, strapping them down on the table next to him. They strapped his head in the direction where his family was being tortured, forcing him to watch as they tortured them to death. They did it one family member after the other. Then, after killing his family, they tortured him until he was nearly dead. They kept him alive to tell the story, though, dumping him and the corpses of his family in the streets of a neighboring village, just to send a message to the other Mujahideen and the villagers who harbored them. I just didn't believe it. I thought it was an urban legend until now."

"Let's fucking get out of here, man. We're all clear," Casey says with disgust, turning back the way we came.

Flipping our weapons back to safe, we walk out silently. As we exit, the lieutenant signals with his hand towards his eyes, holding up the number two on his fingers, then immediately pointing toward the corner of the building.

Without missing a step, my mind is back on mission. I fall back into formation behind Casey and the five of us stack up along the building wall. Repeating the push-back signal, we initiate movement. As we break cover from the compound wall, the five of us fan out into an L-shaped ambush formation behind the men dressed in all black, matching the description from aerial surveillance. Their backs are turned toward us as they watch the activity on our FOB. Having the advantage, we sneak up on them. Nearly ten feet away from them, they hear a rock crunch beneath one of our boots. Both men spin around, each of them holding loaded AK-47s in their hands.

Seeing their weapons, in one single and smooth transition, I raise my rifle, flipping it from safe to fire, placing my finger on the trigger. Without hesitation, I control my breathing as I look down the barrel of my rifle, through the optic, at the red dot I've now centered on the enemy's forehead.

"Drop your weapon!"

"Do it now!"

With only a split-second passing over my flashback, I'm back to reality and sitting next to Peyton.

Sitting straight up, moving my hand away from hers, I feel ice pulse through my veins. Not adrenaline, but the calm, cold, collected ice in my veins, knowing precisely what I might have to do. *You're going to have to come through me to get to her, and I'll be damned if that's going to happen.*

Without breaking eye contact, sitting four feet away on the opposite end of the fire, he breaks the silence forcefully, "You have any money?"

Looking at the man, with my left hand planted in the sand, I subtly reach my right hand behind my back, gradually lifting my sweatshirt up until I feel the rough texture of my Walther 9mm pistol concealed in my belt line.

Tightening my grip on my firearm with my finger on the trigger guard, I say, "Peyton, you said you had to run to the bathroom. I think it's right up there by the stairs. Why don't you head up there now? I'll wait for you right here."

"You sure?" she responds, wondering if she should stay or she should go.

"Yeah, I'm sure. You've been waiting a while. I'll be fine," I say, hiding all concern from my voice.

Standing up, brushing herself off, I wait until she's out of earshot before replying to the man. With my hand still firmly grasping my handgun, left hand in the sand, I look at the man. Without breaking eye contact, in a calm, authoritative, dissociated voice, I say, "Look, dude, this isn't my first rodeo, and it certainly won't be my last. If you're cold and need a few minutes to warm up, you can stay. I'm not giving you money, and if you think you're going to hurt her or me, you picked the wrong campfire. I suggest you move along."

Without breaking eye contact, staring at me for a long, tense moment, he drunkenly considers his options. I remain poised, ready to draw my weapon and incapacitate the man the second he attempts to pull his large combat knife or charge me from across the fire.

Quietly, he breaks the silence, "I'm cold. I've been

homeless six months, since my ol' lady kicked me to the curb."

Releasing the grip, pulling my sweatshirt back down over my handgun, I put my hands back in front of me. "You can stay, man. We don't have much wood left, but I'll leave the rest when we leave so you can warm up."

The man and I talked for a few more minutes before Peyton returned. She and I headed back to the truck to go home. *Of course, when you finally build up the courage to lean over and kiss her by the fire at sunset, it gets ruined. Murphy, you and your law are real fuckers.*

We drive the hour and a half home, getting her back to her car considerably later than I promised. I'm still stuck in my head by the last half of the drive home. *Is this how it's going to be from now on? You evaluating every person as a threat?* I exit the freeway, wishing I could stop the clock and keep the date from ending. *You didn't even kiss her. She probably thinks you don't like her!*

Pulling into the parking lot at her work, the radio quietly plays in the background.

"I had a good time tonight, Steele. I was really nervous. Nobody has ever taken me on a date like that before," Peyton says quietly, playing with her keys.

"Me, too. Thanks for coming," I respond, unlocking the doors.

Sitting in silence, she continues rolling and jingling her keys back and forth in her hands for a few very long seconds.

"Alright, I'll see you later then?"

"Yeah, I'm sure I'll see you around. I don't live far!" I respond, playing it cool.

Opening the door, grabbing her purse, she takes one more look at me as if she were waiting for something before shutting the door.

Sitting in the truck, I think, *Oh, you fucked up. "See you around"? What the hell is that?* Reaching over, turning the volume of the radio up, I immediately recognize the song. It was as if the big man himself were giving me a swift kick in the ass.

I should have kissed you, just like I wasn't scared at all. So, I turned off the car, ran through the yard, back to your front door. Before I could knock, you turned the lock and met me on the front porch. And I kissed you goodnight, and now that I've kissed you, it's a good night.

Immediately, I look down at the radio, displaying the song played. *Great timing. I get it. Thanks.* Looking over and seeing Peyton's car lights on, reaching up to the gear shift, placing it in drive, I hesitate. Without thinking, I throw it in park, unbuckle my seatbelt, and step out of my truck.

"Hey, Peyton, wait a minute," I say over the sound of my diesel engine.

Opening the door, getting out of her car, "Yes?"

"I planned on kissing you back at the beach. Obviously,

my luck is just that awesome," I say, pulling her closer, hugging her.

Leaning in, I kiss her. "I lied. I don't want to see you around. I had a really good time. I want to see you again."

"Me, too. Tomorrow?" she responds, with blushing cheeks and a smile.

∗ ∗ ∗

I WANTED TO TELL HER THEN THAT I LOVED HER, but I didn't want to scare her away. At the same time, it was overwhelming, because I had never fallen in love at first sight or been so sure of something. For the first time in my life, I wanted to get married and have a family. Not at that exact moment, but I knew she was the one I had been searching for all along.

About two months later, riding the gondola down the side of Crystal Mountain Resort from dinner on top of the mountain, I couldn't hold it in any longer. I nearly yelled to her mid-sentence—and very off topic—that I loved her. When she said it back, I kissed her and held her hand the entire drive home. About halfway home to Portland from Seattle, I had a realization. I realized that all the trials and tribulations I had experienced—all the pain, the years away from home—now all made sense.

I decided that it happened because I had to go through trials and tribulations that made me a better person. It had to detour me through the long backroads of life before eventually leading me to her. Had I not deployed and been away from home for so long, I would have never gone to the doctor's office that day where I met her. I wouldn't have moved back to Oregon, and I wouldn't have made the friends that I now call my brothers.

*"Every warrior of the light has felt
afraid to enter into combat.
Every warrior of the light has betrayed and lied in the past.
Every warrior of the light has lost faith in the future.
Every warrior of the light has trodden
a path which was not his own.
Every warrior of the light has suffered
because of unimportant things.
Every warrior of the light has doubted
that he is a warrior of the light.
Every warrior of the light has failed
in his spiritual obligations.
Every warrior of the light has said yes when he meant no.
Every warrior of the light has hurt someone he loved.
That is why he and she are warriors of the light;
They had endured all this without
losing the hope to improve."*

—PAULO COELHO

CHAPTER 11

MIXING OUR PAST
WITH OUR FUTURE

THE PROBLEMS BEGAN ABOUT FIVE MONTHS INTO
dating. It takes two to tango, and because this book is
about post-deployment issues and how they manifested
into my own issues, I am being candid.

The honeymoon phase of returning from war had worn
off. I was not able to sleep longer than three to four hours at
a time. I was becoming increasingly more depressed and
was still unsure of "what next." By September, the sleep
deprivation was beginning to take its toll. My patience
was nonexistent. I became argumentative and gradually
started to consume more alcohol.

Sitting at my favorite Mexican restaurant, I stare at
Peyton. Many say the honeymoon phase should have worn
off by now; however, every time I look into the sparkle of
her green and copper eyes, at her smile, my heart skips a

beat. Every time she reaches her hand out for mine, I feel butterflies swarming inside my stomach. Sitting across the table from her, I still can't believe this amazing woman is sitting across from me. *How did I get so lucky? I would have never imagined meeting a woman like this,* I think to myself.

"Babe, we need to talk about something," she says, solemn.

"Um, am I going to need a couple shots of tequila for this one?" I say, with a wave of anxiety. One of my admitted issues is trusting my significant other. Unfortunately, every person before Peyton had cheated on me or talked to other men behind my back, so I held back and guarded myself.

Waiting for her to tell me that she started talking to another guy or that she had found somebody else, I take a large gulp of my margarita. Expecting the worst, my mind begins to wander as I stare out the window.

"I'm going on a trip to Colombia, El Salvador, Honduras, and Southern Mexico by foot and backpack with my stepsister."

I couldn't contain the sigh of relief that she hadn't cheated on me. Then, my veins run cold. *Two little American girls in Colombia? El Salvador? Honduras? Southern Mexico?* As if the restaurant were running past me, suddenly I'm whipped through the vortex of an instantaneous flashback to Kabul, Afghanistan.

Attempting to check out and detach myself from the situation, somehow I find myself back *there*.

It's roughly January of 2015, only eight months prior. It's quite cold outside, and I just got into bed after a twenty-four-hour QRF shift with little to no sleep.

"Kelly, wake up. Secondary QRF is getting spun up for a riot outside of the gates, about one kilometer away, in case it gets out of hand or we encounter suicide bombers. Briefing in five minutes at our platoon ops room," my squad leader says.

Hopping out of bed, I pull on my pants, boots, and combat shirt from out of the cupboard. I'm calm, as any combat nowadays seems routine and, quite honestly, mundane. Standing up, I reach over pulling my armored plate carrier up off the ground, whipping it over my head and onto my chest. Reaching for the buckles, I clasp them together. *Maybe you should grab a couple extra magazines for this one.* Looking up into my tactical dresser, as I called it, I grab four extra magazines, sliding them into my left cargo pocket. Looking to the right, I see two fragmentation grenades and a smoke grenade. *Yup, I should probably take you guys, too.* Reaching up, I feel the cold metal of the grenades against my fingers. Checking to ensure the electrical tape is still holding the spoon and pin in place, I hang them off my plate carrier where I can grab them, rip the tape and pin out, and throw them at enemy forces if need be. Reaching for my rifle, I clip the sling to the shoulder harness, dangling my rifle from my armor, heading for the operations center.

"Gentlemen, there is a riot about one kilometer away.

Intel says it's a local disagreement. Supposedly, this woman was burning the Quran, and it has immediately incited violence. Remember, this is the drawdown. Our orders currently are to protect the base, and we are only here to ensure peacekeeping. It is the Afghan Police and Afghan National Army's job to do any enforcement. Is that clear, gentlemen? You will NOT interfere at all. Am I crystal-fucking-clear?" the platoon leader says.

In a synchronized fashion, ten men calmly respond, "Yes, sir."

As we approach the gates exiting the compound, I draw my 9mm Beretta pistol, pulling back and releasing the ice-cold slide from the winter air and racking a bullet into the chamber. To ensure it is loaded, I draw the slide halfway back, ensuring there's a bullet chambered. Without looking, after months of combat, I slide the pistol back into my thigh holster, as if it were an attachment to my body. Reaching for my rifle, I slap the bottom of the magazine with the palm of my hand. Simultaneously reaching for the charging handle, I pull it back, loading a bullet into the chamber. Indulging in my superstitious ritual, I pull my lucky can of tobacco out of my pocket and place a dip into my mouth.

Leaving the gates, the street seems empty. Too empty. As we walk around the compound, snaking through the streets of downtown Kabul, we examine every freshly poured square of concrete that could be laced with explosives, and every man, woman, and child—any of whom could be wearing a suicide vest. Getting closer to the populated section of Kabul, we take notice of the crowd screaming and yelling, punctuated by the sound of bricks and debris being thrown. They are shouting in Pashto, yet there are so many screams, it is impossible to decipher any phrases. Jarringly, there's a burst of flames in the middle of the riot, and we are unable to see anything going on. Standing there, we wait around, ensuring they will not change directions toward the base. While we observe, I can't help but notice a mass in the middle of the flames. By this point, it is so charred, mangled, and burnt, I can't tell what the mass is. The smell of burning feces, tires, and oil is a familiar smell of the country, but this is unusually strong, with black smoke billowing into the air. We are ordered back to base.

Returning to base, I place the muzzle of my rifle into the clearing barrel, tap the magazine release, drop the magazine out of the receiver, and stick it into my pocket. Because this process is so frequent and routine, I pull the charging handle back, ejecting a bullet into the air and catching it in my left hand. I repeat this with my pistol and walk back to my sleeping quarters.

Laying back in bed, attempting to drift off to sleep, I can't help but think back to twenty minutes prior. *What was the mass in the center? It was too big to be a dog, too small to be a car? Was that a person they lit on fire? What were they throwing stones at?* Unable to distract my mind to drift back to sleep, I pull out my cell phone and go to the Live Leak site. Sure enough, there it was.

As the video begins to play, I recognize the surroundings. The familiar buildings, checkpoints, street corners, and the crowd I had just seen. As the video progresses, I watch as a woman lights the Palestinian books (not the Quran) on fire in the middle of the street. Out of nowhere, a man yells in Pashto, "She's burning the Quran!"

Immediately, large flocks of men begin exiting their houses. It was a situation with gasoline ready for a match. The men start screaming at the woman, circling all around her. Trying to escape, she clambers up onto building roofs, attempting to flee the angry mob. The men climb up onto the rooftops, following her as she desperately tries to escape, quite literally running for her life.

As she scurries down the roof line, the men begin to hurl stones as hard as they can toward her. The woman is able to dodge the stones for several minutes, maintaining her speed and escape attempt. But that's the problem. It's only an attempt. Mid-stride, a stone hits her back leg, causing her to trip, sending her rolling across the roof, down toward the ground. At the last second, she catches herself at the bottom of the roof, making for another escape. Except this time, there's no exit. The men chasing her on the roof close the distance, and with one push, they thrust her off the roof down to the ground six feet below.

The angry mob circles around her, repeatedly striking the twenty-something woman with stones. After several attempts, the crowd takes turns gang-raping the woman as her father breaks through the crowd. In Pashto, you can hear her father ask the men questions. Then, as you think the father is about to help his daughter up off the ground and end the brutality, he picks up a brick and begins stoning his own daughter.

After several minutes, I thought the punishment was going to end. Through the crowd, I can see a man carrying a can of either gasoline or kerosene. Making his way through the crowd, he gets to the woman now severely beaten, raped, and nearly murdered, yet somehow still alive. Taking the can, he dumps all of the fluid onto the woman, looking toward her father. The man then sets his own daughter on fire, watching her burn.

Back to reality, I begin to process the words Peyton just told me. I can smell burning flesh and gasoline. I can picture the woman getting stoned, gang-raped, and set on fire. Yet, the only face I see on the woman is Peyton's.

"I'm not fucking okay with this," I respond sharply.

"What do you mean you aren't okay with this? I don't think I asked my dad's permission here." Her tone was equally as annoyed as mine.

"Look, do you know what happens to young women in cartel land? They get tortured, chopped up into pieces, raped, or sold into the sex trade. Can't you go to a different fucking country? I'm not okay with cartel-controlled, politically disheveled countries."

"You can either support me or not, but I'm going.

Your view of the world is jaded, and these countries are very safe."

Arguing in a restaurant was the last thing I wanted to do, so I took a long pull from my drink to buy myself time.

"Anyway, back to what I was saying. I think I'm going to go for enchiladas tonight. What do you want?" I change the subject.

Over the next few days, I began to grow increasingly angry at the thought of her trip. She was excited and thought nothing bad would happen. I was terrified the girls would be kidnapped and sent into a human sex trafficking ring or worse. No matter how accepting I tried to be, how much I tried to think positively, I couldn't combat the fear, and I actively lashed out, asking her to change the location of her trip.

I realized later that this was the first step into her viewing me as controlling. Quite frankly, if I were in her position or the position of a person who had not seen the horrors of the worst people in the world, I would probably think it was controlling too. However, if you are going to get involved with a combat veteran, a first responder, or any other individual who has experienced severe trauma, the "controlling line" must be reevaluated and defined.

A couple of days later, I met up with my old squad leader. Telling him about her trip and my fear, he gave me some advice. He explained that, in life, many people need to go out and find themselves because they have a sense of adventure they want to satisfy. We satisfied that through our military service. He explained that, possibly, her urge to go to those places to find herself was for the same reasons that I chose to enlist and volunteer for deployment. Finally, he hit me with the cold hard truth. He told me that by handling it with anger-based fear instead of concern, all I was doing was driving a wedge between us. Instead of being an ally and showing that I support, care for, and love her, I looked like a controlling asshole.

He realized, after issues in his own marriage, that although it is difficult and a "not-manly" way of approaching situations that trigger your own issues within PTSD, it is much better to explain to that loved one that we are worried or scared. We can do this by calmly giving an explanation of why and how the experiences that led to PTSD have created the fear and worry. Explain that it's hard for you to vocalize concern and fear, so it comes off as anger or controlling the situation, when that isn't your intent.

That night, I realized I had been handling the entire situation with anger because I was afraid of something happening to Peyton. I decided to take her to dinner, giving her a card with a love letter for every week she was gone. In addition, I apologized for the way I had handled the situation. I took my old squad leader's advice and told her that I handled it wrong, that I was wrong, and that I was sorry. I explained why I was fearful and that I was scared of losing her at the hand of violence. Leaving the details out, I told her that every time I pictured the drug cartel controlled areas she was going to be in, all I could see was her face in place of that woman's.

She ended up going on her trip, and I worried about her every day. I prayed for her safety daily. It was excruciating not to let anxiety from my experiences spiral me downward over the month she was set to be gone.

For many of us—the personality type seen in the military—we tend to be alpha males. We often embrace the definition of masculinity and being a strong man. We have a desire to join, leave, and protect the ones we love at home. However, over prolonged periods of time spent seeing behind the curtain and dealing with the "boogie man in the dark," that desire to protect our loved ones back home continues, even after the threat subsides and we're home.

International travel wasn't the only time my PTSD was displayed through fear, anxiety, and control. On several occasions—when Peyton left my house late at night knowing she had to drive thirty-five miles, or when she went out with her girlfriends for ladies' night—I asked her to text and let me know she got home safe and had the door locked. Quite honestly, I didn't care what time she got home. I just wanted to know she was safe.

On a few occasions, she forgot to text me to let me know she had made it home safe and sound. I woke up at four in the morning panicking, jumping to the idea that she was dead in a ditch, held hostage, or in grave danger. In a form of OCD (Obsessive Compulsive Disorder) on one occasion, I called more than six times until she woke up so that I knew she was okay.

The difficulty with this type of situation is that the veteran knows the panic is completely irrational. The odds of something terrible happening to somebody, let alone our loved one, are extremely slim. However, even as I picked up the phone, knowing she probably drank too much and had forgotten to text me, I couldn't stop myself from being convinced, even positive that she was in distress or that something terrible had happened to her. On two particular occasions, the following day, I was extremely upset about it. As if I were speaking to a subordinate, I said, "Really? I don't understand why it's so fucking hard for you to simply text three words: *I'm home safe*. Is it really that fucking hard of a concept?"

Looking back, I can see how destructive this manifestation of PTSD can become when someone is in a relationship. Too many in her support group, and even in my civilian circle, don't understand the panic and sheer terror that washes over us when we think something has happened to the ones we love most. Many people see it as an overbearing form of control, and they can't understand that checking in has nothing to do with trust, infidelity, or wanting to control.

I don't know if the fear of the worst happening to the people I love most will ever go away. What I do know is that many relationships after trauma are affected by this same dilemma. To the person who hasn't experienced the trauma, they can't imagine the horrors running through our mind or the panic that we can't help them. What is most important is that the issue is communicated between the couple. It should not be weighed in on by people outside of the relationship who have never been involved with an individual who has been through heavy life experience. It is the job of the people who are dating or married to each other to communicate their intent and make an effort to reassure the other.

The fact of the matter is, everybody comes with baggage. To some, it's stranger than others. However, when getting involved with a combat veteran or first responder who makes the attempt to communicate fears he knows or understands may seem irrational, it is a commitment for each person to support the other if you want the relationship to succeed. Even if it's as trivial as setting a reminder on your phone that says, "Text him you're home safe." It's one of the smallest things to those unaffected, but the biggest to us.

As individuals struggling with PTSD, it is our job to make an additional effort to ensure that we are not being controlling, recognizing the difference between fear of a situation and manipulation. This is a double-edged sword, relying on our significant other to meet us halfway once we acknowledge the fact that we are being triggered.

"Before my father died, he said the worst thing about growing old was that other men stopped seeing you as dangerous. I've always remembered that—how being dangerous was sacred, a badge of honor. You live your life by a code, an ethos. Every man does. It's your shoreline; it's what guides you home."

—RORKE DENVER, US NAVY SEAL

CHAPTER 12

LOVE AND WAR

——

ONE HAND ON THE STEERING WHEEL, HEART AS full and content as it possibly could be, I'm driving down the interstate with my unicorn riding in the passenger seat. Looking down at the center console, I can't help but notice how perfectly her hand fits into mine. Every finger perfectly placed between mine as if they were meant for each other. I look over at her and, even after nine months of dating, my heart seems to skip a beat every time I look at her smile. I begin to notice how perfectly her blonde hair sits in her ponytail holder as the wind blows escaped wisps of highlighted hair across her face. Without realizing that I'm staring, my admiration is interrupted.

"What?" she says in a flirty and somewhat giddy voice.

"I can't help but notice how beautiful you are. And not just your looks. You have a beautiful personality, too—a real-life unicorn," I say with a shit-eating grin.

"Stooooooop," she says, failing to hide her smile.

"No. I mean every word of it. I love you. I feel lucky to have you in my life."

"Look, babe, the reason I was so intrigued by you was because although you had seen some pretty awful things, you were upbeat and positive without acting like a victim. Men these days just aren't as sexy, humble, kind, and gentle, yet manly all at the same time. You don't feel the need to brag. You're just confident and comfortable with the man you are. You—you, babe—are the unicorn," she says, equally genuine.

Smiling and blushing, I grasp her hand a little tighter. Hiding behind my sunglasses, I look out at the cars in front of us. *Gentle? If you only knew the other side of me.*

The sounds of music and passing cars begin to muffle out as I'm sucked back to only eleven months prior.

"Yeah, man, I'm making a documentary. You got any last words for your wife before the big mission?" I hear, passing first platoon. Although said humorously, I can't help but notice the serious tone inflection in his voice. Shifting my shoulders, I continue walking, feeling the weight of my rucksack compressing the vertebrae in my back.

Whose bright fucking idea was it to bring 700 rounds of 7.62x51 belt-fed ammunition, three spare barrels, four days of food and water, thermal optics, and a tripod? Oh, yeah. The same platoon sergeant who is only carrying a forty-pound pack while the rest of us carry over one hundred. Yeah, the dictator sergeant who has no idea what leading by example looks like.

Picking my arms up a little more, I resituate the M240B twenty-seven-pound machine gun, continuing toward the hangar.

Walking into the helicopter hangar, I can't help but notice the beautiful and brilliant purple and pink colors displayed as the sun begins to set over the airstrip. Getting to my squad, the sounds of crisp guitar notes and drums blasting through the stereo, Five Finger Death Punch's song *Wrong Side of Heaven* fills the air.

Dropping my pack, I hear the clanking sounds of belted ammunition, grenades, and optics slamming together. Pressing the spring near the barrel, I unfold the legs, setting the machine gun on the ground. Walking to my brother Casey, I polish off my third Red Bull for the night.

"Hey, fucker, don't you find it funny the dictator put all the guys he hates on the first chopper? Nothing like fishing for Taliban when you're the bait!"

"Hey, cock gobbler, might as well sacrifice the lambs you hate first!" he responds, laughing.

"Yeah, well, he's a badass, remember? That's why he's on the last helicopter to land," I respond, sarcasm shining through.

"Gentlemen! Gather around for ramp brief!" a voice commands.

Gathering around, you can't help but feel the testosterone and anticipation in the air as salty, seasoned warriors circle up—emotionless, despite the risk they are gearing up for.

"Gentlemen, Allied forces haven't been here in over seven years. Afghan National Army has no idea we're coming, so it may be a bit of a surprise to them. We currently have no idea about their attitudes and opinions toward NATO forces. Until proven wrong, assume Taliban has infiltrated their ranks and they are combatants. However, do *not* get trigger happy, as they may be allies," the commander says calmly.

The hangar is so silent, you can hear a pin drop.

"Chalk One, where are you? Raise your hand."

My hand joins eight others in the air.

"I will be going with you. Chalk One is going to be the first to land. We will be escorted there by Apache attack helicopters equipped with Hellfire missiles, and we will have aerial support for the duration of the mission from B2 bombers and F16 fighter jets. We will be advising the following chalks on the ground situation. We are going to stagger Chalk Two by twenty minutes in case the ten of us come under fire and it is too hot to land the rest of the helicopters.

"Gentlemen, should this be the case, we will consolidate to the tower on the southwest corner of the base. While there, the ten of us will hold enemy forces off until we can get QRF to come help. Unfortunately, if we cannot get the rest of our chalks in by air, they will have to go by ground. That may take twenty-four to thirty-six hours to get QRF by ground vehicles, so be prepared for the ten of us to fight it out for several days. We should have roughly 7,000 7.62 rounds, not including M4 ammunition."

I couldn't think of a better commander than this guy. *He's the real deal, leading by example. My own platoon sergeant can't even do that.*

"Either way, whether we're holding out or the rest of the guys are down there, you guys have rigged up five other body bags full of ammunition, rockets, and grenades for a re-supply drop. They are already pre-rigged for the choppers and can be dropped at any point in time as needed. Prepare for the worst, gents. We may get lucky and be back here thirty-six hours from now, but be ready for the long haul. We could be out there a while," the commander concluded the ramp brief.

Those of us who regularly go to ramp brief prayer with the chaplain conduct services and then head out for the mission. Walking over to my gear, I interlace my fingers around the shoulder straps of my rucksack, heaving with both arms the backpack that weighs more than a fourth grader, slinging it onto my back. Hardly able to bend over, I pick up my weapon and follow Casey toward Chalk One's Blackhawk helicopter.

Are we going to be fish in a barrel? If they've been tipped off, they'll wait until the helicopters drop us to shoot at us with no cover, out in the open. Am I ready for the judgment of my God?

Cutting through the fleeting thoughts of our impending fate, I hear the soothing sounds of our ramp music bringing me back to reality. It seems to echo the feelings many of us have.

I heard from God today, and she sounded just like me—
What have I done and who have I become? I saw the devil
today, and he looked a lot like me—I looked away, I turned
away! Arms wide open, I stand alone. I'm no hero, and I'm
not made of stone—Right or wrong, I can hardly tell! I'm
on the wrong side of heaven and the righteous side of hell.

Sitting for what seems like hours, we wait for the sun to set—waiting for the witching hour to give us the cover of darkness. Hearing the engines fire up, the rotors of the Blackhawk slowly spin to life, it's our cue to mount up. Putting my game face on, I accept my fate. *If it's judgment time, so be it. I'm ready.*

"Hey, Jew Bear, I want to tell you something real quick!"

"Kelly, not now," he says seriously, expecting the typical dirty joke.

"No, I'm—I'm serious," I say, being sure to nix all sarcasm from my tone while still hiding any fear in my voice. "I wear a Saint Michael necklace around my neck, and my dog tags are tied to my belt, draped into my back, right pocket. It'd mean a lot to me, if something happens, if you'd make sure both my tags and necklace get home to my family. I also left a letter for my family on the shelf in my room. It's on top of my grandfather's flag that was draped over his casket. Just make sure they get home for me, brother."

"Nothing's going to happen to you, brother," he replies with uncertainty clearly lingering.

"Just, please...please...promise me. Just in case."

"You got it. I love you, brother."

"I love you too, bro. Catch you on the flip side."

As I wait for the men to fill the seats inside the Black-hawk, I feel a pat over my right shoulder. Spinning around, I see my brother Casey.

"Hey, fucker, if one of us dies, either open the back gate to heaven or turn the A/C on when you get to hell. You know, just in case Big J doesn't want to let in sinners like us!" His comedic relief cuts the tension like butter.

"Oh, you know I will! See you on the other side, fucker! Whichever side that may be, I'll have whiskey waiting!" I shout over the roar of the now fully spinning rotors. Giving a genuine bro hug, we go our separate ways—Casey to the left side, me to the right.

Finally, it's our turn to board the bird. I'm the last guy on and the first guy out of the right side, with Casey the same on the left. Looking through the green view of my night vision, I see nine other courageous men sitting on the chopper. All the nods are on, and each and every one of us have the most serious *don't fuck with me* looks on our faces. The thrust of the rotors lifts us off the ground, and the chopper banks right toward the south, flying over the base. Looking out the window down at our tents, I wonder if we're all going to make it back alive.

Reaching into my left shoulder pocket, I pull out my full can of Grizzly chewing tobacco. Giving it two hard flicks of the wrist, I cut the seal with my fingernail, cracking the lid. Holding my can in my left hand, I reach my right hand over, pinching my thumb and index finger together and pull out the required amount to take the edge of stress off. As if it were the engage switch, I put it in my lip, pop the lid closed, and place the can back in my left shoulder pocket. Without hesitation, my game face is on, fear is gone, and I am ready.

After about ten minutes of flight, I'm looking at the ground, running over all the scenarios of what may happen when we land. Unexpectedly, I'm jolted by the concussion and flash of muzzle fire filling the cabin. Facing the rear of the chopper toward the gunner, I watch as he leans out the window, pressing down on the butterfly trigger of the machine gun. My heart begins to race. I pull my machine gun tightly onto my lap, bracing myself for the impact of an incoming RPG (Rocket Propelled Grenade) that will send us from thousands of feet in the air to our sudden death. Swiftly, he stops, returning to his swivel for the enemy forces lying in wait. *Well, at least it works. No RPG. Would have been nice for a test fire warning. At least somebody is watching.*

After an hour of flight, the pilot breaks the hum of the rotors, shouting over the loudspeaker, "One minute out!"

Calm, cool, and collected, I tighten the night vision mount on my helmet, pulling my weapon tightly onto my lap.

"Thirty seconds!"

Heart racing.

"Ten seconds! Go get 'em, boys!" the pilot shouts in farewell.

The doors whip open with force. Helicopter hovering, without hesitation, I lean out the door, throwing myself out of the helicopter, landing onto my stomach, as if I had done it a million times. I can feel the wash of the rotors propelling air down onto my back in the pitch-black desert. The only sound is the roar of the blades overhead.

Shouldering my machine gun, left hand under the buttstock beneath my right armpit, hand around the grip, my index finger on the trigger guard ready to slide to the trigger in a split second, I scan for enemy targets. The only indication I have that guys are getting off the bird is the rhythmic flop of men jumping off onto their belly, one on top of the other, landing on top of me. In my left eye, the lens displays the green of my night vision. I see five infrared lasers from the men next to me who are searching their fields of fire for enemy fighters. The lens of my right eye shows the white and gray heat signatures from the thermal optic mounted on top of my M240B machine gun.

As swiftly as the Blackhawk came in, I feel the thrust of the rotors spinning faster as the chopper disappears into the night sky, heading back to base. Glancing at my watch, I mark the time, adding twenty minutes.

Within the hour, all chalks had arrived, carrying sixty armed professionals who would neutralize any situation on the ground. While placing snipers and command post, I lean against a wire-laced container filled with dirt and gravel. Pushing forward on the machine gun with the tripod pushing back on me, a flicker in the green hue catches my eye. Silhouettes, headlights, and trucks armed with machine guns are speeding toward us.

"Casey! We have seven armed trucks headed toward the gates straight in front of us. They're coming fast, bro." My voice was mechanically calm.

"Yeah, they are! Get ready, gents!" he orders, equally as cool-headed.

Weapon shouldered, left hand once again on the stock of the rifle under my right armpit, my right hand tightly grasps the grip of the weapon. I lift my index finger up to the safety. Feeling for the rough texture, I push softly, feeling it click from safe to fire. Placing my finger back on the trigger guard, I'm ready to send lead at the cyclic rate of 650 rounds per minute into any of the men who decide to bring me or my brothers harm. I begin to count.

"Hey, Casey, we have seven mounted heavy crew serve weapons, at least twenty to thirty armed men," I say, spitting brown-colored chew spit to the ground, returning to the sights of my weapon.

"Get frosty, gents! Here we go!" Casey orders to the fifteen stacked up soldiers behind the barricade next to me.

The armed men pull into the compound directly in front of the barricades, jumping aggressively out of their vehicles nearly eight feet in front of us. The men on the far side of the trucks exit, taking cover behind the fenders of the trucks, aiming their AK-47s at us. In the back of the trucks, the seven men manning the heavy weapons are now turned toward us, aiming their Russian-made .57 Caliber DSHK, PKM, and RPK machine guns directly at us. The standoff begins.

Without moving a muscle, finger now placed on the trigger, safety off, I'm ready to apply the final four pounds of pressure firing hot lead into any of the men at the slightest movement toward hostile action. Continuing to look over the barrel of my rifle in the green night vision over my left eye, I see thirty perfectly placed infrared lasers on the chest and forehead of every potential combatant. Through my right eye, the headlights of the trucks have lit up every man in front of us. *You may kill me, but I've got a one-hundred-round belt to fire, taking as many of you with me as I can. Little do you bastards know, every single one of you could be dead two seconds from now.*

I can feel the bead of sweat trickle down my forehead from beneath the foam pad of my Kevlar helmet. Tensions escalate as their commander begins shouting at our interpreter. Both sides hold their position while still aiming at each other, attempting not to have a repeat of "the shot heard 'round the world." Everyone is still.

In the background, I can hear our commander say calmly to the interpreter, "Tell him to order his men to put their weapons down. We are here to accomplish a mission. It's need-to-know basis, and he doesn't need to know. We will leave here when our mission is over."

Their commander, agitation laced in his voice, barks

what are unmistakable demands at our interpreter. After nearly thirty minutes of deadlock, he shouts an order to his men, and they lower their weapons. Taking my finger off the trigger, placing my weapon on safe, I straighten my back out, taking a deep sigh of relief.

Interrupting my sigh of relief, the commander shouts, "Where's second platoon? Come here, now!"

Fifteen soldiers, including me, circle the commander as he issues the order, "Gents, one of our support Apache helicopters just made an emergency landing about one kilometer northwest of here. Their wingman is circling at high altitude until you guys get there. They don't have much fuel left, so they don't have long. You guys need to get to them before the Taliban does. They're severely outgunned, and their lives depend on you guys. Leave the compound, recover them, and bring them back."

As we leave the gates, I turn back for one last glimpse of the compound. *Let's do this.*

As fast as it had come, the memory fades away, the sound of music and passing cars fills my mind, and I'm back in my truck. Still holding her hand, I look over at her, grasping her hand a little tighter, smiling, "Thanks, babe. I love you more than you know. Let's go grab dinner."

Silently, I wonder if she would still think of me and love me the same if she knew more about me. *If she only knew. If she only knew the other side of me.*

* * *

FOR A WHILE, I STRUGGLED WITH THIS PARADIGM with Peyton, my family, friends, and coworkers. I felt there was a whole different side of me that they didn't even know about. I felt like Dr. Jekyll and Mr. Hyde. They saw this loving, caring, kind, and gentle man, even passive at times. On the other hand, the side they didn't see or know about was the warrior—the direct man who will accomplish the mission however dangerous it may be, even if it means using violence. The side who could stand up under gunfire and explosions, disregarding personal safety, emptying magazine after magazine of ammunition at enemy forces. The man who is willing to sacrifice everything for the ones he loves most—not only the external comforts or his life, but even his personal ethics, morals, and softness. When it comes to life or death and protecting the ones I love most, there is nothing I won't put on the table of "things I'm willing to lose."

Despite their impressions, I felt the way they viewed me was the way you view a weak individual, rather than the sharp alpha who could push himself beyond his natural physical limitations. This has been a major dichotomy for myself and many other combat veterans I know. We don't want our wives, family, or civilian friends to know what we did, because we want them to see the best and loving side of us. We want to be seen as men who choose to be loving—the warrior in a garden. However, we also want them to know that if evil and harm lurks around the corner, we will face it. There is no limit to the things we will do to protect freedom, the American way of life, and the ones we love. We often feel our kindness gets misunderstood as weakness, and eventually, we feel as though our family and friends view us as weak or mentally broken.

Stuck in this dichotomy, I continuously felt emotional turmoil over who I had become. Was I the ruthless warrior who had a side of violence? Was I the passive individual who preferred peace and love? Am I no longer a dangerous man? I feel this is an issue that many of us struggle with while reintegrating.

A few days before I met Peyton, I had a beer with a longtime family friend and mentor. He had several combat deployments and was undergoing a messy and painful divorce. When the following conversation took place, I was looking for somebody to help me navigate how to return and re-integrate. I absorbed all his advice without looking at it from an objective point of view. However, after meeting Peyton, the advice stuck with me, and it drastically affected my relationship and the things I chose or didn't choose to share with her. After several years of hindsight reflection, I am finally beginning to understand what he meant, in a roundabout way.

"Steele, don't make the same mistake with your future wife that I did with my soon-to-be ex-wife. You and I—we made the decision to join combat arms. Understanding the risks and the extremes of war, we said, 'Here I am, send me.' In doing so, we saw things that the average American will never see or experience in their lifetime. When we come home, we struggle with certain things. In addition, they view us through a lens of innocence.

"They will tell us they want to know what happened; however, based on their life, it's relative. They think of bad things as one thing, because they can't grasp just how bad *bad* can get—it's all relative. By telling them what *bad* really is, we are robbing them of their innocence. This was our choice, and it's our burden to bear, not theirs. If you tell her and others, eventually, they will view you in a completely different way. Instead of seeing you as this loving person who wouldn't hurt a fly, they begin to think of all the things you're capable of, and it will change the dynamics of your relationship."

For a while, this contributed to the "Who am I?" predicament. I wanted to tell Peyton about certain things so she could understand why I got worked up if I didn't hear from her telling me she had made it home safe. On the other hand, I loved her with all of my heart, and I didn't want to rob her of her innocence or have her view me in a negative light. However, I also didn't want her to see me as a passive or weak or controlling individual.

What I eventually realized was that I am entirely both people.

Within psychology, this is discussed and incremental to Erik Erikson's theory of identity and psychosocial stages of development in the stage of *Identity vs. Role Confusion*. This stage is usually experienced between the ages of twelve and eighteen, but can be experienced at different times and revisited in multiple phases of the human life, especially when an intense or traumatic experience happens. In this stage, individuals explore and identify their self and personal identity through understanding what their own beliefs, morals, ethics, and values are. During this period, it is considered normal to have different versions or identities of ourselves, and the versions are situationally dependent. Over time and maturity, we realize all of these traits or identities are us, and they all come together to form one complete identity.

While struggling to determine which identity is ours, it's hard to see that all of these hats we've worn in our military or civilian life are who we are. The key is realizing not all of these traits need to be expressed at all times. Knowing when to display which version of ourselves is the factor that balances us out, making a healthy person. For example, if you present the aggressive side of yourself every day in non-hostile environments, you look like an asshole with an anger problem. Not that you are, but the situation doesn't call for that behavior. The average person around us who hasn't experienced such a stressful situation that would require it, can't understand why we're so "on edge." On the flip side, if somebody breaks into your house intending to do your family harm, it would be ridiculous to be passive and non-hostile, because the situation now requires you to put your aggressive alpha male hat on.

This phenomenon is referenced in several war and military tactic books going back hundreds of years, including Sun Tzu's, *The Art of War*. In the book, Tzu discusses the balance of a warrior. He says in one passage, "He who knows when to fight and when one shouldn't will be victorious."

"It is the Soldier, not the minister
Who has given us freedom of religion.
It is the Soldier, not the reporter
Who has given us freedom of the press.
It is the Soldier, not the poet
Who has given us freedom of speech.
It is the Soldier, not the campus organizer
Who has given us freedom to protest.
It is the Soldier, not the lawyer
Who has given us the right to a fair trial.
It is the Soldier, not the politician
Who has given us the right to vote.
It is the Soldier who salutes the flag,
Who serves beneath the flag,
And whose coffin is draped by the flag,
Who allows the protester to burn the flag."

—CHARLES M. PROVINCE, US ARMY

CHAPTER 13

HORMONES, TRAUMATIC BRAIN INJURIES, AND PTSD

—

WHEN I RETURNED HOME FROM AFGHANISTAN, I experienced roughly a three-month "honeymoon" period. I was happy to be back in the United States and was overwhelmed with joy with the simple ability of having the freedom to hop in my truck, get a coffee, or drive anywhere for that matter. I had an overwhelmingly positive outlook and felt ready to make changes in my life to pursue the Green Berets. I had been training for several years, and I finally had enough experience, physical conditioning, and mental strength to try out.

I felt I would be one of the few who were fortunate enough to make it through hell and back without any major outcomes. It wasn't until the sleep deprivation and depression set in that I realized I was different. For the first year, I lived in a state of denial. I began having angry outbursts, during which I would get aggravated and vocalize my discontent in a destructive way. Little things, such as the towel folded wrong or my socks not rolled up would be enough to anger me. I unintentionally developed a pattern of blaming everybody else for making me angry. If I got cut off in traffic, they were trying to ruin my day and were simply out to be an "asshole." If I got mad at my little sister, parents, or Peyton, I would blame them— because, you know, *it's their issue.* I couldn't possibly be the one who had developed a problem.

I continued to tell myself, despite my loved ones pleading for me to seek counseling, that PTSD, depression, and anxiety were for the weak. I genuinely believed that only emotionally and mentally fragile individuals succumbed to these things. I was a warrior, and I was good at it. I began wondering how to get on the next deployment because life seemed so much happier, easier, and fulfilling over there than it was back home. I wanted to go back, and I wanted to go back so badly I would have given both my left and right testicle to do so.

It wasn't until my medical condition deteriorated that I realized going back wasn't an option. I became increasingly depressed and began losing muscle mass, gaining fat, and had mood swings that would take me from the happiest I've ever been one moment to the saddest and most hopeless place I've ever been a second later, then to the angriest I've ever been. I continued lifting weights and running, but nothing seemed to make it better. I knew something was wrong because I had never been that way. I had always been the optimistic, happy, and rarely a down-in-the-dumps kind of guy. I felt horrible because I physically felt like I was riding on a roller-coaster, and I knew the effect I had on those around me. And yet, I still couldn't control it.

The blessing in disguise, which I didn't realize until after six months of testing and specialists, was that I had enough knowledge of psychology that I was able to critically evaluate myself from a third-party perspective. I knew this was not a depression issue, and I was not bipolar, but I knew there was something wrong with my body.

I met my limit, and I made a doctor's appointment with a general practice physician. Leaving out the profound hopelessness and depression in fear that they would jump to conclusions and seize my firearms, strap me down, etc., I downplayed the situation and gave him the story. At first, he said I simply needed an anti-depressant—that millions of Americans struggle with depression, that it wasn't a weakness—sometimes you just need something to help out temporarily. I stuck to my guns. I nearly begged him to draw hormone levels and any other possible blood work.

Three days later, I got a phone call.

"Hello. I'm calling on your lab results. I have to swallow my pride here. It looks like you're right. Your cortisol levels are off the chart, your testosterone is 340, when at your age, it should be 800–1100, and your estrogen is high, roughly a ninety, which is nearly the same as a pregnant woman. I'm sending you to an endocrinologist for further care. Please let me know if you need any help or have any questions."

I hung up the phone.

Motherfucker. I fucking knew it.

Now, I know to a lot of readers that may sound like gibberish, and it might not make any sense. Hormones are very complicated. However, I will spare you the long textbook answer. I encourage you, if you think this may be affecting you, to do your own research and dive deeper, as the human endocrine system is extremely complicated and I'm barely scratching the surface.

Cortisol is a hormone associated with stress and stress responses. It is secreted by the adrenal glands. Triggering the adrenal glands to produce cortisol is the pituitary gland, which is roughly the size of an almond and is located just behind the eye sockets on the brain. It regulates your body's metabolism and secretion of other hormones, like testosterone and estrogen. If you have high levels of cortisol, it can interfere with learning and memory, lower immune function and bone density, and increase weight gain, blood pressure, cholesterol, and your risk of heart disease. Essentially, it can put your body into a continuous state of fight or flight. It also affects other hormones and chemicals to make room for the fight or flight response.

Testosterone is also controlled by the hypothalamus and pituitary gland. The hypothalamus transmits signals to the pituitary gland to release hormones that regulate the testes and testosterone production. Testosterone is often associated with the hormone that gives men aggression, muscle mass, hair growth, and much more. Testosterone helps the body create stronger muscles, stronger bones, and regulates the sex drive in both men and women. Low testosterone can result in fat gain around the waist and abdomen; chronic fatigue, and the inability to attain or maintain an erection. In addition, it can cause the sex drive to plummet and can increase chronic fatigue, depression, and sleep interruption.

Estrogen is the hormone often associated with women. However, both genders have estrogen. It is essential in balancing testosterone and bone density. Recent research indicates there is a correlation in early mortality from heart-related death in males with low estrogen levels. High estrogen levels in men can be just as destructive. It can make you overly emotional and can cause many other issues. When you couple that with high cortisol putting your body into fight or flight and low testosterone, which also makes you emotionally sensitive, it can lead you into being an emotional wreck.

Now, in my personal opinion—as an individual who struggled through this, a combat veteran with PTSD and a Traumatic Brain Injury (TBI), as well as my professional opinion through my studies in cognitive psychology, neuropsychology, and psychopharmacology—I believe this is where the Veteran Affairs and civilian healthcare systems are failing our service members. This is also one of the many reasons I wrote this book. Before continuing about how cortisol, testosterone, and estrogen affect our service members, TBI and PTSD need to be discussed to understand how the current VA treatment, private healthcare treatment, and psychiatrists may be failing some of our veterans.

Currently, there are several doctors (Dr. Mark Gordon in California, Dr. Frank Comstock in Tucson, Arizona, and several others) who have been doing extensive research, treatment, and advocacy for TBI, PTSD, and their effects on patients. One doctor, in particular, Dr. Mark Gordon in California, has attempted to bring awareness and treatment to veterans through appearances on Joe Rogan's podcast, *The Joe Rogan Experience*, Episode 438, 574, and 700, (I highly recommend listening to the episodes with Dr. Gordon). Dr. Gordon also works with a fantastic foundation called the Warrior Angels Foundation, which is spreading awareness and funding for treatment.

TBI can vary in severity. It can range from a mild concussion all the way to a vegetative state and coma. Even mild concussions can have long-lasting consequences. The blow doesn't need to be severe to affect a person's quality of life.

The brain, which floats in cerebral spinal fluid, is protected and cushioned by the fluid. In war zones, when an explosion goes off, the blast wave hits the body, jarring the brain. It shifts forward, impacting the frontal lobe (which is the primary area for deciding what is socially acceptable, consequences of actions, and risk-taking). The pituitary gland—that almond-size gland behind roughly the eye socket area and partially responsible for testosterone, estrogen, cortisol, and other chemicals—is also injured when it impacts behind the eye socket region. Then, the brain whips back toward the back portion of your skull, impacting with the parietal and occipital lobe, often causing bruising. The parietal lobe is responsible for interpretation of touch, analytical thinking, and understanding of objects, shapes, and space. The occipital lobe is responsible for processing and making sense of visual information.

There have been several private institutions and researchers who have discovered that repeated exposure to machine gunfire, rocket fire, cannon, mortar, and artillery fire can be enough to have effects on the brain. While in combat, an infantry or cavalry scout platoon often expends well over 5,000 rounds in one firefight.

On one occasion in particular, my truck, which was equipped with an auto-grenade launcher known as a MK19 (pronounced Mark-19), fired over 600 grenades at Taliban forces. Our platoon used over 4,000 .50 cal machine gun rounds, over 4,000 7.62 x51 rounds for an M240B belt-fed machine gun, and thousands of M4 5.56 rounds. This was in just one firefight. You can imagine the toll that over twelve to eighteen months of combat can take and how this can affect the physiology of service members' brains. Many of them think that because they may have never been knocked unconscious that there was never damage. Medically, this isn't the case.

Depending on what number you look at, the current veteran suicide rate ranges from twenty to twenty-eight veterans per day, every single day. Not all of them have a damaged endocrine system. However, it is common knowledge and is printed on prescription bottles that anti-depressant medication can induce suicidal thoughts, ideations, apathy, anhedonia, as well as mood swings. As a veteran attempting to get treatment, many of us feel we're cattle being led through the gates waiting to be branded. I discovered many of the providers are incredible people who want nothing more than to give back to our veterans. However, the bureaucracy, politics, and issues of the administration don't allow the doctors to go out of the cookie-cutter style treatment. The administration is so backlogged and archaic that they prefer the providers throw pills at you, get you out, and move on to the next.

It is my opinion, and the opinion of many researchers, that several of the veterans who are living in misery from depression and symptoms of hormone deficiencies, as well as veterans who have committed suicide, may have been treated for the wrong disorder. Their suicides, effectively, are the result of medical malpractice. It is possible that, had the administration been more open-minded to brain injury research, many of these veterans would still be alive—and families would not be broken, disregarded, and thrown away as many of us feel we have been.

Many of these veterans have never even been screened or tested for hormone disorders. It is possible that, by neglecting this treatment or testing, millions of veterans have been prescribed benzodiazepines, opiates, and anti-depressants inappropriately.

Unfortunately, when you prescribe an individual an anti-depressant when it is not a serotonin, dopamine, or norepinephrine problem, it can have the opposite effect, known as the ping-pong effect, throwing these chemicals into a state of dysfunction that may not have been. By doing so, it can potentially induce suicidal ideations in an individual who may never have had them in the past. The drugs ping-pong back and forth, and prescribers often stack more psychiatric drugs to try and treat the side effects. Equally lamentable, many of the people who made the decision to see a psychiatrist or other mental health provider are already in a state of despair, hoping the pill will bring them back to their "old, happy self." I know, because I've been there.

Because the drugs we are prescribed aren't treating the root of the problem, which is often hormonal, many of these people have a hard time when the side effects like suicidal ideations begin. They have no way to realize it is a result of their medication. When taking manufactured serotonin and dopamine, it becomes difficult to decipher which thought is yours and which is a result of side effects. It makes us more isolated, creating more fights with our loved ones, and spirals us down into a cold, dark pit of emotional pain. When you're in it, it's hard to realize that it *will* get better, because it feels like it never will. We lose sight of all the strength it took to get through the experiences that would have killed many others. Eventually, many of us continue down the spiral into alcohol and drug abuse, which damages our relationships. Finally, we are either pulled out of it through a mentor, loved one, or ourselves—or we become another statistic.

I wish I could say that a blood draw and weekly injections are the solutions. I wish it were that easy. If you find the right doctor who is open to research, open to realizing that these hormones are a range and that every human body is different, then it could be. Unfortunately, as I discovered, many of these doctors look at the "range" on a lab slip. In many labs, this range is roughly 370–1100, covering the age range of 18–80. In my case, the doctor at the VA was extremely "within the box." If your testosterone number was 450 but you exhibited every sign of low testosterone and you were twenty-one years old, he would call you within normal range and refer you to psychiatry.

Logic would dictate that a twenty-one-year-old should not have the same testosterone level as an eighty-year-old man. If the majority of men in that age range are between 800–1100, the patient sincerely says he is symptomatic, and you can visually see the pain in his eyes and struggle, then he probably is symptomatic and should be treated as such. Unfortunately, we could discuss for an entire book the issues with the current medical system, drug-seeking behaviors, and the inundation of malpractice lawsuits that our medical professionals face, complicating the job and making them less likely to think outside the box—and who can blame them? It must be hard taking on that kind of stress.

I went on to see an endocrinologist in private practice at the Mayo Clinic in Arizona. Ultimately, the doctor placed me on Testosterone Cypionate once weekly through intra-muscular injection. About six weeks in, I felt marginally better. Unfortunately, this doctor who was great for diagnosing was still extremely conservative and did not pursue recent research and treatment for low testosterone. As a young male in his twenties, I would like to get married and have children in the future. Testosterone Replacement Therapy (TRT) can cause a male to go sterile. By artificially giving your body testosterone, whether prescribed by a doctor or buying anabolic steroids illegally, you can completely suppress your endocrine system, damaging your testicles and causing sterility. The risk is that the treatment will cause your body to be unable to produce sex hormones like testosterone and estrogen normally.

In the last few years, TRT has made leaps and bounds in treatment and research progress. There are two medications formerly used as fertility drugs for women that have been discovered to help men maintain fertility while artificially taking testosterone. These two drugs are Human Chorionic Gonadotropin, and Clomiphene or Chlomid. If these drugs are not taken in conjunction with testosterone injections, eventually the male's testicles atrophy, shrinking in size and firmness, and ultimately sperm production can cease. This happens because two hormones, LH and FSH, are suppressed. In essence, your body becomes lazy because it is getting testosterone without having to work for it.

HCG and Clomiphene trick your body into forgetting it is getting testosterone artificially. In the right dosage, testicular side effects are avoided, and reproduction ability is preserved as your body still creates sperm and testosterone naturally. In addition, many men need an estrogen blocker when on TRT. Now, this does not block estrogen to zero. As I explained, even men need estrogen for bone density, heart health, and other things. It simply does not allow your estrogen to soar sky high with the synthetic testosterone. Unfortunately, many doctors refuse to treat this way with HCG/Chlomid or even an estrogen blocker. This is their prerogative, but their treatment regimen did not work for me. I know several men in their twenties, thirties, and forties for whom it does work. As I said, it is different for everybody.

When I found Dr. Comstock in Tucson, Arizona, my life was changed about a month after treatment. In fact, he saved my life. I felt like my old self. I was happy. The depression lifted. The hopelessness disappeared, and my mind felt clear. I could think and rationalize things again. I no longer had the emotional roller coaster from the mood swings, I began putting muscle on, lost all the fat I had put on, and felt the way I did before the testosterone issue began.

Unfortunately, this was a private doctor, and since the issues began in service, I wanted to get VA treatment and service connected for compensation and pension, especially since it is a condition that will require treatment until I die. I was referred to endocrinology at the VA Hospital.

* * *

AS I WAIT IN A CHAIR NEXT TO THE EVALUATION table with the student doctor in the room, the doctor whips the door open. Without closing the door, while patients and nurses walk past the room, the doctor derogatorily says, "So, what's the problem? Can't get a boner? I'll just give you some Viagra and get you out of here."

Caught off guard, I say, "Um, excuse me?"

Responding to something within the extent as if he was the one who discovered medicine, "Well, you're too young to have a testosterone issue. I haven't drawn your labs, but you're a fit young man. Seems like you're looking for other reasons to get it."

"No, actually. I'm currently being treated by providers at respectable hospitals and practices, and I was initially diagnosed by a Mayo Clinic doctor. And the Mayo Clinic and Dr. Comstock's practice both have a lot better track record than the VA," I spat back at him.

With the door still open, he says, "Fine, drop your pants."

Flabbergasted at his unprofessionalism and treatment, I respond, "Uh, the door is still open. I'm not going to give a show to everyone."

The next fifteen minutes are a blur, as I was engulfed in rage. However, the last thing I needed was for this egotistical know-it-all-man to accuse me of having an anger problem and send me to anger management, despite the situation being reason enough to make any person angry. At the conclusion of the appointment, they wanted to do an MRI to screen my pituitary gland and ultimately go off testosterone for a battery of testing, and to ultimately, "see what happens." They were convinced I was a steroid abuser and declined to take my diagnosed TBI into account. If I wanted treatment from the VA for compensation and pension, since the entire testosterone issue began in service, I would be forced to go off all testosterone treatment for six months to a year for "testing."

In that period, they did an MRI telling me I had a pituitary adenoma, which is essentially a small tumor that can affect your hormones. Then, a month later, they reneged that diagnosis. There were several circles on the merry-go-round with this department. Unfortunately, at the end of the year off testosterone, they had only run two blood tests and refused to explain why their reference range was different than OHSU, the Mayo Clinic, Lab Corp, and several others. They didn't perform any of the other tests promised or research the cause. In addition, they ignored several respectable specialists in the field who concurred with each other that I required testosterone replacement therapy, even offering to prescribe. However, I still had faith the VA would help me, since that's what they claim to do—help veterans.

My emotional roller-coaster from the hormonal imbalance had begun to take a serious toll on my family and friends. The most substantial impact was on Peyton. While off TRT, every small issue felt like the end of the world. Since resuming TRT, I can see how I made mountains out of mole hills. I can see how my emotional swings took a toll on every relationship around me, and how hard it was on Peyton. I certainly wasn't the best version of myself.

With time, however, I realized that the foreboding comment I had made to my mom about meeting my future wife was an early prediction of the battles I would have to fight within myself.

"The truth is that the more intimately you know someone,
the more clearly you'll see their flaws.
That's just the way it is.
This is why marriages fail,
why children are abandoned,
why friendships don't last.
You might think you love someone until you see the way they
act when they're out of money, under pressure, or hungry.
For goodness' sake.
Love is something different.
Love is choosing to serve someone and be with
someone in spite of their filthy heart.
Love is patient and kind.
Love is deliberate.
Love is hard.
Love is pain and sacrifice,
It's seeing the darkness in another person
and defying the impulse to jump ship."

—UNKNOWN

CHAPTER 14

THE SILENT
TREATMENT

———

IT HAD BEEN NEARLY NINE MONTHS OF DATING ONE of the most amazing women I had ever met. It had also been over nine months of sleeping four hours per night if I was lucky. I had become extremely short-tempered and grumpy, and I still refused to believe that I was struggling with issues of PTSD, depression, and anxiety. Following the VA's request, I had been off all testosterone medications nearly four months and was severely feeling the side effects. I once again began having mood swings, my emotions were all over the map, and I had lost nearly thirty pounds. To add to my frustration, the VA still had not done much testing and were convinced my testosterone level as a male should be between 90–240 and being 160 was not an issue. This range is inconsistent with every respectable civilian health provider that ranges male testosterone from 370–1100.

After roughly three weeks of being off testosterone cold turkey, I began to have abnormal heartbeats and rhythms. I literally could feel it racing, slowing, and skipping a beat. I had read some research correlating certain heart conditions to low and high testosterone levels. By this point, my endocrine system was crashing as a result of the artificial source of testosterone being removed from the equation without weaning me off the medication. One night in particular, I woke up with severe chest pains and palpitations, unable to feel my arms or legs. Initially, I figured I slept awkwardly and pinched a nerve. Attempting not to wake Peyton, I quietly rolled out of bed trying to shake my limbs out and regain feeling. This happened three more times throughout the night, and I realized it was my heart causing the issue.

The next day, I felt as if I had run a marathon all night. I was run down, unable to think clearly, and felt as though I had the flu. Peyton and I left, driving three hours home. By the time we got home, I told her about my heart and that I was getting concerned. She took my blood pressure and resting pulse, which was abnormally high for my age. I decided to try to sleep it off.

I woke up at 5:30 a.m., once again feeling as if I had run a marathon. I reached over and grabbed her pulse oximeter off the nightstand. Still lying in bed without moving, the meter read, "148." *That can't be right.* I turned the machine off and turned it back on once again, placing the clamp on my left index finger. Beeping, indicating completion, it read "152" as Peyton came back into the room.

"What does it say, Steele?"

"Ohhhhh, 152."

"Are you kidding me? You haven't gotten out of bed. It should be down around mid-60s or 70s." Concern was evident in her scowl. "You're calling the doctor. You are going to go get seen at the hospital!"

"Look, Peyton, I'm tired of dealing with those assholes. I keep telling them something is wrong. They continue writing me off and pushing psychiatry. I'm telling you, it's not psychiatric. Something is physically wrong. They blame the easiest thing so they can move on to the next patient and don't have to pay out." I was annoyed and didn't want to deal with another VA doctor ever again.

"I don't care how tired of them you are. You're going."

Knowing she was right, I was still hesitant. "Yeah, okay. I will later if it acts up."

"Steele Kelly! Don't you fucking play games with me! Don't make me call your mother and send her after you!" she said as jokingly as possible, a hint of a smile on her face, but I knew she wasn't bluffing.

Later that day, the heart palpitations began, and I could physically feel my heart out of rhythm, slowing down and speeding up. Reluctantly, I drove myself to the doctor.

"Excuse me. I need to see a nurse immediately," I express calmly as if nothing is wrong.

"And what would it be about?"

"Something is wrong with my heart. I don't know what, but something is definitely wrong," I say, wiping sweat from my forehead. *Why am I sweating? I'm not even hot. Why is my heart off to the horse races when I haven't done anything today?*

Immediately, a nurse walks out, accompanying me to a room with an EKG machine and equipment to take my vitals.

"Um, I'll be right back," the nurse says calmly, masking her concern and removing the paper from the EKG machine as she exits the room.

Pressing recall on the vital equipment, I see, "Blood pressure: 180/110. Heart Rate: 248." *Woah, that's kinda high. Your maximum heart rate is 220, subtracted by your age.*

Interrupting my thoughts, the nurse barges back into the room. "Mr. Kelly, I've consulted with the doctor. You need to go to the hospital. You have an abnormal heart rhythm and are in what's called Supra Ventricular Tachycardia or SVT," she says, attempting to say it in an anxiety-easing way.

"Well, that's weird. I'm not stressed about anything. It's actually been a good morning. How about I just drive myself?" I say in the most nonchalant, unconcerned way.

"No, I really think you should go by ambulance."

"Oh, no. In fact, hell, no. I am not going to be *that* guy. I do not want to make a scene," I say, emphasizing every word.

"Well, Mr. Kelly, that's your choice, but it's not safe for you or others on the road. If your heart stops, there will be no way to help you. It is not the smart thing to do."

"But—"

"Mr. Kelly, I've already called an ambulance. It's arriving now."

Well, that kind of eliminates my options. Thinking of Peyton and the last few weeks of high tensions, I did not want to tell her anything until I knew exactly what was wrong. I did not want to add any extra stress to her plate. I figured I would get to the hospital, do a few tests, and once I knew those answers, I would let her know.

Pulling my phone out, knowing somebody had to pick up my car, I text my mom: *Hey, no big deal, but my truck is in the parking lot of my doctor. I need you to go pick it up. They're sending me to the hospital. I apparently need to go by ambulance. Don't worry, no big deal.* I hit *Send*. Immediately, I get four messages in response, communicated with anxiety. I respond: *Don't say anything to Peyton yet. I want to wait until I know what's going on.* Before I know it, I'm being lifted onto the bed, IVs are being placed, and I forget to hit *Send*.

Wheeling the stretcher through the hallway, down the elevator, and into the lobby, there she is—Peyton. Of course. She works in the same plaza, and my mother decided to be "helpful," texting Peyton, saying I was going by ambulance. Immediately, I can see a pissed off look on her face. The look that says, "You're so in the fucking doghouse, Steele."

"Steele, I'll find out where they're taking you and be down there as soon as I get my shift covered." She was concerned, yet unmistakably irritated for not finding out from me.

Well, I'm definitely in the doghouse. Not only for not keeping her in the loop, but also because it took me over eight hours after I said I would go to the hospital that I actually did. I can't blame her in the slightest. I would have absolutely been irritated if I were her.

When I got to the hospital, they ran several tests and ultimately told me I had to follow up with the VA. They had no idea why it happened or what had caused it. Reluctantly, I went back to the VA and was issued a pocket heart monitor that activates when your heart does something abnormal. I wore it for the next thirty days. It had beeped several times throughout the month, indicating activation. By the end of the thirty days, my general physician read the faxed over response from the Portland VA Cardiology department.

"Looks like nothing. Cardiology says you should get follow-up care with psychiatry for anxiety and PTSD," he says.

"That's bullshit. I want to see the monitor reports. This is not a result of PTSD or anything like that. You guys keep doing this because it's easier to pawn me off and get me out the door. I'm going to end up dying because the system is so fucking broken," I say back in a calm yet clearly irate tone.

This common VA issue caused many fights with my parents, with Peyton, and with others. I continuously told them it was a physical problem, yet because of the VA's lazy behavior, it appeared as if it were all a mental problem that I was in denial about.

As I said before, it takes two to tango, however, I made several learning mistakes along the way that I would like to address so other vets who are either in denial or haven't realized their own PTSD, anxiety, or depression issues can change and repair the shortcomings before it's too far gone.

On one particular occasion after this incident, Peyton and I got into a disagreement over a VA appointment. I wanted her to go with me so she could see how Doctor Know-it-all treated me. Unfortunately, emotions were so charged and heated that a simple miscommunication meant she didn't submit a time off request to go to the appointment, which turned into a major explosion. In past relationships, I had hurt others' feelings from verbalizing frustration and anger in the heat of the moment. When I met Peyton, I never wanted to repeat those mistakes. I didn't want to say something in the heat of the moment and cause harm.

In my attempt to cool off and take space, I didn't realize it had become hurtful and destructive in the opposite way. I ignored her text messages and phone calls for most of the day. When she got home, I answered very shortly and to the point, without looking at her, hugging her, or asking how her day was. I was so frustrated and wrapped up with the VA system, doctors, and the way I was being pawned off by these doctors that I took out my frustrations on Peyton. Unintentionally, I made her the scapegoat for my frustrations because of our regular miscommunications. I convinced myself that her not going to the appointment meant I wasn't important to her.

Looking back, I don't believe not caring was the case, and I overlooked how stressful the situation was for her, too. Everybody handles this differently, and something that could have been communicated, let go of, and moved on from, was stewed upon and unsolved, causing more damage.

Over the next three weeks, I ignored Peyton for the majority of the days. I would respond with one-word answers (mostly no response at all), ignore her phone calls, and only communicate that I was upset she didn't go and "blew me off." It wasn't until the third week that I realized that, in my attempt to "cool off," I was hurting and stonewalling her.

* * *

IT WAS A TYPICAL WINTER MORNING IN JANUARY of 2016. I woke up early, attempting to get my coffee and beat the traffic to my early morning Psychopharmacology class in downtown Portland. My heart was broken, I missed Peyton, but my thoughts nagged me. *How can I be with somebody who wasn't going to be there when I needed her? I need a two-way street, not one-way. You should just get over it and call her. Clearly, you miss her. You're miserable without her here. No! She needs to make an effort to work things out. She should come to me,* I decide.

As the traffic gets worse, the freeway quickly turns into a parking lot. I look down at the clock—7:15. *Are you fucking kidding me? A fifteen-minute commute is now an hour and a half?* To pass the time, I scroll through my podcasts to my favorite show, *The Joe Rogan Experience*, clicking the most recent guest interview, Aubrey Marcus. I begin listening to the conversation through my car stereo as if I'm sitting in the living room with the guys.

The timing was divine—Mr. Marcus and Mr. Rogan begin discussing relationship dynamics and disagreements or fights with significant others. Listening, thinking back over my relationships with previous girlfriends, none of it seems to apply to my situation with Peyton.

"You know, Joe, it's a funny thing. My girlfriend and I got into a fight recently, and I realized over reflection that I handled the entire thing wrong," Mr. Marcus says.

"Yeah? What happened, man?"

"Well, we got into a pretty big disagreement, and I began ignoring her text messages and not responding. This went on for quite some time—a couple of weeks, I think. Well, one day while clearing my mind, I realized the only reason I was ignoring her was because I felt she had hurt me. Subconsciously, I wanted her to hurt as bad as she hurt me. Deep in my subconscious, I knew that by ignoring her, not responding, and not answering calls, it was deeply hurting her," Mr. Marcus confesses.

Immediately, my heart sinks down into my stomach, and a wave of shame comes over me. *You. Are. Such. An. Asshole.* I was doing precisely what Mr. Marcus just explained. Over time, my space turned into the desire for Peyton to feel the level of hurt that I felt for her not going. *That's not you or the man you want to be.* I knew I owed her an apology for holding her emotionally hostage, which, no matter how you dice it up, is a form of emotional abuse.

Almost ironically, I receive a lengthy text message from Peyton several minutes later. "Steele, I can't do this anymore. I can't handle this roller-coaster or having my emotions held hostage. I can't be in a relationship with somebody who feels that's acceptable, nor do I want to be. I appreciate what you've done for me. However, I think it would be best if we met up this weekend to exchange each other's stuff."

"How about we go get breakfast on Sunday instead?" I rapidly text back. Over several text messages and hours later, she agreed. Understanding that it might be too little too late, I attempt to drag breakfast out as long as I can, knowing this may be the last time I see her.

"Can we go talk for a little longer without people around?" I ask, expecting a *no* response.

"Steele, I don't really see the point. I can't be in a relationship with somebody who gets upset and holds my emotions hostage. That's considered emotional abuse, and you know it."

"I didn't realize that I was doing that until now. I guess it's a learning experience. That was never my intention. I didn't realize it until the other morning listening to Aubrey Marcus and Joe Rogan. Can we go talk, and then if you still want us to go our separate ways, we can?" I say, swallowing my pride.

"Okay." She's clearly reluctant.

Leaving the restaurant, I guide my truck up into the back roads deep into Oregon wine country. Placing my truck in park, overlooking the vineyards, there is an awkward silence with feelings of tension. She broke the silence, and it becomes clear that she has already made the decision to leave. Her eyes begin to glisten, her voice begins to quiver and crack, and I realize at that exact moment that I'm watching her heart shatter to pieces.

"I love you, but I can't be with somebody who does that," she says between tears.

Without knowing what to say or how to say it, Mr. Marcus's message hits closer to home with every makeup-covered tear streaming down her beautiful face. I feel a ball welling up in my throat as I attempt to hold back my heartache at the realization that I was the one who caused her heartache. *It takes two to fight, yet I took it to the extreme by ignoring her for three weeks. Intentioned consequences or not, I was stonewalling her, and it was my actions toward the one I love that caused all of this clearly visible pain in her.*

Without saying a word, I pull her over toward me. Putting her arms around me, she begins to cry, this time without words. Unable to hold it back anymore, tears begin to roll down my face too.

Stuck in my head, I think: *I should have handled this situation differently. I can't go back and change this, but I can certainly change future interactions by remembering this mistake and the heartache it caused.* I promised myself never to repeat my actions that caused such heartache for both of us. This was one of the many painful growing experiences I had to go through; unfortunately, it came at her expense.

"Peyton, I can't change things. All I can say is that it started off with good intentions to cool off. I didn't realize until the other day that I was stonewalling, and it was abusive emotionally toward you. I was holding your feelings, heart, and emotions hostage. All I can do is genuinely say I'm sorry, and I love you with everything I have. I'm not perfect. I will never be perfect, but I can certainly do my best to learn as we go and do everything I can to become the man I want to be."

We made up and got back together. However, the relationship was never the same after that. I never repeated that mistake, but the damage was done.

Many veterans, first responders, and people in general have a hard time expressing their feelings. Many see it as a weakness to talk about their feelings. However, the real weakness is not having the courage to talk about your feelings until it's too late.

It is very challenging at first to realize that we may be the problem. That our experiences—which forced us to detach and dissociate, making decisions and calling the shots—now force us to shut down and carry on, disregarding the complaints or problems our loved ones see. Because of our "drive on" attitude and frequent need to be authoritative for survival, it is difficult to see that our way of thinking is wrong, we're wrong, and our experiences in the world have transformed our minds to see or expect the negative and harmful things, treating others poorly as a result of our threat evaluation. We have essentially become a monster from fighting monsters.

At first, recognizing you may be the problem is uncomfortable and difficult to see. However, our responses and self-reflection are a sort of psychological muscle group—it must be exercised regularly in order to be healthy and robust. When you get back in the gym lifting weights after several years off, it hurts. It feels uncomfortable, and our strength doesn't have much endurance. However, after practice, time, and effort, we become stronger and stronger until we have more stamina.

If you find yourself saying, "Oh man, this is me. I've been doing this to my kids, my family, my significant other, etc.," then the first step is admitting the problem. The possibility that your actions and thinking may be the problem. The second is apologizing and owning your actions. Believe it or not, a sincere and heartfelt apology and putting yourself out there for rejection goes a long way in the healing process. The third is committing to change. An apology, no matter how heartfelt, sincere, or kind, is worthless if you continue repeating the action. The final step is actively changing our negative behaviors, knowing you may stumble. Luckily, it's a marathon, not a race.

A mentor of mine once told me, "Before saying anything when you're angry, make the choice to temper your anger with determination. It's hard in the heat of the moment, but a method that works well is to look at your loved one, take a few deep breaths, tell them you love them very much, that you're committed to them, but you need to go cool off, and that you will be back in a little while. Give them a hug and a kiss. Then go somewhere quiet to think—somewhere you can write everything you want to say in your state of anger. Re-read it several times and notice how constructive it is. How would this make *you* feel if your loved one said this to you? Is this issue big enough to cause destruction in your relationship? How important is this in the real scheme of things?"

Psychologically, physiologically, and logically, there are several reasons for this practice. First, the three to five deep breaths you take forces your fight or flight (sympathetic nervous) system in your body to slow down. It gives your parasympathetic nervous system, (the system that reduces fight or flight chemicals) a second to catch up and calm you down. It does this by allowing more oxygen into your body that permits you to think more clearly and rationally. By telling them you are going to go cool off, it demonstrates that you acknowledge your frustration, and most importantly, that you are working on changing the way you handle disagreement or conflicts that will inevitably arise in any healthy relationship.

By expressing your love and commitment, it does two things. First, it reassures the other person that you still care. You aren't going anywhere permanently, and it gives them a chance to calm down as well. Second, it would be awful if the inevitable happened and one of you got into a car accident or something and this was the last exchange you two had. Take it from me—living with survivor's guilt is very painful. In this case, it is entirely avoidable by knowing you didn't leave in a fit of rage or nasty words, or without telling them you loved them.

By hugging the person, your body releases oxytocin, which is known as the "love drug." It is known to reduce depression and anger and is one of the major factors in creating intimacy. Although you might feel hesitant, reluctant, or that this idea is seemingly crazy, this is the first step in fixing the disagreement at hand in a healthy manner.

Lastly, by writing your initial thoughts down in your anger, it allows you to vent without hurting somebody. It allows you to get all your frustration vocalized onto paper to read. When I do this myself, I realize that it's my frustration speaking and not something I would say while calm, cool, and collected. It allows me to take a step back and think of a more constructive, healthy way to communicate with the other person without hurting their feelings. There is a tremendous difference between a disagreement and a fight with somebody. A disagreement is finding out *what* is right, while a fight is figuring out *who* is right. By having a disagreement and communicating with another person, it allows resolution and finding out what went wrong and how to make it right. By fighting for who was right and talking *at* somebody, it simply breeds more anger, usually making the situation worse and more explosive for everybody involved.

If you find yourself in the same realization I did—no matter what you do, say, or change, the relationship has come to an end—they don't want to be with you. It's a position I understand, and it sucks. All you can do is learn from the experience and find a way to come to peace with your actions and eventually accept them. Take the time to reflect and come to the realization that the person we were yesterday does not define the person we are tomorrow. It is never too late to learn from the experience and write an email or send an apology.

Focus on the things you did wrong rather than everything they did wrong. If you focus on everything they did wrong, you won't take responsibility for your faults to make changes. If you don't make changes, you will continue this cycle of relationship failures. Advice I recommend, that worked for me, is to find a good counselor. Then, discover the underlying issue that you may not have realized was there in the first place. Lastly, I would encourage you to work on daily interactions that irritate you, frustrate you, or get you worked up. By practicing some of these techniques, it will make a more immediate response in the future when you become emotionally involved in another relationship. That being said, it probably isn't a good idea to attempt to tell your boss, coworker, or random grocery store person you love them and go in for a hug and kiss. I would probably save that for the future romance.

"But you loved her?
Yes.
And she loved you?
Yes.
Then why did it end?
Because love and compatibility are
not always the same thing."

—SUE M. ZHAO

CHAPTER 15

THE FINAL STRAWS WHILE RUNNING FROM THE TRUTH

—

SITTING IN THE TRUCK, I COULD FEEL THE HOSTIL-
ity in the air. Peyton and I had been in a rough patch for
over a month and a half. I was frustrated because I had
been asking her to move in with me for over eight months,
and it seemed she was half in, half out. I couldn't help but
compare myself to her ex-boyfriend whom she had moved
in with less than two months after dating. We lived thirty
miles apart, and she worked full-time and went to school
part-time, while I went to school full-time. I felt we had
grown to a point in life, our relationship, and growth as
a couple that it was time for us to grow closer together. I
felt we had been stuck in a state of limbo, like a casual
relationship where I would stay the night a couple times

a week, and there was no progress toward marriage and a life together, which I wanted.

I was frustrated because our schedules were so busy that we were lucky to get two or three nights a week where I would stay the night and talk for an hour before going to bed. On the weekends, we tried to make plans, but our schedules had grown so busy that by the time the weekend rolled around, it was more of a recovery day on Saturday, then homework and preparation for the coming week on Sunday. We had typical disagreements that normal and healthy couples have, but we didn't have the regular day-to-day interaction where we could pack the other's lunch, make breakfast, or have any of those positive daily interactions that could help get us through inevitable disagreements.

Additionally, the drama from our parents, siblings, and friends was beginning to take its toll. I felt it was time to begin the building blocks of a future together, but our relationship was growing more and more volatile. Over the next ten months, our relationship was completely hot and cold, and we fought over everything. We fought over our friends, over my behaviors (which she viewed as controlling and I viewed as trying to keep her safe). We fought over schooling, work, vacations—you name it, we argued about it.

Eventually, we were both more unhappy than happy, and toward the end, I spiraled into a depression. Still in denial that it had anything to do with my past. Over the weeks we were breaking up, what little emotional stability I had was rocked when I lost another friend to suicide.

One night, we got into one of our on-again, off-again fights. I was pressing the issue of why she wouldn't move in or commit, in my eyes, to the level of commitment I wanted. At the time, the conversation impacted me because it was painful to hear. It was painful because I knew she was right. In it, she called me out on my very real character flaws. She said I was pessimistic, suspicious, and that I consistently saw the worst in people. She also laid into my tendency to score keep—punctuating those as the reasons she never wanted to move in with me. She knew I was trying and had been trying, but the progress was too slow and not dramatic enough, and she wasn't wrong.

Her words accurately depicted how I viewed people, the world, and everything else. I knew it was jaded and pessimistic, and I didn't want to view the world that way. I just didn't know how to stop or change it. Despite the volatile nature of our arguments, we remained hot and cold for a while longer.

The next week, for Valentine's day weekend, I set up a mystery date in Vancouver, B.C. I knew we were in a rut, so I planned a long weekend, knowing Peyton always wanted to visit Canada. I knew I needed to start the process of rekindling and repairing our relationship. I knew we were both on thin ice, and I wanted to make an additional effort to show that I was changing and making an effort to recognize behaviors that needed improvement.

The weekend went better than I could have dreamed, and we both agreed to work toward a future together.

Things remained good for the rest of the trip. However, when we returned home from the trip and went back to our separate living arrangements, I reverted back to being jaded, short-tempered, and nitpicking the trivial things. And as always, I fell back into my old patterns and behaviors of the push-pull without making the changes I promised I would. We continued to argue over her next backpacking trip and my fear of her traveling abroad. She had her fill with my push-pull and inability to see the issues I was struggling with, and we split up for a month.

After stewing on the idea that she was going back to Central America and panicking over the idea of her being sold into the trade or worse, I met up with her after a month of no contact. I wanted us to leave each other on an amicable note, just in case the worst happened. The visit was emotional, and we both admitted to still being in love, despite our poor communication and many other issues.

While she was away backpacking for the month, we emailed back and forth, trying to work through our problems. While she was gone, family tensions with my parents escalated as my alcohol consumption increased, and I couldn't even be greeted by family without responding in anger. I realized while she was gone that the only way for me to change without continuously going back to the person I used to be was to completely leave the surroundings, the people who remembered the old me, and every other subtle reminder. When she returned, we were overjoyed to see each other. We began temporarily communicating more effectively.

I decided to move to Montana while we were apart, and when we got back together, I asked her to move with me. I had applied to Montana State University during the time we were apart and chose it because they had programs for us both, in hopes that, when we got back together, she would come. Our relationship had drastically improved. We still had disagreements, but we were headed in the right direction. When my moving day came, she agreed that she wanted to move from Oregon to Montana with me and that we'd figure out the logistics soon. It felt like life was finally falling into place.

Once I packed up, I hugged my family goodbye and loaded my Labrador Lucy into the truck. It was hard for me to leave. I looked at the empty passenger seat and the open palm of my hand. *What are you thinking? You shouldn't be leaving without Peyton next to you. You should be holding her hand as you wave goodbye to your families together.* Throughout my trip to Montana, Peyton and I exchanged multiple texts. She was just as unhappy as I was about the prospect of me moving out before she could join me, and she assured me she'd follow me soon.

Over the next two months, I missed her every single day. The lack of daily interaction was beginning to take its toll. It became increasingly difficult for me, emotionally, due to my insecurity and fear of her having the power over my heart and emotions the way she did. Fear crept in when I opened myself up to the thought of losing another person from my life, except not by death this time, but because I wasn't the best version of myself.

Counterproductively, we began to go days without really talking or bickering. Initially, I thought I could change my location and that would change me completely. What I didn't realize at the time was that, even if I changed locations, without a mindset and destructive behavior change, I would never change at all. For the next few months, we were equally hot and cold—hot when we were together, desperate to make it work, and then cold once apart again.

We met for a weekend, missing each other since it had been several months. I had finished the year-long VA testing, abandoned the VA, and gone back on testosterone with Doctor Comstock two days prior. We had an amazing dinner and night together. We went to sleep, feeling like we were first dating again, eager for the holidays to come. It felt as if nothing was wrong, and the tides were turning.

Still in complete denial that I had any form of PTSD or repercussions from my time in Afghanistan, our last night together demonstrated that it was impossible to remain in denial that I was affected. As I laid down next to Peyton, for the first time in several years, I felt right at home being next to her, and I had the feeling that everything was going to be alright. I fell rapidly into a deep sleep, straight into a nightmare that had been reoccurring several times a month since I returned home, except this time Peyton was in it. It is a nightmare that has been explained by most of the combat veterans I know. Each of them are unique, but they carry the same theme of being separated from your unit and either out of ammo or unable to fire your weapon.

* * *

PATROLLING ON FOOT WITH MY PLATOON THROUGH an enemy village, I can feel the heat through my armor. Looking at my feet, through doorways, and scanning every corner before I turn down an alley. *Why are we alone in the village? There aren't any villagers, and the campfires are still burning with pots left boiling on the stoves.* Suddenly, machine gunfire and rockets impact all around me and my platoon. Dust, gunfire, and explosions fill the air, and I'm knocked off my feet, unconscious.

Coming back to, I'm face down in the same alley. I have my rifle still slung to my vest, ten full rifle magazines on my plate carrier, two grenades, two radios, and my pistol in the holster still strapped to my leg. Pushing myself off the ground slowly, ears ringing, I look around. Everybody in my platoon is gone, and I'm alone. *Where is everybody? How long have I been separated from my unit?*

Suddenly, the gunfire begins again, and I run down the alley looking for a door. I try kicking several doors open, but they won't budge. Sprinting down the alley, blasts impact my path, spraying dirt into my face as I continue running. Reaching down to the transmission button on my radio and gasping for air, I yell over the sounds of explosions and gunfire, "Saber Main! Saber Main! This is Butcher 9-2. I'm separated from my unit taking heavy fire, over!"

Getting to the end of the alley, I take cover behind the dirt wall and turn around, aiming at Taliban fighters. Controlling my breathing, I place the crosshairs on the forehead of the enemy. Pausing my exhale, I pull the trigger.

Click.

Nothing.

Looking down, I pull the charging handle back to clear the jam. Aiming as the fighters get closer, I pull the trigger again.

Click.

Nothing.

Looking down again, the magazine from my rifle is gone, and all of the magazines that were on my armor are missing. I'm out of ammo.

Pulling my grenade off my plate carrier, I kneel down behind the corner wall, pull the pin, and count *one, two,* and on *three*, I roll the grenade down the alley, turning away from the blast, taking cover behind the wall. The blast eliminates the fighters, and everything is silent once again.

Standing up, I reach for my radio again, "Any unit this net! This is Butcher 9-2. I say again, I am separated from

my unit. I am in village Zulu 3-4, need immediate QRF.
I'm out of ammo, and I don't know how much longer I
can hold them off!"

Suddenly, two familiar voices screaming for me catch
my attention, "Steele! Steele! Help me!"

Throwing my rifle to the ground, I draw my pistol,
running toward the voices into the main street of the village. On one side lies my brother Casey with two gunshot
wounds, one in his leg and another in his chest, puncturing
his left lung. Blood froths and bubbles out of his mouth
as the air whistles through the hole in his chest with every
quiet syllable. "Bro, I need help. I lost my med-kit and
tourniquets. I'm—I'm—dying."

On the other side of the alley is a villager's house made
of mud, with flames rapidly engulfing the house and door.
Inside the hut, I hear Peyton's voice, "Steele, the fire is
spreading in here! Please help me! There's a lot of smoke
and it's getting hot in here!"

Tossing my tourniquets at Casey, I holler, "I don't
have a med-kit either! Hold on, bro! I'll be right back!"

I run toward the door that is now fully engulfed in fire,
throwing all of my body weight with force into the door.
It won't budge. Backing up, turning away, I kick back as
hard as I possibly can to break the door down. Still nothing.

"Hang on, Peyton. I'll get you out!" I yell, running
around the building to a window.

Finding the window, I jump up to pull myself through.
Except the fire blows the glass out, shooting fire down

the front of me, burning my hands. Climbing back up, I struggle to pull myself up, when the fire blows me out the window, once again burning me.

"Peyton, lay on the floor. I'm coming!" I yell, running back around to the door.

"Peyton, I'm going to use my last grenade to blow the door down. Back as far away as you can and lay down on the floor behind something!" I command.

Looking around for a heavy object to deflect the force of the blast directly toward the door, I see a boulder. Sprinting over, I pick it up, throwing it in front of the door. Running over, I wedge the grenade between the rock and the door. Pulling the pin and spoon, I jump out into the alley onto my stomach as the blast rains shrapnel down around me.

Standing back up, the door is still there.

Looking at Casey still on the ground and knowing Peyton's inside, I quietly mutter, "I can't—I can't save you guys." Muddy tears begin flowing down through the dirt covering my face.

"Steele, please!" she cries out.

Dropping to my knees in the middle of the dirt alley, between sobs and gasps for air with every word, "Peyton, I'm so sorry. I love you. I can't get you out. I'm sorry."

Suddenly, my dream takes me back to the alley where it all began. I'm sitting down with a broken leg, back against the dirt wall with my pistol in hand. Rockets and gunfire continue hitting the wall spraying rock and dirt all around me. Looking down the alley, I lift my pistol up in my right hand, aiming at the group of Taliban closing in on me from every direction.

Click.

Nothing.

Looking at the fighters now fifteen feet away, *I'm out of ammo. There's nothing I can do.* Dropping my arm to my side, pistol still grasped tightly in my hand, I rest it in my lap. Looking down at the gun, I realize the gravity of the situation. *I don't even have one last bullet for myself. There's no way to spare me from the torture that is about to ensue.*

Hanging my head in my lap, my plate carrier presses firmly against my neck. Slowly, I release my grip on the pistol, allowing it to slowly tumble to the ground next to my broken leg. Resting the back of my hands on the ground, defenseless, hot, muddy tears once again flow down my face. I know I only have a few more seconds before they take me away.

"Steele! Steele! Wake up! You're having a bad dream!" Peyton's voice breaks through, and I'm awake.

Sitting up, gasping for air, I feel around me. I'm soaking wet, the sheets are sweaty, and my heart is pounding.

"Babe, it's okay. You had a bad dream, I'm right here," Peyton says with concern in her voice.

"I know, it's nothing," I say, still struggling to catch my breath.

"Babe, I'm worried. This is the worst one yet. Was it a dream from over there?" she asks, genuinely concerned.

"No, I don't remember what it was. Can I get a hug?" I say, attempting not to cry.

Leaning over and putting her arms around me, I hold onto her.

Breaking the silence, "I love you, Peyton."

Still hugging me, she says, "I'm worried, babe. You were sobbing in your sleep, saying you were sorry that you couldn't. I couldn't make anything else out. I think you need to go talk to somebody. I love you, and this is hard for me to watch."

"No, I'm fine. There's nothing wrong, I promise".

Laying down with her head on my shoulder, my arm around her, we fall back asleep.

That next morning, we went to breakfast, followed by a trip to the dog park to take my dog to play ball before our six-hour drive home. After I loaded Lucy into the truck, I turned around and walked toward Peyton, pulling her into a hug. I can't explain why, but I had a gut feeling *this is the last time you will see her.* Holding each other outside her car in the cold fall morning air, I hold her tightly, knowing in my gut it was over. *You won't ever hold her in your arms again.* After a few minutes, leaning backward, I use both hands to slowly put her hair behind her ears. With one continuous motion, I softly put my four fingers on her neck just under her earlobes with my thumbs resting softly on her cheeks, looking deep into her eyes.

Through a cracking voice, I whisper, "Peyton, I love you. I wish I had met you at a different time, different place, and was already the man I wanted to be for you. I wish I could go back in time and change things, but I'm starting to think it's too late even if I did. I want you to know before you head home that no matter what, I'll always love you. I'll always be there for you if you need something, no matter how much time has passed. Even if I had everything, like the Kip Moore song, it would have *Everything But You*." Softly kissing her forehead, I back away from the embrace and turn around to get in my truck.

With one last gesture before saying goodbye, she reaches her hand out for mine. Softly grasping her hand, I put my thumb over the top of hers, rubbing it softly. Quietly, sadly, her voice breaks the silence, "I love you, too."

We begin to cry as we say goodbye—goodbye to go home. However, I think in both our hearts, we know this is our goodbye for good and the reason for the unusual waterworks. We know this is the last time we will ever hold each other and the last time we will ever say, "I love you."

Getting in our cars, we begin driving away. As I turn right onto Interstate 90 East, she turns left onto Interstate 90 West. I look in the mirror one last time as her tail lights fade away, and the woman of my dreams drives out of sight, eighty miles per hour away from each other, for the last time.

I knew in my heart she was driving out of my life, but I tried to convince myself that in December I would wake up to her every day. My heart broke for the last time, knowing the inevitable end was almost here, and this time there wasn't the time or an apology that could fix it.

After a few more days of volatility, a week passed since I heard from her, then I received a break-up text. This one, I knew, was for real.

To make matters worse, and as if my grief weren't enough, another friend and mentor of mine committed suicide the following day. He had succumbed to his battle with depression and PTSD. The worse part was that none of us saw it coming. He had left the military, started a new career, and got a new girlfriend.

My grief was multiplied over Peyton, and my tendency to over-drink got worse. Over the next several days, I had messaged her several evenings while blackout drunk. I wanted closure. I wanted to hear her say that she didn't love me anymore, that she didn't want to see me again. I didn't want to change her mind. I just wanted her to look me in the eye and tell me it was over, and to admit she wanted to conclude such a long, serious relationship.

Immaturely, I sent so many text messages while intoxicated and grieving, it was actually pathetic. On one of the drunken occasions, in a series of heated texts, I asked her to just admit that she never loved me or had any feelings for me at all. Looking back, I cringe knowing that I was a grieving man with many more issues than Peyton. She wasn't the reason for all the grief or the last straw to severely plunge into alcoholism. She was just the outlet for it all.

I felt lost because I thought only weak men crack, that strong men can move on and don't let the things they have seen or done affect them. I bought into the idea that real men don't cry, they don't struggle, and that because others had it worse, I shouldn't be struggling.

After packing Peyton's stuff up from my apartment, I headed home for Thanksgiving. I dropped her stuff off on her porch at her request. I hated the lack of closure.

The following day was Thanksgiving, and that's when the totality of survivor's guilt hit me. The friends I had lost to the war, my friend who had just committed suicide, and how I was eating dinner with my family, upset about Peyton when they would consider that trivial compared to the grave. I felt guilty for feeling bad that Peyton wasn't at my dinner table when they would never be able to sit at their family's dinner table again.

Everything compounded together, and I fell into a pit of despair and grief over the next three weeks.

I was struggling with so many different things, including the last several years of my experiences. I was drinking heavily every night, failing all of my classes, and unable to concentrate on anything besides my own grief and problems. I had a hard time making friends in the new place since I was one of the oldest kids in my classes. After traveling around the world several times and with all of my life experiences, I struggled to connect with eighteen-to-twenty-year-olds. I felt extremely isolated, especially while living in an apartment Peyton and I had picked out together yet never really lived in together.

As pathetic as it was, I continued to message Peyton

every couple nights. In my drunk "good ideas" state of mind, I was asking for an in-person closure over Christmas break. I wanted to know how it was so easy for her to walk away when I was struggling. I created a toxic cycle. I would begin drinking around 2:00 p.m., text or message her around 8:30 p.m., go to bed, and wake up in the morning regretting ever messaging her. I even had flowers sent to her house, which remained "undelivered" because they were rejected at the door. I can't blame her in the slightest as I appeared to be a desperate and struggling man with no personal sovereignty.

I was hurting pretty badly. One day, my phone whistled with an iMessage notification from Peyton.

I understand that you need closure; however, at this point, I'm not willing to meet up to do it. Yes, we've dated for a year and some months. However, I don't know what there is to talk about and honestly feel it's unnecessary. I really do wish you the best. I appreciate everything you've done for me, as I've said before. I'm sorry I'm not able to give you the closure you need. I am moving on, and I'm asking that you please respect me. I don't want you to contact me again. I wish you and your family well and that you'll have happy holidays.

At this point, I realized this was the only closure I would get. There was nothing left to be said, and what was felt and thought about me was never going to be overcome or worked out. The only thing I could do was leave her alone and fix all the things I promised I would, but never did.

I continued to drink over the next several months. At first, it was a couple of beers a night, and by the following spring, I was drinking nearly a gallon and a half of whiskey per week, plus a couple beers throughout the day. I spent more time intoxicated than I did sober. I was drinking over Peyton. I was drinking to try to escape the stuff I had suppressed before Peyton. I was drinking because I felt guilty for surviving, and because I didn't have a better way to suppress the grief that consumed me.

I tried opening up, to work through my issues. The problem was that once I opened up all the issues I denied and suppressed, I couldn't put the cork back in the bottle. I began trying to process all of these things I had stuffed down deep over the years. I was at a point where I didn't experience much. I was suffering a deep kind of anhedonia where you don't feel happy, yet you don't feel sad. You just feel numb. I had tried several different hobbies— working out, running, snowmobiles, dirt bikes, and many other activities—yet nothing seemed to make me happy anymore. The harder I tried, the harder I failed, unable to find them.

This phenomenon hit me especially hard when my dad came to visit and we went out on the snowmobiles in February. Before leaving the parking lot, he and I took a picture together. In the picture, he looks so happy to be going out and having fun with his son who had spent the last nearly six years away. But my smile and eyes are checked out as if there's nothing inside.

These kinds of incidents grew and strengthened my survivor's guilt. I felt guilty for not feeling the same level of happiness those around me did. I felt guilty for not feeling it when my brothers who died would love to have a day with their father or loved ones. I felt like I was an ungrateful kid who had no reason to feel numb the way I did. I felt so many other people had much worse experiences than I did and that I was weak. I had my arms and legs still, so why was I down on myself?

This conundrum continued and contributed to my increasing drinking problem. The truth was, I didn't drink because it made me happy. I drank because it was the only time my guilt, remorse, and regret went away. It was the only time I felt I could get a reprieve away from all of those things and feel like the old me. The problem was, the more I drank, the shorter the reprieve from my issues was. Over time, I could drink all night with enormous volume. However, by April, I couldn't even get myself drunk. I would simply vomit from the amount of alcohol with no reprieve at all. My final coping mechanism wasn't working anymore, and the times I wasn't drinking, I felt more depressed than ever before. I was in a downhill spiral that I couldn't escape from. I tried to go more than a day without a drink; however, by the afternoon of the second day, I couldn't go without one. I would get the sweats and a tremor, and all of my struggles would come back out of hiding. I continuously tried to push them back down deep, but I didn't have the coping skills or ability to handle them. And every morning they came right back to the surface.

This was my rock bottom. I realized they were right. I was impacted by PTSD with the way I worried about Peyton. It wasn't a car backfiring or a movie; it was this overwhelming fear of an atrocity happening to the woman and people I love most in life. I learned with all of the damaged relationships it was easier for me to point the finger at her and everybody else for my frustration and the reasons for being distant. It was easier because, by blaming them, I didn't have to accept my role in creating the wedge between us, or everybody else I cared about.

In reflection, I realized I couldn't point the finger at myself or see my own issues because I would have had to admit that I was somehow emotionally weak or damaged. I realized, too late, the weak man puts his sufferings onto others, and the strong man admits his sufferings to get help and support to become a stronger man than before.

After taking a year of reflection, I now fully understand why I was on-again-off-again—the roller-coaster of "let's be done." I cringe every time I look back on this chapter of my life. I, in no way, ever wanted to be *done*. The truth of the matter is, I was afraid of allowing another person to have control over my heart and emotions. I had never allowed myself to fall so head over heels for anybody, nor had I ever wanted a relationship to work so bad. With every person, every circumstance, every life event, I adhered to the philosophy of one of my drill sergeants, "Gentlemen, never expect or even hope for the best to happen. Only expect and hope for the worst to happen. By doing so, you'll never be disappointed or surprised when a mission goes bad, or your wife fucks Jodie back home. Hoping for the best makes you weak, because it won't ever happen the way you hope it will."

The thought of her having the power to hurt me caused me to feel out of control over myself. I had grown to be a man who didn't leave much up to fate or destiny. I was, and still am, very plan-oriented. I have a plan, followed by a plan B and plan C, followed by an exit strategy if all of those go up in flames. I wanted to be in control over my emotions and heart, because I felt a man who can't control his emotions, heart, and actions is a man with no control at all. In addition, with my time spent in an emotionally checked out combat environment, I had stopped feeling emotions and wasn't able to pinpoint or decipher emotions like frustration, sadness, hurt feelings, stress, or vulnerability from anger. In a combat zone, you can only have one emotion—anger—no matter how sad the situation. This manifested as my outlet for all emotion.

In a combat zone, if you go around sad or impacted by every little thing, you will be unable to perform your job. However, if you react to everything with anger and hate, you'll stay alive and you'll keep your men alive. It is truly the only way to survive a war. Unfortunately, that's what makes the reintegration difficult and what, I feel, impacts veterans the most. When we get home, we don't know how to explain anything other than anger to our loved ones, whether that be family, friends, wives, or girlfriends. We cannot recognize the dysfunction of this coping mechanism because we're in it. We don't realize until it's too late that we hurt the ones we loved most because of the people war made us become.

This is why people have heard so many veterans explain that we feel we have become a monster through fighting monsters. We leave for combat to save and pro-tect the people and country we love most, yet when we get back, these are the people we hurt the most. It stacks on top of our weight of survivor's guilt and everything else. Many of us, including myself, struggle so badly with these things because, deep down, we have extraordinarily loving and kind hearts.

Now that I am working through my issues, critically evaluating myself over the years, I can see that I wasn't ready for Peyton. I could hardly communicate anything. I continuously looked for the worst, trying to find rea-sons to put her at arm's length or push her away with unattainable standards. I was struggling with the things I had done, unable to see even one good quality or thing about myself anymore. As a result, I often asked her to "stop seeing the negative and the worst in me," because I just wanted somebody to see something good in me again. In actuality, she had many valid points.

It was very immature of me. By putting her on the roller-coaster the way I did, I felt worse, knowing I was living as a man I didn't want to be. I was cold, shut off, angry all the time, pessimistic, and messing with her heart and emotions. I can see why Peyton didn't want to live with me. People like me, who have high-risk, high-stress careers, have different relationship needs than someone who hasn't endured the same stress, decisions, and sorrows.

I realized after Peyton left that I needed to get back into church as well. For me, my faith in God and God's plan has kept me going in even my darkest hours. I had been reading *The Art of Happiness*. In it, the Dalai Lama explains that when we hold onto toxic emotions, it makes us toxic individuals. He explains that we must let go of pain, hate, anger, and the wrongdoings of others. In one practice, he recommends, "If you're religious, pray for the prosperity of the people whom you hate or have hurt you the most. If you're not religious, meditate for good things to happen to these people. Picture in your mind during meditation all of these good things happening to that person. If you're neither, then think good things for the person."

This has been one practice that has really helped and even changed my life. When Peyton and I broke up, I felt nothing but spite and anger because I had grown into the inability to process sadness and grief. I was carrying around all this weight on my shoulders. I spewed negativity to everybody in my life, especially in regards to my old platoon sergeant, and the people I viewed as wearing down my relationship with Peyton. Ultimately, it was only hindering my own happiness.

Every night and every morning, I started praying for good things and prosperity for the people in my life who had brought me the most anger and pain. At first, it was incredibly frustrating and painful. I didn't see the point. However, after about two months, I didn't feel the hate, anger, or rage toward any of them. I began wishing and genuinely hoping these good things would happen to them.

Also, to combat my pessimistic and jaded views, when I'm driving or out in public, I actively seek out positivity. Instead of looking for a hostile individual, I look for happy things such as a couple holding hands, a couple laughing, a group of people smiling, walking around. What I've discovered over the last several months is at first it was difficult, and my optimism throughout the day didn't last more than a couple hours. However, now I see these good things more often than I don't. Instead of thinking the world is doom and gloom, with somebody around every corner wanting to kill or harm myself or the ones I care about, I see the inherently good side of people. Now I'm left with a longing for that same love to come back into my life. I want to be the one holding my lover's hand, laughing while walking down the street, and I would take that over my previous view any day of the week.

I realized that the most miserable times I felt toward myself after the war, while dating Peyton, were when I was focused on my own emotions, my own needs, and making myself happy. Right or wrong, I was acting very selfishly by trying to find fulfillment any way I could, without success.

I have so much love, respect, and admiration for the strength Peyton had to go against her heart, knowing it was best for us both. Looking back, I feel she gave me the gift of insight into myself. Her ability to challenge my ways of thinking and call out my faults and unhealthy behaviors, as well as her courage to leave the way she did, led me to realize I hadn't been the best version of myself toward her, my family, and my friends.

Peyton's exit from my life forced me to confront the demons from my past that I otherwise wouldn't have. Even with the sadness, mistakes, and everything in between, I experienced a great deal of love, compassion, trust, and happiness with her. The growing pains I experienced with Peyton taught me what kind of man I don't want to be, and they shape the man I strive to be every day.

The man I am striving to be is one who recognizes that crying or emotional pain isn't a weakness, admitting that you're hurting inside and asking for help isn't the weak thing to do; it's what a strong man does. He is willing to work 140 hours a week to provide for the family he loves. He is the man who, no matter how awful his day was, shows his family nothing but love and strength. I want to be that man, similar to my father. I want my kids to look up to me the same way I look up to him. I want to be the man who is able to positively impact all of the people I come in contact with, regardless of who they are or what their life situation is. Most importantly, I want to be the man who makes his wife feel like she is lucky to have him. I want her to feel like every single day is the first day we met—the man who she snuggles up to every night, feeling as if there's no place like home. I want to be the man who admits he is wrong, fixes his mistakes, and isn't afraid to apologize. Ultimately, I want to be the man who turns all of his weaknesses into strengths and helps others make it through all the things that nearly killed him.

That's the man I want to be, the man I wanted to be for Peyton, but the man I didn't know at twenty-two how to become.

"It is easy to hate, and it is difficult to love.
This is how the whole scheme of things works.
All good things are difficult to achieve;
and bad things are very easy to get."

—CONFUCIUS

CHAPTER 16

JUDGMENT CALLS

———

ONE NIGHT A FEW MONTHS AFTER PEYTON LEFT, I was sitting on the couch with a glass of whiskey attempting to drown out my own issues, when my phone went off with a text from a buddy I deployed with. Although I was polishing off my fourth glass of whiskey, I knew he was severely intoxicated. He had told me several times that he wanted to go back to Afghanistan and that things had gotten worse since his wife took the kids and left. This time was different though.

"I am going to go buy a gun, then go to the woods and think about things for a while, Kelly."

"Well, I'm here if you need a hand in the dark, man. I've been there. Still am," I respond nonchalantly, thinking it was just another drunk conversation from him.

"I shall be alone, brother," he replies back less than thirty seconds later.

"You aren't, and you know it," I say, beginning to grow concerned.

"I will be tomorrow!"

"Just don't do anything you'll regret," I say back, beginning to realize that he is planning on committing suicide tomorrow.

"Well, if I'm not around, I can't regret it, right?"

"You're right! Leave your kids behind, that's a much better fucking idea."

"I can't even see my kids because of my cunt ex-wife!"

"TEMPORARILY—THAT'S NOT PERMANENT, DUDE—YOU KNOW YOU AREN'T THE ONLY MAN IN THAT BOAT, DUDE!" I hope the all-caps will emphasize my concern.

"Idk bro. Fuck it all man," he says, disregarding my anger.

"Brother, your kids WILL come back around in a few years. Trust me. I'm watching it happen now. They'll get older and realize they were lied to by their mother about you, and they will seek out a relationship with you," I respond, thinking about some other fellow soldiers who had time for that scenario to play out.

"I love you, man. Just remember that. You're a good dude. You're a smart person. You'll go far—just don't get married or have kids!"

"Dude, I swear, with God as my witness, if you do something stupid and make me for the rest of my life wish I called to stop you from doing it, I'm going to piss on your grave," I say attempting to defuse the situation with some humor.

"I'll count on your piss watering the flowers on my grave."

"I'm serious. Don't make me regret not calling somebody to check on you," I respond back hastily.

"Wouldn't make a difference and you know it."

Continuing, "Kelly. You're like a brother to me man. But I'm going to do what I need to. And right now, it's drink this bottle of liquor. Tomorrow I'm buying a gun. We'll see what happens from there. Good night, brother," he responds in a farewell.

I go to bed that night sick over what just happened. *Fucking asshole. He's drunk. He has said some crazy stuff from guilt and remorse, but he's always fine when he sobers up,* I convince myself. Waking up the following morning, I immediately text, "How are you feeling, bro? Hungover?"

No response.

Later in the afternoon I get in a dirt bike crash. I send him a text, "Bro, I just broke my hand, cast and all!" I say, sending a picture.

No response.

Anxiety growing, I know that he is clumsy and most likely broke his phone throwing it against the wall while drunk and angry, or he felt embarrassed by what he said the night before. I brush it off as if it's nothing.

The following morning, it had been two days without hearing from him. I couldn't shake the nagging feeling:

He's in the middle of the woods, dead inside of his truck, and I never called.

Pulling my phone out on the way to class, I text, "Brother, I'm getting worried. Text me."

No response.

Deciding that I wanted to get another opinion, I text my old squad leader.

"Hey, brother, I want to send you some screenshots. I'm worried about my buddy from deployment who is struggling. I can't decide if it's drunk babble or if it's legit."

Immediately, my phone vibrates with a text, "No problem. How long has it been since you've heard from him?"

"Two days."

"Just got them, give me a minute to read them."

What felt like twenty minutes, while only two minutes actually passed, my phone vibrates again. "Bro, Brent is going to kill himself if he hasn't done it already. You need to call right now. You know better than that with the guys you've already lost to suicide! You should have called that night."

Realizing he was right, I pick the phone up, calling a battalion commander and mentor from a previous unit I served with.

"Sir, I'm sorry to bother you, I know you're busy. I'm worried about one of the guys from my deployment. He said some stuff the other night. I want to send you the screenshots. I think he's going to kill himself or already did."

"Send them to me. I'll get guys on it now," he says, hanging up the phone.

About an hour later, I get a text from Brent, "Fucking great, thanks!"

This was the last text message I received from my friend, *my brother*. He feels I betrayed him, his trust, and our brotherhood. I felt an extraordinary amount of guilt that day over the judgment call I made. In the story in the preface of this book, Casey, Cat Daddy, and I were pinned down by machine gunfire. Brent jumped up on the .50 cal M2 machine gun, laying down hundreds of rounds, disregarding his own safety to provide cover fire, protecting me as I ran across the open area several hundred meters to my truck. He earned a purple heart that day for taking shrapnel in the face from Taliban forces. I love Brent, and I know that had it not been for him, I would be dead. Although I knew I made the call out of love, I still feel as though I betrayed my brother's trust. I hope similarly for him as I do Peyton—that he realizes I never intended to hurt or betray him.

This is something many veterans and first responders like myself have had to face or make difficult decisions and judgment calls on. Brent, myself, and those like us never speak of our pain or demons that we wrestle inside. Many of us find the only time it is possible to talk about the hidden feelings and sufferings inside is while intoxicated. It becomes a vicious cycle where everything is bottled up, so you drink to escape, and it works for a little while. Over time, however, it harms your relationships and everything else in your life, so you bottle up more and try to escape for longer periods of time. The length of time you're sober rapidly decreases, and soon, the alcohol is adding more problems than you ever had before. Although alcohol and other substances once let you escape your troubles and worries, now they imprison you. What is often overlooked is the fact that alcohol is a depressant. Sustained drinking can often worsen the symptoms of depression, leading to worse coping skills, increased drinking, and eventually sending you into a relentless downward spiral. Once in it, it's hard to see any way out other than ending the suffering experienced in the moment, and it often removes all hope of your life getting better. Eventually, the continuous cycle runs out of momentum, and many succumb to the battle before they see that life *will* get better.

*An old Cherokee Chief was teaching
his grandson about life...
"A fight is going on inside me," he said to the boy.
"It is a terrible fight, and it is between two wolves.
One is evil—he is anger, envy, sorrow, regret, greed,
arrogance, self-pity, guilt, resentment, inferiority,
lies, false pride, superiority, self-doubt, and ego.
The other is good—he is joy, peace, love, hope,
serenity, humility, kindness, benevolence, empathy,
generosity, truth, compassion, and faith.
This same fight is going on inside you and
inside every other person, too."
The grandson thought about it for a minute
and then asked his grandfather,
"Which wolf will win?"
The old chief simply replied,
"The one you feed."*

CHAPTER 17

TRIGGERS

IT SEEMS ON A REGULAR BASIS SOCIETY REVEALS
new "triggers"—things that may cause emotional scarring
or bring up emotionally traumatic events. The list has
become so long that it seems as if any and every word
could be considered a trigger. Unfortunately, this has created a stigma around even mentioning the word "triggers."

However, this is a very real topic that needs to be
discussed, especially for veterans, first responders, law
enforcement, and others with hazardous occupations.
Contrary to popular belief, besides the stereotypical triggers such as an unexpected boom, blast, gunfire, etc.,
many of the actual triggers are things you would not expect
or even realize are triggering to your loved one.

For example, to this day, I can still picture the first suicide I ever saw. This individual hung herself from the attic
space in her garage. Because this was the middle of winter
time, there was not a terrible aroma, even though she

had been hanging there for over a week and a half. Upon entering the garage, I saw that her neck had stretched and elongated to between a foot and foot and a half long. All of the soft tissue had stretched in joint spaces, and she looked like a stretchable action figure, where you can stretch every limb and it eventually shrinks back together. That was eight years ago. To this day, I will never look at elastic action figures the same.

The difficult part is that many of the triggers that get guys like us worked up are often things we don't realize for months or even years. For the first year and a half home, I couldn't figure out why certain things would send me sky high. Eventually, I learned that when someone addresses me or anybody else unsuspecting with a hostile, accusatory, or aggressive tone, it sends me from zero to sixty in about 0.2 seconds. It still, to this day, puts me immediately on the defensive, and I'm ready to fight.

Unfortunately, I did not have this realization of my triggers until long after I'd hurt many of my friends and family. I had been struggling, and Cash—a man I consider my brother—and my sister-in-law Jenny had convinced me to fly to Arizona for spring break. They thought a Tatum sand car with over 1,000 horsepower would be the trick to snap me out of my depression. Although I wanted to go down there badly, I felt so bogged down by depression that I couldn't find my way out of a paper bag if I had to. Forcing myself to get out, I bought a flight to spend my spring break in the sun. I was excited to get down there and see them; however, it took about every ounce of energy in the tank to get down there.

Stepping out of the RV, I stretch out. *Nothing like nearly thirty-six hours being awake, driving two states to Oregon, leaving the dog with my parents, and then flying three hours to Arizona. Worth every second to be down here for five days.*

Without skipping a beat, I beeline for the whiskey and Coke. After pouring vacation amounts of alcohol, I head out of the RV with Cash to meet their friends, Chris and his wife, Janet. Immediately, I could tell both were the kind of people that are easy to get along with—genuinely good people. Eventually, the women wandered off to bed, leaving Cash, Chris, and I to continue drinking. We discussed the long list of horsepower upgrades that none of the vehicles needed, but they "needed."

The following day, starting at the crack of dawn, before the Yuma heat turned the dunes into an oven, the sound of a combined 2,000 horses roared to life. Climbing into the sand car, ducking my head under the roll bars, I fasten the four-point harness, cinching my body down to the seat.

As the suspension of the car absorbs every bump at nearly fifty miles per hour along the US-Mexico border fence, a border patrol agent is spotted observing the fence line. As if they were two teenage boys, both drivers give the cars just enough throttle to make a statement. As both vehicles squat down accelerating, the parked Tahoe blurs passed. The wind sends sand onto my face and into my mouth, and I still can't stop smiling. *Maybe they were right. Maybe the trick was adding over 1,000 horsepower to my life.*

Later in the day, we decided to take a trip out into the dunes. Unfortunately, Chris's new sand car had its maintenance serviced incorrectly by a mechanic who put an extra three quarts of oil into the engine, blowing the seals and leaking into the transmission. However, this just meant that Chris was my new drinking buddy for the weekend.

Since it was almost four in the afternoon, I was pretty well liquored up. Because I was riding in the back seat, I figured I might as well pack a couple of beers for the "guys' ride."

"Hey, I'm opening a beer to chug real quick, guys," I say through the headset.

As if Cash thought I were joking, I crack the beer open, raising it to take a sip. Without warning, before the can even meets my lips, I'm thrown back into my seat with the front tires off the ground, riding a wheelie with more thrust than a commercial airliner taking off. Meanwhile, as if somebody turned a garden hose on full blast in my face, I am wearing my now half-full beer. With one motion, the front tires slam down, and the car veers left, shooting suds of beer out the right side of the car. Before I know it, the vehicle is airborne off a jump. In slow motion, I watch a stream of beer leave the can, shooting up into the air. As I attempt to catch it back into the can, the car lands on the downside of the dune, sending ice cold beer over Cash and Chris.

"Hey, guys—I told you I wasn't kidding about opening a beer. Unfortunately, it's gone now. The three of us are wearing it."

I barely get my words out between hysterical laughs. Slowly, I begin to forget about Peyton. I forget all the things that have been bothering me over the last three years. And most of all, I forget about the nightmares that seem to catch up with me when I least expect them.

Continuing our day, we're laughing, telling jokes, and hanging around the camp. Interrupting the casual hangout, my nine-year-old niece comes up to Cash.

"Daddy, can we take my Razor out?"

"Sweetie, the cars are broken. I don't think we can get everybody out there."

Jenny chimed in, "Hey, we have the quad, Jeff's car, and a couple of dirt bikes. Let's just go up to sand hill!"

"Sure, why not? Guys, what do you think? We still have a couple hours left on the crock pots!" Cash says to everybody.

"Might as well!" I shout, and everyone agrees.

Wrangling everybody up, we get ready to leave the campsite. When Chris pulls up on a dirt bike next to me, he says, "Dude, last time I was on a dirt bike I crashed, had several feet of intestines removed from internal bleeding, and nearly died. I'm shocked my wife didn't blow an artery seeing me hop on this!"

"Dude, no joke! Maybe you should ride in a car!" I say lightheartedly.

"Nah, it's just a quick trip out there! I learned my lesson last time!"

Taking off through the sand, we leisurely ride through. Taking turns in front, I look back, and Chris is gone. Downshifting, I slow down, cranking the handlebars to the left while hitting the gas. Sand flies into the air as the quad spins around. Taking off back down the trail the way I came, I see Chris standing up, picking the bike up off the ground.

"Bro, you didn't see shit!" he says jokingly.

"Nope, not a thing! Like I said, maybe your wife was right!" I shout back.

Heading back down the trail, I follow Chris the remainder of the way to sand hill, waiting for everybody else. Sitting down in the sand, the typical dirty jokes ensue, and the five of us guys each drink a beer. Wrapping up to head back, I suggested a friendly wager.

"Alright guys, one beer out here isn't going to cut it for my night. The last one back makes the other a drink?"

"Works for me, man," Chris says, already halfway to his dirt bike.

As I put on my helmet and walk toward the quad, I see Chris take off, headed up the large, steeply sloped sand hill.

Starting the quad, I hop on taking off after him. Hearing the RPMs climb, I shift through the gears, zooming up the hill. Getting close to the crest, I see Chris whip around and dart back down the hill past me. Realizing I don't have paddle tires—*if I downshift, I'll go over backward*—I hit the gas, spinning the quad around. Following Chris's tracks, I'm headed down the hill. Speeding back down, I can see him hitting the bottom of the hill when the back of the bike begins to hop and buck him around.

He's losing control, and there's nothing I can do. I hit the gas, knowing he's going to crash, riding as fast as I can in his direction. With one last buck, the back of the bike comes up off the ground. Riding on the front wheel, it digs into the ground and Chris goes over the handlebars. To my left, I see everybody scrambling to run nearly two football fields to where Chris lay.

Coming in fast, I slam on the brakes, spinning the quad sideways while hitting the kill switch to the engine. Running over to him, I can hear audible semi-conscious groans of pain. Without moving him, I snap into combat medicine procedures, feeling his neck, spine, and arms. Immediately, I palpate several broken ribs, vertebrae, and collarbone. By now, everybody is around me when I hear one of the women speak.

"Does he even know what he's doing? He can't be moving him!"

"Shut up! He knows what he's doing. Let him check him out!" I hear Jenny shout.

As I continue assessing Chris while holding him stable, I freeze.

Oh, fuck. I don the role of makeshift-medic like it hasn't been over a year since I'd been around such injuries. Barking out orders to Janet, I sprint over to Cash.

"Hold him. Don't move him an inch!"

"Cash! I need you to drive as fast as you fucking can to the Border Patrol station. Tell them we need life flight. He's got a collapsed lung, broken collarbone, several broken ribs, and I don't know how long until the other lung collapses. If they don't hurry, he will die. GO!" I say, quiet enough for only him to hear.

Following my orders, the 1,000-horsepower engine roars to life, and he's shooting across the open dunes. Running back over to Chris, I continue to hold him stable. Cutting his shirt off along the chest plane, I can easily see that he has full-blown tension pneumothorax—a condition where your entire airway shifts to the strong side of a working lung if the other lung is punctured or collapsed.

Knowing he might need an emergency tracheotomy, I holler out an order, "Janet! I need you to help support his chest and head as we get the helmet off. I'm going to hold his neck and head in place while you pull the helmet off!" I order to his wife.

"Alright, start slowly pulling it off," I say calmly, without a hint of concern or worry in my voice.

As she slowly pulls the helmet off, I support all of the weight and tension of his head in my hands without allowing any movement of his neck. As she pulls past his jawline, I feel his jaw fall out of socket and into my hand. *Fuck, it's completely shattered.* In a combat situation, I would immediately be doing a NCD (Needle Chest Decompression).

However, mine were at home in the trauma kit in my truck. His trachea begins to shift, which is an indication that his other lung is starting to collapse. *Okay, you got this, Steele. Get a knife and a ballpoint pen, take the ink out and improvise for the NCD.* Attempting to improvise quickly, I'm waiting as a last resort, since this would be a harrowing, extremely painful, very invasive version of a needle chest decompression, but we're running out of time.

"Hey, does anybody have—" I stop mid-sentence when I see an EMT scrambling out of a Park Ranger truck.

"Here, put your hands over mine, hold Chris's head like this, and don't fucking let him move," I say running toward the EMT.

"Dude, glad you're here. Twenty-eight-year-old patient, tension pneumothorax, shattered jaw, broken collarbone, broken ribs, and one, soon-to-be two, punctured and collapsed lungs. He has a history of internal bleeding from a motorcycle accident two years ago. He needs life flight now," I say calmly.

The EMT looks at me like a deer in headlights and pushes his bag into my arms.

"Here's my bag. I need your help to save him. You clearly know more about this than I do!"

Running back over to Chris, I cut the rest of his clothes off. In harmonious timing, the EMT comes over, and we place the C-spine collar on. The EMT moves out of my way so I can strap the head pieces onto Chris.

"Hey, I need two more guys, lift on three and place him

in the truck!" I order to the guys from the group watching. On the count, we lift Chris into the truck.

Sliding him into the bed, slamming the tailgate closed, "You—get in the back of the truck. You—drive and radio. I'll take care of him," I bark out to the EMT and Janet.

In the back of the truck, I can feel every bump and bounce of the sand dunes. I know he is suffering through it, the gurgling from his collapsed lung unrelenting.

"Keep him talking, tell him you love him," I say quietly.

Through her makeup-covered smears, she says, "Chris, I love you. Hang in there, please!

Chris's responsiveness slows. He is growing silent, and the groans of pain are beginning to stop. He is going into shock, and if I let him go unconscious, he risks a coma and never waking up again.

Knowing I have to do what is best, I make a fist and begin rubbing as hard as I can on his broken sternum bones. This technique is used in the medical and law enforcement fields to generate a pain response from the unconscious or overdosing. It's painful enough without a broken sternum, but it's excruciating with one. With three hard rubs, I hear a slight groan.

The groan is followed by, "Babe, I love you. I don't think I'm going to make it. You and the girls will be taken care of, I promise," he sputters, beginning to lose consciousness.

I continue sternum rubs between groans, to keep him awake and alert. It quite literally pains my heart to do it because I know I'm sending excruciating pain through his body. Out of nowhere, in-between groans of pain, he puts his left hand up toward me, with his palm open. I don't know this man particularly well, but I know that I won't ever let a person die feeling alone. Opening my hand, I grasp his, our thumbs together, palms around the backs of each other's hands. I'm beginning to believe he's right. *He's not going to make it.*

Suddenly, his grip releases from mine, so I grasp it tighter. *Fuck, I'm losing him.* "Chris! Stay with me, buddy! We're almost there!"

A rush of overwhelming sadness and grief comes over me as a memory I had suppressed and forgotten about washes down over me. Listening to Janet's cries, I look down into Chris's eyes unable to break eye contact, except it's not Chris's eyes or the dunes I see. Everything goes silent, and I'm back to four days before deployment.

Walking downtown Phoenix, I'm twenty years old. I can feel the warm summer air against my face. Despite being 7:45 in the morning, it's already a toasty ninety-four degrees. It's the last leave I would get before deploying to Afghanistan, and I want to spend it drinking beer by the pool and hanging out with friends. While my friend is in class, I go out to drink coffee and appreciate America for what I am convinced would be the last time. Mid-stride, I hear a distinct "thud" followed by screams. Immediately, I'm in combat mode. *Where's the shooter? Where are the shots coming from?*

Looking to the east, I see a man in his mid-fifties lying

on the ground. Without hesitation, I drop my bag, sprinting across the road, dodging oncoming vehicles. When I get to his side, I see a cut on his forehead, *probably a seizure*. Rolling him into the recovery position, I feel across his clammy skin toward his carotid artery, looking for a pulse. Feeling a faint "thump," I begin counting beats while counting the seconds on my watch. *One, two, three...* Abruptly, it stops. I roll him onto his back realizing he needs CPR.

Immediately taking action, I begin to work on him, tilting his head back and attempting to open an airway, when he swallows his tongue. The older adults, who evidently have no idea what they are doing, begin pushing me away, attempting to physically pull me off him. They are saying, "He's too young to know what he's doing!"

My friend begins screaming at the top of her lungs, "He does know what he's doing! He's been training for the last three months to go to Afghanistan! PLEASE! PLEASE, LET HIM SAVE HIM!"

Luckily, an off-duty firefighter sees me struggling to help this man with everybody in my way. Running over to me, he says, "Hey, bud, I'm off duty, what's the situation?"

Quietly whispering so his frantic daughter over my shoulder wouldn't hear, "No pulse, CPR."

"Get us an airway. I've got chest compressions," he orders as if we worked on the same rescue crew daily.

I stick my fingers in the man's mouth, pushing my hand between his teeth as far as I can, reaching with my index and middle finger. Grasping what I can feel is a textured and dry tongue, I pull it out of his throat, opening the airway. My hands and forearms are now covered in dark blood from the man biting his tongue and cheek as he fell to the ground. Disregarding the blood, I arch his head back into a modified C-spine hold. My hands are resting below his ears on his neck, allowing air to move freely in and out. Kneeling above, still holding his head in my hands, I look deeply in through his eyes to the depths of his soul. Locking eyes, I can literally see the fear in his eyes as he begins to panic.

Without breaking eye contact, I can feel his twenty-five-year-old daughter standing so close behind me that her legs are pushing against my back.

She's screaming, "Daddy! Daddy! Please, save him!" through tears and a pleading voice.

Eyes still locked, I see the water begin to build up in his eyes as he slowly begins to cry. I can visibly see the man knows he is nearing his final moments. Tortuously, tears ball up near the eyelashes on the outside corner of his left eye, and a single tear is released. The tear glides down his cheek onto my hands, mixing with the blood. I continue holding him, looking into his eyes as his body ripples back and forth from the chest compressions fracturing every rib in his sternum. In one fluid transition, I watch panic in his eyes turn to fear, the fear turn to acceptance, and the acceptance turn to peace. Unable to break the intimate eye contact, I watch the light and electricity glistening in his eyes seconds before fading to complete darkness. The once human being, full of life and electricity, turns into a seemingly inanimate object.

Just like that, with a flicker of light being extinguished, he is gone. No amount of resuscitation is going to bring him back. I realize over the last five minutes that I shared a more intimate moment with him than anybody in his life. More than his wife he made love to, more than his child being born. I held the man, gazing into his eyes, attempting to save him, and ultimately held him and provided comfort as he crossed to the other side. We continued CPR until the fire crews arrived. We both knew he was gone. We just didn't have the heart to stop as his twenty-five-year-old daughter's cries ripped through the air, begging and pleading, "DADDY! DADDY, PLEASE DON'T GO! I LOVE YOU!"

When the fire crews arrived, we exchanged the professional eye glance. Without saying a word to each other, they knew as well as us that he was dead. Standing up, I look down at the open palms of my hands and forearms covered in the man's blood, wishing I could have saved him.

With a bump of the truck, I snap out of it. *I'm not going to let him die on me too.*

Unsure of how far we have to go, I pound against the back window of the truck, "Bro, we need to go faster right fucking now!"

Holding Chris's hand with my left hand, sternum rubs

with my right, I'm no longer even evoking a wince or groan from him. As I begin to grow increasingly concerned, I see the ambulance and fire truck now waiting nearby.

Hopping out of the truck, I fill the paramedics in while helping them unload Chris from the bed of the truck and into the ambulance. I can feel myself beginning to break, and I don't understand why. I just know I don't want anybody to see it, not a soul, because "grown men don't cry," and neither Cash nor Jenny have ever seen me cry. Walking away, I can't help it. I begin shaking and silently sobbing. It isn't only about Chris. It's everybody along the way who has died or been terribly injured in my hands. I can't help but think of all of them, including the feeling I had in Afghanistan, watching my friend get loaded into the medevac, as it all hits like a ton of bricks.

Facing away, refusing to look in the direction of anybody, I continue silently sobbing, attempting to suck back and hide any of my tears. Before I realize it, Cash is giving me a giant bear hug.

"Bro, you can't hold it all in, man. You've been doing that for as long as I've known you, and that's been six years. You are one of the toughest men I know. It's okay, bro. If you weren't here today, Chris would have died. Do you realize all you've been through has led you to be able to save two girls' father?" Cash says, attempting to hold back his own emotional pain at the sight of mine.

"This is what I mean, man. I told you and Jenny, my soul is tired. I can never go anywhere without these situations happening. I feel this world—God if he fucking exists, karma, I don't fucking know—never cuts me a break. You look at it as me saving his life. Do you know every time you grab somebody's hand as they're dying, a small piece of your soul dies with them, too? I'm tired. My soul is exhausted. I don't know how much more I can take," I say, fully sobbing.

I continue, "Can you please just take me back to camp before you go pick everybody up, so I can have a few minutes to collect myself—pull myself together?"

When we get back to camp, I pull my phone out to call my mom. "Mom, it happened again. I don't know why this always happens to me."

Without even having to ask what I was talking about, she knew. "Oh, no, honey, I thought this was going to be the spring break that you could get a break from stuff like this. What happened?"

Unable to hold back the pain of everybody I had lost and all my experiences, I tell her the story, trying to hold back the sound of my crying.

"I just don't understand, Mom. Clearly, I'm dealing with survivor's guilt and other stuff. I have to save somebody everywhere I go. Then to add to it, every couple I see holding hands, I think of Peyton. I just don't understand why I can't ever catch a break to at least tread water."

"Honey, things happen for a reason. There's a reason these things always happen to you. You're calm under pressure, and you have the know-how and skills to save people. Just think what would have happened if you weren't there. God isn't giving you anything you can't handle. He's giving you enough pain required to spark a change. What that change is, I don't know. I love you, honey. Keep me posted."

Hanging up the phone, I push the pain and sorrow as far down as humanly possible, attempting to hide any indication that anything was wrong. Seeing the group turn into camp, I pull my sunglasses on and throw on another fake smile.

"Who's ready for a drink?" I ask, in a fake, yet perfectly disguised optimistic tone.

That day, I saw clearly for the first time that I will always be impacted by PTSD. I will always have triggers, things that bother me, and situations that will arise and trigger memories of my past. For me, it isn't movies, music, or anything stereotypical that triggers me. For many of us, situations as described above, as well as harsh or aggressive tones from loved ones, send us from calm to completely irate. We will always relate critical incidents with our time in the military—the current trauma forcing us to relive previous events. I could be having a perfect day, yet the second a trigger is flipped, my fight or flight is activated, and I get extremely confrontational and authoritative.

As veterans, first responders, or anybody for that manner, it is important to figure out what it is that triggers us. It is essential to communicate with our loved ones how situations like hostile tones or arguments can trigger that confrontational and authoritative side of us, just like it is equally important for them to tell us when they feel we are treating them like a service member or criminal. This is a two-way street.

In my experience, I have made the effort to explain to my significant other or family that the aggressive tone amps me up to an authoritative person. When I try to calmly tell them, "Your tone is beginning to amp me up, can you please talk to me like a normal, calm person?" I have heard, "No! I'm not! It's you getting angry for no reason." This two-way street works if both parties are able to communicate. If your veteran or first responder spouse is making an effort to work on their issues and communicate with you, it should be a good sign of progress. You should put aside your ego and recognize the effort being made. Maybe you do have an attitude? Perhaps they're being sensitive? Either way, is it worth closing the communication gap they're clearly attempting to create?

*"Those who are hardest to love
need it the most."*

—SOCRATES

CHAPTER 18

ACCEPTING FATE

——

IT'S PRETTY CRAZY HOW THINGS HAPPEN. I LIKE
to believe that everything happens for a reason. These
struggles and experiences lead us from one door to the
next. We can't see this or make complete sense of it until
we view our mistakes and decisions in retrospect. While
making sense of this concept and my decision to fly to
the Himalayas, I watched a video with philosopher Jason
Silva. He said, "Follow your bliss and the universe will
open doors where there once were only walls. Everything
has been figured out in life except how to live. So perhaps
the better question is not *what we do with death*, but *what
we do with life?* Life exists in moments that are up to us to
individualize and enhance—to chain together so many of
these moments that we would want to live that life again
and again."

Growing up, I was the adventurous one. I had some
pretty crazy spiritual experiences in my life that have

led me to follow whatever calling it is you want to call it (universe, religion, spirituality, fate, karma, your gut, etc.). It made me the man who will up and leave somewhere without caring what anybody else thinks.

My Himalayan journey was my last-ditch effort to find whatever was lost before I was out of ideas. I felt the most excruciating survivor's guilt, remorse for things I did, regret for the people I've hurt, and the void all of that left, in addition to losing Peyton.

The journey started on May 4, while sitting at my favorite restaurant with my parents. Sitting in the restaurant, I could no longer smell the fresh tortilla chips and salsa. I could hardly even taste the alcohol in my margarita that made my mother cringe from strength when she tasted it. Looking around the restaurant at all the colors, people, and sunlight through the windows, it seemed dim, dark, and dead. It seemed to portray how my heart and soul felt inside. Nothing was vibrant, healthy, or even positive in my life anymore. I felt like I was standing in the sunlight of people, yet nobody could see the rain clouds above me. It wasn't from a lack of trying. I had tried five anti-depressants, a diet change, an increase in exercise, moving across multiple states, changing careers, and changing friends. It seemed the harder I tried to empty my boat that was filling with water, the faster it sank. Several loved ones repeatedly tried throwing me a life jacket, except none of the jackets fit, and I continued to drown.

Sitting in silence, I listen with not much to add. I'm

stuck in my thoughts. *Is God calling you there because that's the end of your journey? Should you say goodbye or leave a letter in case everybody is right and you die in a crevasse or avalanche?*

Interrupting my thoughts, my mom says, "Steele, why are you going? We just want to understand why you are headed to climb to just shy of 21,000 feet over a dream. Why do you have to go?"

"I don't know. I can't explain it. My heart just tells me to go. I feel like it's some message from the universe that I need to follow," I respond in the same numb monotone that fills me.

Dinner continues while everybody else talks. With the meal winding down, I glance at my watch, reading 2030.

"Well, guys, I have to go. I have to be up early to finish packing to catch my flight across the pond tomorrow," I announce somberly to everybody who is joyously laughing and enjoying dinner.

"Alright, bro. I want to drive you home. Let's have a cigar, just in case that mountain swallows you," John says, making light of the situation.

"Sounds good, man."

As we walk into the parking lot, John unlocks his car and we slide in. It's hot outside, but it doesn't feel different to me, and I hardly even notice.

"Brother, I've known you since we were five. It's been twenty years. I know when my best friend is in pain. You're in pain like I've never seen, man. I love you, and I'm beginning to worry. I want to get you out of it—I just don't know how. Will you please just level with me before you go? Give me the reason why you feel the need to take these risks all alone?" John says in the most loving, brotherly fashion.

"I'm tired, man."

"Dude, all of us are tired. I've worked my ass off all week installing solar panels on rooftops. You went days without sleep in Afghanistan. So don't lie to me right now," John snaps back in an irritated tone.

"Bro, I'm tired. And not in the physical sense. I feel like I've put eighty years of hard miles on my soul." The tears begin to breach the dam. "I have been around the world twice. I've seen the beginning of life with a baby born. I've seen death take people from my hands. I've saved a life and I've taken some. I've seen the largest mountains on earth and the greatest oceans. For the first time in my life, I've loved another person who isn't family with every fiber of my heart and soul. I've been the student, and I've been the teacher. I feel like my time here on earth impacting people is coming to an end. I feel I've learned just about everything there is to learn, and I feel like I've taught and given everything I have to give," my voice cracks.

"Bro, I didn't—"

"I hurt, I'm tired, and I feel like the last year I've lived white-knuckled, clenching my jaw, and holding onto a rope as hard as I can. The rope is beginning to fray. My palms are sweating from holding on so tightly, and I don't know how much longer my grip will last." It's the first time

I've talked to anybody about what's going on emotionally and spiritually.

"It hurts me to hear you say that. You mean so much to so many of us. You hide it behind your smile and laugh. But now I can see it as visible as daylight. I don't think you realize how many people look up to you for your strength and courage. You hide everything so well that nobody can see any cracks in the concrete of your foundation. I think you've learned a lot. Maybe you have learned everything there is, but I certainly don't think you've contributed everything there is to contribute to the world. You don't see it, but you light up the world for everybody around you. Every single time you walk into the room, you fill it. You are a big man, way bigger than your physical appearance. You walk in commanding and controlling the room. You brighten the room for everybody inside. I just wish you could see it."

"I truly feel like I try to put so much positive energy and love into the world. I try to help every person I can, genuinely, without expecting anything in return. I help and try to be kind, because I feel the world needs more of that, and it makes me happy to put a smile on another person's face. I just feel like I continue to do all these kind things for people, treating people with love. Literally the only things I've asked for in my prayers and life are happiness, making peace with the things I've said or done wrong, and to become a better man. To learn from my mistakes and have a family one day.

"I've never asked for money, material things, or fame. Just happiness. I continue trying to brave the storm and show kindness, yet everything I've asked for is gone. I feel more survivor's guilt, guilt over the things I've done, and remorse over some of the ways I've treated the people around me than ever before," I barely mutter through the cracks of pain in my voice.

"I support your decision, brother. You'll come back from the mountain with a whole lot of lessons learned and ready to change the world like I know you will one day. This isn't the end; it's simply the start of the next chapter. I'll see you when you get back."

I give him what could be the last hug and pull myself together by stuffing the emotions and pain back down as far as I can before walking into my parents' house. Walking inside, I'm greeted by both of our yellow labs licking me and attempting to gain my full attention. Walking like a zombie toward the fridge, I open the door, plucking a cold beer out. With a pop of the cap, I lift the bottle up, chug it down, and toss it in the trash. Opening the fridge again, I grab another beer and walk toward the living room.

"How was your time with John? What'd you guys talk about?" my mom asks lovingly.

"Oh, not much, you know, John getting into woman drama and stuff," I lie.

"Honey, I just want to understand why you feel the need to go. It breaks my heart seeing you hurt. You hide it, but I know you're hurting badly, and there's nothing I can do. It just hurts to watch, and I want to make it go away."

"Mom, I don't fucking know why I need to go, as I've told you fifteen fucking times! I had this dream, and I feel like the big man upstairs is sending me there for reasons I don't know. I just know I'm going to find out when I get there," I say, thoroughly agitated.

"I just don't understand. Why there? Why alone? It terrifies me to think of you all alone out there taking your final breaths in the cold and the dark, scared and alone! I don't want that to happen to you!" my mom says, now holding back tears of her own.

"Mom! Do you think Moses knew why he was called up to that mountain? No, probably not! But he went anyway! I told you, I'm being called there! I don't know why! I just know that I'm going, and I'm not scared of what I'll find!" I fire back.

"Okay, honey. I understand. I hope you know that you mean everything to us. You're the greatest gift to so many of us. You don't realize how many people in this world love you. You don't see how many people see you and instantly their face lights up. I have to go to bed," she says, crying, walking toward her bedroom.

I stare back at my reflection in the dimly lit window, the same window and couch I had stared into almost exactly two years prior. Once again, I am unable to recognize the man in the reflection. This time, I don't see a tough, unbreakable, unshakable man. I see a broken man from years of suppressing painful experiences. The lines on his face are still clearly visible from the stress and burning sun of the desert. I take in the hollow shell of his eyes. There is so much pain, sorrow, and sadness. I want to help him. I want to put my hand out and pluck him from the ashes, allowing him to rise above. But I can't. I continue staring at the man, once again beginning to cry—the words my mom just said and my response to her ringing guilt into my ears.

My phone buzzes with a text message from an old mentor who has since left the sheriff's office: *Brother, come over. We need to have a beer and a serious conversation before you fly out tomorrow.*

What I didn't realize was that he could see through my tough exterior shell. He knew I was waging an internal war on myself, sitting on the brink of no return. He could see it because he had been there himself. When I showed up, I cracked a beer, expecting to hide behind more raunchy jokes and guy talk. What I wasn't prepared for was an intervention.

"Hey, brother. Grab a seat," Corey said.

"Uh, okay?" I respond, realizing what is about to come next. I do my best to smile and hide what he already knows. *Maybe I need another drink for this one?*

"I'm worried about you. You laugh, smile, make jokes, act like everything is okay and like nothing is bothering you. But I've known you since you were fourteen. I've watched you grow up and become the man you are. When

I found out you were joining the Army, I wanted to say something. I wanted to warn you about fighting monsters. Once you see them and know what's out there, you can't unsee those things. They change and darken you for the rest of your life, and it is something that is difficult to escape. However, I knew you had seen many of those events before the Army, so I didn't say anything. Now that I see how it all compounded, I feel guilty for simply watching. I feel partially responsible for the pain I can see that you're in."

"It's alright, brother. It's really not your fault. Had you warned me or not, it was my calling, and I would have gone either way."

"Look, you're like a little brother to me. I love you, man. Others probably can't see it because you hide it so well, but in your eyes I can see the level of pain you carry. I can see through it to the level of desperation you're at. I can see it because I remember the optimism and hope you had before you experienced the world. Now, ten years later, I look into your eyes, and there's not much in there. I see myself two years ago, perfectly. It hurts me to see, because I know what I felt, and I would never want you to go through that. I already know you've contemplated suicide to escape it, but you aren't the kind of guy who would go out that way. I know what you're looking for in all of these high-risk activities, like climbing mountains, racing dirt bikes, skydiving, and all of that. You aren't going to find fulfillment there anymore, because your life is different. When I was your age, I did the same thing. But I'm worried you're headed to the mountains because you know there's a good chance you won't come back."

Still denying Corey could see it, I tried a classic technique of admitting just enough to hide the truth. "Yeah, I don't know. I think things are fine. The problem is my family and Peyton wanted me to find things I enjoy doing. I have, to an extent. I enjoy riding my Harley, I enjoy wakeboarding, but I can't find an activity that brings the same gratification it used to. I mean, for fuck's sake, look at the picture of my dad and me in February. He looks so happy, and I look like I've got nothing inside. I feel guilty, and I can't find anything that makes me happy anymore. I feel dead inside. It's certainly not a lack of trying. I believe I'll find it one day. I just don't really enjoy anything anymore."

"You know man, I don't know if you know this or not. I met my wife really young. I was the exact age you were when you met Peyton. I was extremely close with her brother, and she left damn near the same way Peyton left you—it was without warning, and I felt left holding the bag. I waited around for several years, dating casually, but I still thought of her and missed her. About four years later, I accepted the fact she had already moved on, wasn't coming back, and I had to move on. Well, one day four years later, I'm on vacation in Hawaii, and I've got a new girlfriend. And my now-wife, the one I had waited on, called and told me her brother had died in a motorcycle accident. I dropped everything I was doing, got on a plane, left the girl I was dating in Hawaii and came home to her. Shortly after, we got married and had my boys."

"Really? Did you just feel like she was your person, or do you feel like you missed out on four years of your life waiting around for her?" I ask inquisitively.

"You know, man, the heart is a tricky thing. Sometimes timing isn't right, and we can't see that we're right for each other and just not ready for each other. Society today has a funny way of telling the people that if it's not 100 percent perfect, you aren't right for each other. You know, my wife and I were on the brink of divorce a few years ago. There were some really shitty and hurtful things we said and did to each other. Eventually, I realized that I'm not perfect. I was routinely emotionally checked out and contributed to a big part of the problem. It wasn't all her or my fault, it was both of us. What I do know is that each and every day of my life when I wake up, she makes me want to be a better version of myself. She makes me want to break my back at work every single day to provide for her and my boys."

Continuing, "She is my person, and I realized that my life is better because she and my boys are in it. We have fights, and she pisses me off to no end at times. But ultimately, it's my family that makes my world go 'round, and I think you've already found what it is you're searching for."

"What in the fuck are you talking about? Clearly, I can't fucking find it, or I wouldn't be in this God-forsaken place!" I respond angrily, grabbing another beer.

"You do know what I'm talking about. The happiest I've seen you was about a month after you got home from deployment. We met for lunch, and you had a spark back in your eyes, and you told me about this woman you had met. You had told me and everybody else for years that you never wanted kids or marriage, yet you had been on two dates with the woman, and you told me you found your future wife. You explained how watching her hold a baby actually made you want to have a family with her one day. For the first time in our life, I heard you tell me that you no longer wanted to go back to a high-risk job or pursue the SWAT team. You wanted to give the career of door-kicking, plane-jumping, and gunfights up so you could become a better man for her and your future family."

"I remember that. I meant it. Are you saying that fulfillment or contentment was with her?"

"Not exactly. You see, all the activities I used to enjoy that I no longer did after violence, became fulfilling in my next stage of life. The adrenaline and excitement I was chasing, like you are, was a former phase of life. I found those needs and feelings of emptiness were filled when I became a coach to my sons' sports teams. After all that violence, I had stopped enjoying so many things in life. But when I took my kids to do the activities I used to love and thought I'd never enjoy again, I found they had become fulfilling again. I think you will find what you're looking for one day. I remember hearing about you—through the grapevine from one of my younger siblings who's

Peyton's age—how excited she was to meet and date you. If Peyton is and was as sincere as I believe she is and was then, I don't think her telling you that she felt you were her person and wanted to marry you one day was fake. I just think that she knew you were struggling with personal demons, and she had no way of helping you. She knew deep down she had to let you go so you could go out and struggle in life to figure it out and she could struggle in life to figure herself out.

"Honestly, dude, I find it hard to believe any of what you just said. I'm not sure I ever want a family again. I think I was right the first time not believing in the white picket fence bullshit of marriage and family. If she had thought of me or missed me, I would have heard from her. She would have said goodbye in person, not over text," I say, holding back heartache and tears so he won't see.

"Look, man, you're one of the toughest men I know. However, I think you've tried to lie to yourself and hide the fact that you have a very loving and soft heart. That is one of the reasons you and she had so many problems. You can still be a badass, tough, courageous motherfucker and yet still be a loving, soft-hearted marshmallow to your significant other, kids, and family. That's what I love about you, you've always been both. I think that's what Peyton loved about you from the beginning. That was the real you that she fell in love with before the reintegration phase started, when you lost that side of yourself. Unfortunately, your bottled baggage came back up, hardening you and making you a man she didn't love or even want to be with. I think you do need to go to the Himalayas. My hope is that you will find that loving, soft side of yourself again—the real you that has always been there. The you that a woman will grab onto one day and never let go of. When you do find that part of yourself again. The universe has a funny way of working things out. I know you'll find a woman you'll love completely and who feels the same way about you—a relationship where it will all make sense."

"Honestly, man, I'm not sure I believe in the idea of fate, the universe working itself out, or even God anymore. I find it hard to believe that a God who is supposed to be all loving and kind allows so many bad things to happen to good people around the world," I say back, a little quieter, trying to figure out if that's how I feel or just what I'm saying.

"One day, ten or fifteen years from now, my wife and I will pass through the state you're living in to take my oldest boy to college. You'll sit me down with a beer looking over at your beautiful and amazing wife in the kitchen talking to mine, and you'll look at your kids and say, 'Corey, you were right. I found the missing piece with my wife and kids. I no longer feel that void that I tried to fill with those crazy adrenaline things. Now, I love being a football coach and a good husband and father,'" Corey says optimistically.

"I don't know, man. I don't know," I say quietly, finishing my beer.

"I know. I know that you've lived a whole lot of life in

the few years you've been alive. You have reached the next phase of life early because you went all out so early on, whether that's from God's plan or luck. Work on yourself for a few years, better your flaws that you've refused to see, and you will become the man you want to be for them. You never know what the future has to hold."

When I left, I didn't understand a thing Corey had said. I felt he was out of his mind, because where my situation sat, I couldn't see tomorrow, let alone a decade down the road.

* * *

THE NEXT MORNING, WAKING UP, REALIZING MY bag weighs eighty-five pounds and will be way too heavy to carry above 10,000 feet, I empty it out.

Alright, what can you offload? We need to get this bad boy down to about sixty-five pounds maximum. You need two pairs of long socks, two pairs of insulation socks, four pairs of underwear, two shirts, and Under Armour for the cold. You can remove your sub-zero sleeping bag and waterproof liner. The down mid-weight bag goes down to zero Fahrenheit, and that should be good. You'll be in tents and teahouses, so you won't have to worry, since your backpack is waterproof. I zip my bag up, carry it to the car, and place it in the trunk.

"Alright, guys, I'm ready to go to the airport."

Getting in the car, I don't feel sad or eager. I feel numb. Reaching over for the radio dial, I turn the volume up when

I hear my favorite band from my time in Afghanistan, Five Finger Death Punch, and the song *I Apologize*. As I listen, I think about all of their music linked to vivid memories of missions and the time I spent training for them. This time, the lyrics seem to foreshadow my impending fate.

One day, I'll face the Hell inside me. Someday, I'll accept what I have done. Sometime, I'll leave the past behind me. For now, I accept who I've become. And now I see clearly—all these times, I simply stepped aside. I watched but never really listened as the whole world passed me by. All this time, I watched from the outside. Never understood what was wrong or what was right.

Since I went to war and came home, home doesn't feel like home anymore. I find myself homesick for a place that no longer exists, and I want to go back to Afghanistan worse than ever before. It's the only place I can remember where I felt alive and like the person I was destined to be. At the same time, I want to be home with my family. I know where home is, but I can't find my way back there. I've seen so many people and loved so many people in this world, listened to their stories and dreams, and yet, just like my own, they all seemed to be shattered, and I'll never see them again.

Continuing to listen to the song, everything fades to silence, and I'm back over *there*.

It was a cold November day, yet standing in the Afghan

sun, it feels hot. It was the day we were set to withdraw all American forces from the base in conjunction with former President Obama's downsize strategy. A terrible foreboding and sadness filled the air because we didn't want to leave. We felt there was still lots of work to be done. As we loaded our trucks with our few personal belongings and prepared to do one last convoy of trucks up north, the ANA soldiers we worked with side by side came to say goodbye. Over the last several months, I had grown to respect and admire these young men, often still teenagers.

They believed in a better version of their country. They believed to their core that, one day, they could have a loving, peaceful, and prosperous Afghanistan.

When I see my favorite ANA soldier, Sgt. Adelle, I give him a big hug, thanking him for everything he did, the help he gave, and his willingness to always be the first man through the door. His personal motto was, "If anybody dies for my country I love, it should be me, not you."

Attempting to hide my fear of his impending fate once we left, I use my typical humor to break the tense situation, "Well, brother, it's been real, it's been fun, but it ain't been real fun!" punctuating the tease with a swat on his ass.

"Thanks, Kelly!" Sgt. Adelle responds, his English accented but perfectly fluent.

"Brother, how much longer until you earn your American citizenship? Where are you going to move when you get there?" I ask, genuinely concerned.

"Three months, bro! I move Texas. Best state in America!"

"Fuckin' A, bro! It's my favorite state! You've earned it, my friend. You've done more for America than most of the Americans I know! I'll be moving to Austin, Texas, shortly after I get home, and I fully expect you to bring your wife and kids over to my house for a BBQ and some American beer! My home is your home!"

I truly felt—and feel—this man lived the American values. Regardless of your opinion on giving citizenship to foreigners, especially those from countries we are at war with, this man embraced the mottos and values of everything America stands for. He had been shot twice, his family had been threatened, and he lost more friends than I can count for the war on terrorism. If anybody deserved a green card to this beautiful country, it was a man like him and our interpreter, Ahmed.

"Kelly, I want you to have this," he says, pulling a patch embroidered in Pashto off of his uniform.

"What does it say?" Confused, I look it over.

"For God and country, we must fight."

"Ah, you know your Ronald Reagan! I love it, bro! I'll put it in my shadow box when I get home. When you meet me at my home in Austin, I'll get it back to you!" I say, fully intending and believing every word.

As we finish our mission preparation, we do a final ramp brief of emergency procedures in case of a rollover, IED, or firefight. It is different than other missions.

The platoon leader chimes in, "Gentlemen, this mission is different. We are *not*, I say again, *not* to maneuver and engage or do any BDA. We are to return fire, neutralize the threat, and continue moving. We will have B2 bomber planes, fighter jets, and Apache Attack Helicopters supporting our entire movement. They are armed with Hellfire missiles and J-DAMs, and Central Command has made our mission top priority. They will do any BDA if necessary."

Before loading the trucks, we pull as much machine gun ammunition, water, and MREs as we possibly can to leave with the ANA. Unfortunately, it's only about 1,000 rounds total and would not last more than a ten-minute firefight. We wanted to leave them with more, but we needed to ensure our own safety in the event of a gunfight.

Rolling out the gates, we literally leave the locks off and continue driving. The air is filled with anticipation and the overwhelming feeling that we are leaving the place we now called home. It feels like moving away to your first day of college, waving goodbye to mom and dad.

* * *

WHEN WE ARRIVED UP NORTH, WE BEGAN UNLOADing our trucks, and men were shuffled to barracks shared with the Spaniards and Italians. They were extremely hospitable, stuffing four of their guys per room so we would have a bed to sleep on instead of the concrete floor of a

5°F airplane hangar. They took our laundry, fed us, and allowed us to shower for the first time in several weeks. I have a great deal of gratitude and respect for both nations.

Before loading my gear and heading to my temporary housing, I walked over to say goodbye to Ahmed and the other interpreters. I had grown especially fond of Ahmed, as we had many long talks about religion, life, the difference in romantic relationship traditions in our respective countries, and the politics of the war-torn country. Ahmed was going to earn his citizenship after returning home to his respective province. He had saved all of his money and was preparing to move his new wife to America with him a few weeks after getting home. He had spent almost eight years risking his life in the American Infantry units, and he was finally done.

"Ahmed! You weren't going to leave without saying goodbye, were you?"

"I don't know, Kelly, you all so busy!" he responds quietly, seeming a bit stressed. "Goodbye, Kelly, thank you for being so nice to me and making sure I was taken care of," Ahmed says, extending his hand.

"Bro, you're family. Like the rest of the soldiers. Put your hand down and give me a hug!" I say in an orderly tone. "This isn't goodbye, my friend. It's a *see you later*! I'll have you and Sgt. Adelle over for a BBQ. We'll sit on the back porch drinking beer and laughing about the good ol' days! Find me on Facebook when we get home, and I'll make it happen!" I say with sincerity.

"Okay, Kelly, I will."

"You fucking better! Somebody needs to make sure the American dream is alive and prosperous when you get there!"

Over the next several days, I began to wonder why I had not seen the interpreters. There was one dining facility, and our barracks were next to the airfield, yet I had not seen the interpreters fly or eat a meal. I began asking all the guys around me if they had seen the "'terps." Puzzling enough, none of them had.

Grabbing my dinner at the dining facility, I see a first sergeant I had frequently bantered with. Spotting him across the hall, I walk over and sit across from him and a commander I barely know.

"Hey, Top. None of us have seen the 'terps. I was just wondering if they were able to get on their flights back home? We figured command got them out early, and we just didn't see them?" I ask, expecting a quick, "Yeah, they got out late the other night."

Suddenly, I realize things aren't what they seemed. Without a word, the first sergeant looks out of the corner of his eye, locking eyes with the commander, indicating something was off.

"Um...Top...why are you looking at Sir that way? What am I missing?" I ask, with a cold pit in my stomach.

"I better not hear this repeated. It was not my decision. It was not my boss's decision. It was the decision very high up the chain. After you guys went to your barracks, it was decided we didn't have room for them here on this outpost. They were escorted out with their belongings and uniforms to the main road at about 2200 hours (10:00 p.m.) and left on the side of Route 1," he says in a quiet and somber tone.

Hot rage consumes me, "What the fuck? You're telling me these guys who go by fake names because Taliban kills their families if they don't, the men who saved our lives on missions, interpreting and gathering intel, were fucked over on the promise from America to be escorted by military flight to their homes? The promise of citizenship revoked? And they were thrown out in military uniform on top of it, like trash?" I say, losing my professionalism and respect for rank.

"Specialist, I don't know what to tell you. I had no part in it. I couldn't change it. It's way higher up the chain than any of us sitting in this dining facility. Truth be told, I agree with you," he says in a man-to-man, regardless-of-rank fashion.

"With all due respect, Top, this is how terrorists are bred. This is how we lose wars, not win them. What happened to American values and doing the right thing because it's the right thing? Whoever made that decision broke the greatest promise. They used them and threw them away, and whoever made that call should be ashamed to call themselves an American."

"Specialist, I can't say anything either way. This conversation is over, and I don't want to hear it spoken of again."

"Roger that, First Sergeant. I'm not hungry anymore. I really appreciate your honesty."

Several months later, we discovered one of the interpreters had made it out because he had family in the area. However, many of the interpreters did not.

In a twist of fate, the day before we left Afghanistan, our platoon leader got a phone call on his disposable Afghani cell phone—it was Sergeant Adele. I was told secondhand that Sergeant Adele had been granted his citizenship but moved checkpoints and decided to stay a couple more months to train the new guys.

Unfortunately, about six months after returning home, I discovered our interpreter Ahmed was executed by Taliban forces sometime after the interpreters were left on the side of the road. In addition, Sergeant Adele and almost all of the twenty ANA soldiers we said goodbye to that day had been executed when their checkpoints were overrun by Taliban fighters.

Supplies never made it to them from the capitol, and they were brutally murdered while weaponless. I still feel a sense of pain and loss that two fellow warriors—*Americans in everything but name*—were lost that day. This is a prime example of how we exited the war too soon, and the withdraw came too early. Had we stayed a couple more rotations longer, the Afghan National Army could have sustained with longevity. Unfortunately, politics got in the way, leaving a power vacuum filled with death and sorrow.

I still have the patch Sergeant Adele gave me. It's

collecting dust on a shelf next to the bottle of whiskey I picked up, intending to drink with him and Ahmed when they got to America.

* * *

SNAPPING OUT OF MY DAYDREAM, I REALIZE I'M AT the airport and it's time to say goodbye to my family. However, this time it feels different. It doesn't feel like the "see you later" goodbye. It feels more like the goodbye Peyton and I shared in Coeur D'Alene, where we knew we wouldn't see each other again. I can't help but wonder: *Will this be the last "I love you," the last hug, the last glimpse of my family just like it was with Peyton?*

I pass through security, headed for one last drink and meal before flying the nearly twenty-seven hours to Kathmandu, Nepal. Pulling my phone out, I begin reflecting on the last couple years. I order several beers, and with each one, I become more and more intoxicated. After half a dozen, I thought it would be a good idea to send a letter to Aubrey Marcus at Onnit and *The Joe Rogan Experience* podcast. Knowing it would most likely not reach him, I sent a kind message explaining how his words in the podcasts had positively impacted my life. How it changed my relationship with Peyton, and how he and Mr. Rogan were one of the sparks igniting my trip to the Himalayas.

Boarding the plane, I walk past passengers and find my seat. I recline my seat back, close my eyes, and say a little prayer. *Hey, Big J. Been a while yet again. I'm out of options. This is my last-ditch effort to find happiness and peace in my soul. I don't know why you're calling me here or what I'll find. I just hope I find it, because I don't know what is next if I don't. I'm scared of coming back in the same state I am in now.*

Roughly twelve days into the hike to my climb, I was above 12,000 feet, and the pack weight was becoming increasingly more difficult the higher I climbed in elevation. On one particular day, I was falling behind my group of Canadian and New Zealander friends that I had met along the way. I had come to a fork in the trail where I could go left, following the main path, or go right and walk up a goat trail "shortcut" to the main trail, cutting almost a half mile off, catching up to my friends. I decided to take the right turn, following the shortcut path, despite it being less traveled. After walking about fifteen minutes up the steep incline, I am stopped by a rock face that is roughly thirty feet up, with small rocks riddling the path. It isn't so steep that I have to climb straight up, but it's steep enough that if I slip, I risk falling off the face, sliding off the goat trail, and falling into the shallow, rapid river several hundred feet below.

Recognizing that I have two options: *Turn around, walk fifteen minutes back to where you were, or tighten the straps on your nearly sixty-five-pound pack and not slip.* I decide to go for it. Climbing up the wall, rocks slip from under my feet tumbling and bouncing down the rocks to the icy river below. With every step, I reach for a rock, ensuring the rock is a strong foothold. Finally reaching the top, struggling to round the lip onto the trail, I take one last step, heaving myself up to grab the hand of my Canadian friend, Komo. He pulls me over the lip of the main trail, and I flop flat on my back, breathing heavily, struggling to catch my breath.

Getting up, I walk over to a boulder and sit down, attempting to catch my breath. While bent over drinking water, I see two men from India, whom I had routinely passed over the last few weeks. We had made jokes about how slow the other group was moving, despite the weight of my pack and their ages (roughly forties or fifties).

One of the men I had several short conversations with walks directly over to me after seeing me climb the face of the goat trail. Pointing to it, he says, "You very brave, very strong man."

I respond, laughing, "Well, I don't feel strong right now! The pack is heavy at this elevation! And I don't know about brave. It's just a couple hundred feet of rocks—no big deal!"

"No. No, not talking about rocks. You brave man in life—you take path less traveled. Take very strong, very brave man."

Pausing for a second, I think about everything I had done, and how, at times, the path less traveled had been very lonely, very difficult, and very sad. I thought about the path that got me to where I am, and the reason for the Himalayas in the first place.

"Thank you, I appreciate it. Sometimes I don't feel very strong on that path. And sometimes I don't feel all that brave. Sometimes that path is very hard."

Nodding, he says, "Is not supposed to be easy. That's what makes it brave."

Two days later, when I arrived in Dingboche, I took a rest and recovery day. I decided to go to one of the tea shops to drink tea and continue reading *The Art of Happiness*. The owner, who was also the town doctor, struck up a conversation with me. We were talking about the helicopter that just landed, evacuating a woman who had High-Altitude Pulmonary Edema (HAPE), and the severity of the condition. We were talking about how many of the trekkers fail to properly recognize the seriousness of altitude acclimatization and how many deaths occur as a result.

"You see, two night ago, two Indian men come here. Hard breath, lips blue, I tell them need oxygen. I get porter to bring for fifty American from Phakding. Men proud, no oxygen. Say they be fine. I tried to tell them you go down if no oxygen, no good health," the shop owner says.

"Well, did they go down? Or did they get flown out?"

"No, man die four hour later in sleep because no oxygen," the owner responds solemnly.

Wait—I knew exactly who he was talking about. The trekking groups were small, and I repeatedly ran into the same trekkers. "Did you say two East Indian men two nights ago in their fifties?"

"Yes!"

I verified, several weeks later, that the man who gave me those words of encouragement was the man who died that night from HAPE.

* * *

IT HAD BEEN ROUGHLY NINETEEN DAYS SINCE LAND-ing in Kathmandu. I had hiked to approximately 17,600 feet, and it was the morning of the day I was headed to the base camp of Imja Tse to make my climb. Sitting on the broken-down foam bed, I shift my weight back and forth, attempting to gain feeling in my legs. The hard plywood beneath the foam presses through continuously, making my legs fall asleep. I scroll through my phone, trying to check my email on the snail speed of the Hima-layan internet.

With shock and awe, I see an email response from Mr. Aubrey Marcus. I couldn't believe he actually responded. Like a giddy teen on his first movie date, I screenshot the response, saving to read it and think on it at the base camp of Imja Tse. With impressive timing, this would be the last message I would read before struggling to keep the Grim Reaper at bay.

When I got to base camp, I wasn't able to sleep due to the elevation. Worse, there were some loud campers who weren't climbing. Disrespectfully, they sat up all night joking, running around, and yelling, and I didn't get any sleep. Due to the amount of vertical feet we had to cover, we were forced to start the climb just after midnight.

Shortly into the climb, I can feel the air getting thinner and thinner. The only light is the beam of my headlamp illuminating the fog and my puffs of breath against the rocks. Hearing rocks slide, tumbling down hundreds of feet, I carefully place every step in the darkness with the realization: *I'm walking on a cliff face; don't take the wrong step off.* With every step closer to the final ascent, I can't help but have some anxiety thinking about the incident a few days prior.

I met the guide in Dingboche as instructed. I brought my own harness, carabiners, and tie-off ropes from home. Unfortunately, I couldn't fit the other gear into my bag, so I was forced to pre-negotiate the gear rental of the ice axe, crampons, dry ropes, and a helmet. When I arrived, I met the boss who attempted to scam me out of a couple of hundred American dollars.

"You must pay for all of this equipment," the boss instructed.

"No. I already spoke with your boss in Kathmandu. I paid for it there, and I was told you would give it to me."

"No. You pay or no gear."

After several minutes bantering back and forth, I decide to play my ace card. "Look, man, here's the deal. I'm going to call your boss and tell him you're trying to scam some money off me and you're changing the agreement. How does that sound?" I say in the calmest, yet angriest tone imaginable.

"No. No. No need bother boss. I get gear for you," he responds, walking away.

Several minutes later, he returns with crampons, a helmet, and one ascender.

"Dude, where is my ice axe?"

"No need ice axe; non-technical mountain," he responds, looking at the ground.

"Uh, no. I have friends who climb Mt. Hood in Oregon that is half the elevation, and they use an ice axe. It's used for breaking ice to establish footholds and a safety brake in case of a crevasse. I want my ice axe," I demand.

"Your friends no climb Imja Tse. No need axe," he responds, failing again to make eye contact.

At this point, my gut is telling me this is bad—that I'm in the middle of being screwed. However, I was still reading the book *The Art of Happiness* by the Dalai Lama and Howard Cutler. So, I figured I needed to embrace peace, compassion, and trust. *When in Rome.*

"Here, one ascender," he says, handing it to me.

"Umm, if you're above a 50 percent slope, you want two. Where's my left-handed ascender?"

Looking me dead in the eye, he says, "No need two; non-technical mountain."

By this point, I am ready to lose my temper with the man, because every part of my intuition is screaming, *This fucker is screwing you! He's going to get you fucking killed!*

However, once again, I figure they climb this mountain every day for a living. *If they say it's non-technical, it's non-technical. If they say you don't need an ice axe, you don't need an ice axe. Maybe it's more of a difficult hike than a climb?*

Interrupting my reflection, I see the twilight of the sun coming over the horizon. I look down at my watch, I see *0330, 18,400 feet.* We continue walking until the rocks change to snow and ice.

"Sir, time put crampons on—we get snow," my guide says.

Pulling my crampons out, I fasten into them, while struggling to catch my breath in the thin air. I can feel every muscle burn as if I had just run a marathon, and we're only halfway there.

As we're about to start walking, I see my guide pull out an ice axe as he tethers a rope from my harness to his harness. Immediately, I realize I've been had. *Non-technical, huh? No need for an ice axe? Well, if an ice axe isn't needed, why in the hell does he have one? Well, fuck it. You're already halfway. You didn't come all this way not to make it.*

Trudging through deep snow and ice, I'm forced to walk bowlegged like I have spurs on my boots to keep from catching the spikes from my crampons. As we continue to ascend, we turn, and I see a roughly fifty-foot span of the open crevasse with several hundred feet below. Ahead, a rickety aluminum ladder looks as if it has been there for nearly a decade. Resting on top of the ladder was another ladder with some parachute cord lashing the two together.

The ladders have roughly six inches of grip on each side of the crevasse, and my guide begins to cross.

Looking down, I expect to see a safety line to clasp my carabiner onto, and there's none. *Well, fuck it. At least if you do fall, you won't feel it.* I set out across the rickety ladders. Continuing to blaze a path, snaking through open holes in the crevasse, it dawns on me: *I'm safety corded to my guide. If he goes through the ice, you have no way to stop because you don't have an axe. And you don't have a knife to cut the rope.* Now, I don't condone cutting a cord on your climbing buddy in any way. It would not be my first choice, obviously. But if I had to cut the rope to keep from both of us dying, because they wouldn't give me the ice axe I paid for, then that's the cost of doing business.

Crossing another crevasse hundreds of feet deep, I climb another rickety ladder over an eight-foot span, ten feet up to the top ledge. Reaching the top ledge, I stop, gasping for air, taking another glance at my watch, it says *0445, 19,000 feet*. Looking straight up at the pitch in front of me, I realize I've been screwed with no axe and one ascender. By my guesstimation, it is a 70–80 percent slope with fixed ropes, almost 1,100 vertical feet, and I can't even see the summit.

Approaching the fixed ropes, my guide pulls out two ascenders. *Why am I not surprised?* He begins scaling the ropes, waddling up the side, sliding right and left hands back and forth, scissoring up the line. By this point, I can feel the effects of thin air, and I'm completely exhausted. Fortunately, I'm stubborn and determined to make it.

Grabbing the rope, I am surprised. *Why is it nylon and not a typical dry rope? Nylon can become brittle and isn't meant for fixed lines, especially ones that are in such severe elements like this one.* Casting my doubts aside, I lock my right-hand ascender onto the line, grabbing the line with my free left hand. I apply tension to the line, sliding the ascender up, while simultaneously taking a step. It doesn't work. I get the ascender about six inches, and because my crampons aren't sharpened to the required amount, I'm unable to gain traction, and I slide back down. Realizing this, I now have to put twice the effort into pulling my entire body weight up the rope with my free hand, while attempting to apply tension so I can slide the ascender up the rope with my right hand. It's two steps up, one step down, all 2,100 feet.

As a result of having to do twice the physical exertion, about halfway up the mountain, a wet winter cough sets in. My lungs are filling with fluid, a condition known as High-Altitude Pulmonary Edema (HAPE). Knowing that I have medication in my bag and that I am now only about 500 feet from the summit, I press on.

You've never climbed before. Why couldn't you pick a beginner mountain like Mount Hood or Sisters, first? But no, you're Steele Kelly. You had to start in the fucking Himalayas. I'm struggling to catch my breath at 20,000 feet. *One more step. Push yourself.* Reaching up, I slide my ascender along the fixed rope, fighting to take another step.

An hour later, I unhook from the final fixed rope, hooking on to the anchor at the summit. Looking down at my watch while gasping for air, I see *0745, 20,305 feet.*

"I did it, bro! I did it! That was way harder than I could have imagined. I'm mentally and physically drained from it!" I say to the guide and another fellow climber and his guide.

"Yeah, bro, it's tough. I think one out of five make summit? Most people underestimate and don't condition hard enough," the European climber, who is roughly my age, responds.

"Bro, can I borrow your ice axe? There's something I've got to do."

"Yeah, here!" he says, handing me his axe.

The dream I had six weeks prior is now a reality. I feel the wind on my face, the cold ice on my knees, and the early morning sun beating down on me. I begin swinging at the ice near my feet on the summit of the mountain. I continue swinging and digging. I swing the ice axe one last time, leaving it in place next to the hole. Seeing my breath in the air with every fast, shallow exhale, I reach up to the zipper hidden by my Carhartt face mask and beanie. Hearing every click of the zipper, I unzip my jacket to my waist, pulling my right-hand glove off, revealing my bare hand that is now steaming from the physical exertion of the climb. I reach into the chest pocket, removing the picture of me and Peyton that I kept in my wallet for so many years.

I hesitate letting go. Holding the picture, I close my

eyes. *She looked so beautiful that night. We looked so happy. What a shame it had to come to an end. I knew it would. I just didn't think it would happen for another eighty years. I miss her, and I wish it ended differently.* Opening my eyes, I let go of the picture as it falls like a feather into its shallow grave.

Reaching into my pocket again, I feel for the metallic item. Finding it with my steamy hand, I pull it out with my thumb and index finger, revealing a shiny platinum diamond ring. Holding the ring at eye level, gazing at it, the sun's rays hit the diamond, illuminating the clarity and precise edges of the princess-cut diamond.

With one smooth motion, I slowly move my arm toward the grave. Hesitating, I picture all the laughs, love and vacations, and those nights I laid on my back as she snuggled her head into my shoulder, arm over my chest, asleep. The nights I felt at home for the first time in years. Pushing through the hesitation, I open my hand, allowing the ring to somersault into its final resting place.

Reaching over, I pull snow over it, covering the grave, holding back my aching heart and the tears of finally saying goodbye.

Standing, I feel a bit dizzy and drunk. At first, I brush it off. *It's probably low blood pressure at elevation, or a flood of emotions.* However, the cough begins, and this time I can feel a wheeze in my lungs. *Oh, no, you have full-blown HAPE—the drunk feeling is the beginning stages of High-Altitude Cerebral Edema (HACE).*

Looking at my guide in the most critical tone, I order,

"We need to descend, like right fucking now. Something is wrong."

Looking back, he's puzzled and says, "We only been here twelve minutes."

"I know, something is very, very wrong. I need to get back to my pack at base camp. I need drugs. If I wait too long, I'll need life flight."

Hooking back onto the line, the guide begins repelling down the line first. Walking to the line, I squat down, rigging my carabiner and descending device. Hooking onto the line, I lean backwards off the line dangling over the cliff. Looking to my right, I take one last look at the mound of snow.

Thank you for all the positivity and love you brought into my life. I know some people can't stay in your life forever. I just wish you were the one who could. I'll always love you.

With one swift motion, I pull back on the rope, repelling down the line, switching every couple hundred feet to a new offset line. At the bottom, I see my guide. However, he isn't waiting. He's walking without me. Struggling to get air, I attempt to speed my pace up to clip the safety line on to him. However, my lungs have so much fluid, I can feel the gurgle of water beginning, and I bend over coughing. I can't walk a straight line. My head is floating, drunk with dizziness. With every step, my crampons catch my pants, ripping them wide open. Getting closer to him, I struggle to maintain the pace. I can barely manage coordination and balance, yet I still have to cross all of the open crevasses, without a safety line, essentially drunk.

Beginning to comprehend how severe my condition is, I attempt to keep moving. My body continues to scream at me to stop and wait—to stop for just a minute and take a nap or rest. *You have to keep moving. You can't stop, or you'll die.*

When I arrived at base camp, my guide had been waiting several hours for me. I can feel the anger building up. *He saw I was in trouble and left me. You're a Sherpa; you've supposedly guided on Everest! You should know what HAPE/ HACE looks like. Why did you take off?*

By this point, time was not on my side. It was 3:30 in the afternoon, and there was so much fluid in my lungs, it sounded like a straw submerged in a cup of water, blowing bubbles with every breath.

"Hey, man. I need to get back to Chukkung before 6:30 p.m. I'm not well, and I might need life flight to a lower elevation. Here's 130 American dollars to get me there by dark," I say, calm yet stressed, to the man.

With wide eyes, he nods his head, saying, "I understand. We can hurry. You no good."

To put into perspective how far 130 American dollars go, a one-liter bottle of water there is roughly twenty American cents. Unfortunately, the HACE had grown incredibly severe. It took me almost an hour and a half to pack five items into my pack. I couldn't process information or think clearly how to pack my bag. At this point, I knew I was reaching the critical point of no-return.

Pulling my bag to the side, I'm grateful that I had

prepared for this before leaving America. I Sharpied the use on the top of each medication bottle cap, knowing I wouldn't be cognitively functioning enough to decipher which was which if I needed them. I pull three medications out. Popping 250 mg of Diamox, I swallow it down with a gulp of water. The second bottle of medication is Nifedipine, a congestive heart failure drug used to expel fluid out of the chest cavity—*10 mg, 3 times daily as needed*. Opening the bottle, I swallow down two 10 mg capsules. My third medication, Dexamethasone, says 2 mg every 4 hours as needed, and I place it in my pocket, knowing that Dexamethasone is an immunosuppressant. I decide to hold off, not wanting to risk an infection. Before prescribing, the doctor warned me it was a "last resort" medication, simply used to buy me time to get to a hospital. *Nifedipine and Diamox should buy you time to Chukkung.*

Crawling out of my tent, I pull my pack onto my back, strapping it on. This little effort alone induces a cough so severe I begin to vomit. As I scramble myself together, I walk to my guide and say, "We have to go, man. Now."

Setting out, I can see the sun setting over the mountains. It is now roughly 4:45 p.m., and I am completely out of life flight options because they don't fly at night or in the clouds. After a couple of hundred meters, I can see the guide about 200 feet in front of me. He is walking fast and not looking back at me. Stumbling over, I begin coughing, trying to get air between a cough and vomit. Bloody foam fills my hands as I cough up some of the fluid.

Looking at my hand, hunched over, *Oh, shit. This is bad. Your symptoms are bad. You HAVE to make it to Chukkung.* Standing back up nearly fifteen minutes later, I look up. He's gone. *Motherfucker! Motherfucker! Motherfucker! He took your money and left! How are you going to get back?*

"It's alright. You got to base camp alone, and you can get back," I say out loud to myself.

Continuing to walk, I see the familiarity of the river I walked in on. However, nothing else seems familiar, and I'm confused. Looking to my right, straight up a hill, I can see stone trail markers stacked like IED markers in Afghanistan. *Oh, shit! You took the east river when you should have taken the west! You zigged when you should have zagged! Cross the hill and you'll see the trail!*

Hiking up the rock face, the boulders are the size of cars. They're loosely settled and roll with the slightest pressure in the wrong direction. *Okay, man. Check the footing first. If you get your foot or leg pinned, there's no way other than cutting it off to get it out. However, you did bring tourniquets, so at least you're prepared.*

As I get to the top of the rock, I see more rock markers. It's getting dark, and I'm attempting to pick up the pace between coughing up blood and cough-induced vomiting. I still feel dizzy, and I'm struggling to maintain balance across the rocky hills. Resisting, I can't hold the tickle in my throat anymore, and I start coughing and vomiting. Except this time it's different. There's bloody foam coming out of my lungs, *and* I'm beginning to vomit blood.

Attempting to stand, I hear a familiar voice, "Bro, please be careful. Me and the lady are having a kid, and you have to stay around in case it's a girl to scare the future boyfriends!" Casey says as if he is standing next to me.

The sound of a cassette tape running out of tape with another familiar voice chimes in, Sergeant First Class Joslin, "Gentlemen, if you're ever lost in the mountains, separated from your unit and alone. *Stop*, dig in, get in a sleeping bag and shelter before the dew points hit, or you will die of hypothermia!" I stop in my tracks.

I snap my head back around behind me, looking for the trail markers I had been following. They were nowhere to be seen. Shaking my head, I close my eyes, snap them open, looking again. Nothing.

Oh, no. Your HACE has gotten so severe you are in full-on delirium. You didn't know you visually hallucinated those trail markers. Casey and SFC Joslin aren't here. Your brain swelling must be bad.

Looking around, there is no vegetation. It is dark, and for the first time in my life, I can't tell which way is north. *You're lost, man. Joslin is right. You have to stop and dig in.* Looking into the dimly lit valley with the setting sun, I barely make out the snow clouds rapidly blowing up into the mountains from the valley. Pulling my jacket sleeve back, I see my watch: *1913 hours, 18,000 feet, 20°F.*

Thinking about my options, I remember my sleep system. *Just pull your bag out, cover your gear, and crawl in your sub-zero bag and your waterproof line—Oh, shit. You took your waterproof liner out to shed weight. You only have your down system. If it gets wet, you'll freeze to death. You have to walk until you find shelter. God, if you're out there and you can hear me, PLEASE, PLEASE help me find a shelter.*

The gravity of my situation sets in. My health is still rapidly deteriorating, and I've never been symptom-free at this elevation. I continue walking for another ten or fifteen minutes under the light of my headlamp.

In my last few minutes of hope, I see a dark rock shadow. *Could it be? Please, Big J. Please God, hook me up. Otherwise, I'm going to die. I've been awake for thirty-six hours. I'm exhausted, and I don't know how much farther I can push.*

Stumbling closer, I see the rocks stacked, each boulder the size of a Honda Civic. The top rock is propped up with roughly an inch overhang. The hole is about a foot and a half tall and two feet wide, just big enough to squeeze my body into.

Interrupting my thoughts, I hear SFC. Joslin as if he were standing next to me: "Steele, take your ArcTeryx Goretex out, and line the outside of the roof over your head. Take your waterproof rain cover out of your hiking pack and line the other side of the roof by your feet. Stack rocks on both to hold it down from the wind tonight."

Listening to the hallucination, I begin following orders. Between each rock picked up, I cough more bloody foam. By the time I finish, I'm starting to feel light-headed from oxygen deprivation, and I'm barely clinging to life. Picking up where he left off, "Steele, take all your loose layers of clothing off. Put on both pairs of your remaining Under Armour, your Carhartt neck gator and beanie."

Growing even more urgent and rapid, I hear SFC. Joslin, "Take 40 mg of Nifedipine, 250 mg of Diamox, and 20 mg of Dexamethasone."

Realizing that I had just taken a double dosage of Nifedipine and 250 mg of Diamox two hours prior, I hesitate. *You're severely dehydrated and at elevation. That's four times the recommended Nifedipine dosage and almost ten times the recommended dosage of Dexamethasone. You might risk death by shutting down your kidney and liver. Not to mention, 20 mg of Dex is more than enough to stop your immune system. Those dosages might kill you. Then again, if you don't take them, you're guaranteed to die.*

I contemplate this order. *Well, your hallucinations have been correct so far. You must have read this somewhere during preparation and it's buried deep in your subconscious.* I decided to take the pills.

After frantically choking down the pills, SFC. Joslin gives another order, "Steele, take your down jacket out. Zip it up, place your feet inside and tie the arms and hood together so you don't lose your feet tonight when you go hypothermic and the blood rushes to your core." Following commands, I do exactly as I'm told.

"Alright, buddy, that's all the help I can give you. Get your sleeping bag out, climb in the bag, wiggle in-between the rocks and make peace for your judgment."

I look at the rocks, hesitating. *I'm on a moving glacier. By climbing into the tight space, if anything shifts, I will be crushed to death. If I don't get in the shelter, I will die of exposure. Either way, I'm dead.*

Inching my way into the rock, I'm so close I can only move my head about two or three inches upward until I'm pressed firmly against the rock on top. Lying in my bag, the water gurgles in my lungs with every ounce of breath sending me into a panic. *I'm drowning—I can't lay still—I'm drowning!* Uncontrollably, I begin to hyperventilate in the tight space, slowly drowning, as I begin to have a panic attack for the first time in my life. *STEELE, control yourself! You are a man with self-control! Control your thoughts, control your breathing, if you have a panic attack, you will die. This panic is all in your head, push it out, shallow breaths, focus yourself!* Calming myself, I'm shaking uncontrollably. I'm still soaking wet from the climb and hike, and I'm entering the early stages of hypothermia. Taking one last look, barely able to read my watch from the violent shivers, I see *1930 hours, 15°F, 18,000 feet.*

Flashing back to what I read the day before, I recall the words from the Dalai Lama, *If there is no solution to the problem, then don't waste time worrying about it. If there is a solution to the problem, then don't waste time worrying about it.* Realizing I've done everything I can, I accept the facts of the situation. *You have done everything you can. You found a shelter and you took the medications. There is nothing else you can do but wait for the morning light. Except, at this point, you most likely won't make it to morning. You are going to die a very cold, excruciating, and slow death. You will drown in your own fluids while battling hypothermia, and they are going to find your body in a couple of months.*

Sliding into physical shock, I'm using every last ounce of energy to remain awake, out of fear of falling into a coma or death. I lose the battle, hearing SFC. Joslin order one last command, "Brother, use your left arm to elevate your head and lungs. If you don't, you will die by drowning in your own fluids when you go unconscious." Following his command, I move my arm out of the bag, fully exposed, lifting my head. With one last glimpse at the sliver of moon overhead, I wonder if Peyton is looking at the moon at the same time. Swiftly, I lose the fight to stay awake, and everything goes black.

While unconscious, I fly through hallucinations from every emotionally traumatic experience from childhood to present day that got me stuck in life. Except this time, they had the ending or goodbye that I'd never gotten, bringing peace to all the internal conflicts—until I got to the most difficult one.

Pulling up to Peyton's mother's house, I knock on the door. Her mom answers the door and points me back to place Peyton's belongings in her room. "Don't you think this has been hard enough for Peyton? I think you need to just let her go and move on. Just let it go so she can move on with her life."

I storm out silently, walking back to my truck. Opening

the door, I'm about to step in when I hear Peyton's voice as she runs toward me, "Steele! Wait!"

Crying, she jumps into my arms in a loving embrace. "I love you, Steele. I just can't be with you right now. We aren't ready for each other. We both have a lot to learn about ourselves. I want you to know that I love you with all of my heart and soul."

Holding her, I feel an ice cold wind whipping past me, blowing the fall leaves violently off the trees and street around us, as the surroundings of her house, neighborhood, and street zoom past us, fading to black. I hold Peyton as tightly as I can with my head buried in her shoulder. Closing my eyes, "Peyton, please! Don't go—I don't want to die alone," I say, crying, knowing she's fading out of my grip.

"I can't, Steele. You have to go back. I'm here to remind you how strong and courageous you are. If you face death, stand with courage before God, and please don't be afraid. I'm here to say the goodbye we never got. I love you, I always will, and I forgive you for hurting me," she says sweetly, rubbing my neck affectionately with her fingernails.

Still clinging to her, trying to hold onto her for as long as I can, "Please, don't go. Peyton, please." The icy wind speeds up, slowly disintegrating Peyton through my hands like sand in an hourglass, blowing her peacefully into the wind, grain by grain, from her feet to her head.

Catapulted back to the rock shelter, I'm alone. Coming

back to, I'm sobbing still, knowing my time has come. Her loving embrace was nothing more than a hallucination caused by physical shock and potential organ failure. I'm drawn back to the reality of my situation—my heart rhythm is irregular and beating much slower than normal, and I'm trembling so badly I'm nearly convulsing from the cold air rushing through my shelter with sideways snow. Clenching my jaw to keep my teeth from chattering, I glance down at my watch—*0230 hours.*

I begin to hear the snow crunching and the sound of footsteps. Left *crunch*, right *crunch*, left *crunch*, pacing toward me. Realizing there might be someone out there, I attempt to yell out for help. Nothing comes out, and I begin coughing the foamy blood again. Swallowing its iron taste, my vocal cords are paralyzed from the cold air, frostbite, and coughing. I know if somebody is out there, this may be my only hope of not having my body found a month from now, wedged between these rocks.

Barely able to muster words through a nearly silent, raspy breath, "If you're real. Please, please, help me. I'm not going to make it. I'm—I'm dying," I whisper out as a hot tear trickles down the side of my face.

The footsteps stop at my words, then I hear them continue toward me. As when the thermostatic heater in a house kicks on, I feel the rocks begin to get physically hot to the touch. A cloud of peace settles around me, and I accept that my mother was right. Her worst fear was coming true. *This is it. You are going to die a very slow, very painful death, cold and alone. This is why you were brought here, I guess. This is the punishment for the people you've hurt. This is your karma.*

With my last thought of clarity, *the warmth I feel isn't real. It's the effects of severe hypothermia and borderline paradoxical undressing, one of the final stages of severe hypothermia. This is why they find people in the winter time naked in the snow. You aren't hot; you're freezing to death.* With my last bit of energy, I reach up, drawing the head strap to my sleeping bag as tight as possible, attempting to burrow in and survive the rest of the night.

Maybe it's the reaper outside. They say if you've been a good person, he'll make you feel at peace as you die. Overall, you've been a good person. Maybe it's time to accept the facts of the situation you're in. Maybe it's time to find your demons and make peace with them inside yourself before the judgment of your God.

As I lay silently, shaking, shivering, teeth chattering in the rocks, tears glide slowly down my face as I close my eyes to say my final, silent prayer to God.

God, I know I've made mistakes. I know I've hurt some people. But, I have never passed a cry for help, and I've done my best to add value to the lives of the people around me. If you have a place up there for me, it doesn't need to be elaborate or amazing. I'll take a corner shed. I realize now why you called me here—to call me home. All I ask is that you take me quickly, stop the suffering I'm in currently, and allow me to go peacefully. Will you please make sure they find my body in a timely fashion so my family doesn't have to go without closure for very long? Will you bring them strength and the understanding that it was my decision to come here? Will you please not leave Peyton with any survivor's guilt, knowing how our last exchange went? And God, will you please have Grandpa, Uncle Mark, Uncle Lee, and my brothers come to take me so I don't have to cross alone?

THE FINAL INSPECTION

The Soldier stood and faced God, which
must always come to pass.
He hoped his shoes were shining, just as brightly as his brass.
"Step forward now, you Soldier. How shall I deal with you?
Have you always turned the other cheek? To
My Church have you been true?"
The Soldier squared his shoulders and
said, "No, Lord, I guess I ain't.
Because those of us who carry guns, can't always be a saint.
I've had to work most Sundays, and
at times my talk was tough.
And sometimes I've been violent, because
the world is awfully rough.
But, I never took a penny that wasn't mine to keep...
Though I worked a lot of overtime when
the bills got just too steep.
And I never passed a cry for help, though
at times I shook with fear.
And sometimes, God, forgive me, I've wept unmanly tears.
I know I don't deserve a place among the people here.
They never wanted me around, except to calm their fears.
If you've a place for me here, Lord, it needn't be so grand.
I never expected or had too much, but
if you don't, I'll understand."
There was a silence all around the throne,
where the saints had often trod,
As the Soldier waited quietly, for the judgment of his God.

*"Step forward now, you Soldier, you've
borne your burdens well.
Walk peacefully on Heaven's streets,
you've done your time in Hell."*

—UNKNOWN

CHAPTER 19

FINDING OUR DESTINY

———

OPENING ONE EYE, EVERYTHING IS BLURRY. SQUINT-
ing, attempting to comprehend where I'm at, what is going
on, I hear one last audible hallucination. It is the email
response in the words of Mr. Aubrey Marcus, "My friend,
you won't find enlightenment in the Himalayas, but you
might find enlightenment within yourself while in the
Himalayas." Looking up, I see a ray of light from the sun
shining through my Gore-Tex jacket roof.

Squirming around, I can feel the crust on the zipper of
my sleeping bag blistered into my face. With one motion,
I rip the sleeping bag off my face. Pain shoots through my
face. Reaching up, I feel water and blood from the blisters
running down my face. "Well, that's certainly a start for
the day," I say, surprised to have woken up.

Shuffling out of the rock, inching my sleeping bag
like a caterpillar, I make my way out. Feeling the burn of
frostbite on my arm, hands, and face, I can feel the fluid

still bubbling in my lungs with every breath. Looking up at the sky: *Okay, the sun rises in the east and sets in the west. If that's east, then south must be that way*, I point to the right of the rocks.

"Okay, Lhotse and Everest are north of Chukkung. That means," I say, scrolling my finger over the map, "Shit. That means you're anywhere from four to six kilometers out onto the Lhotse Glacier."

After packing my gear up, I pull a Snickers bar, Clif bar, and my last bottle of water out of my bag. Sitting on a rock, I force myself to get as many calories as I can to rescue myself. I didn't think I would be able to survive another night out in the elements. While sitting there, the most out-of-character thoughts began to occur. The night before, I felt furious at the guide who I paid to get me to Chukkung. By taking off the way he did that night, he practically signed my death warrant.

However, I thought of the brief message from Mr. Marcus and one of the teachings of the Dalai Lama on compassion, love, and how everybody is inherently good and wants happiness for themselves. I choose to believe that, rather than him intentionally bringing me harm, there may be a better explanation. *Maybe he had a death in the family, financial concerns, his wife or kids were sick, or he just had a lot on his mind. He didn't mean to leave me.* I no longer wanted to report him to the ministry of tourism. In fact, I was thankful it happened. It was exactly what was meant to happen. It was the entire reason I was called to the mountains in the first place—to face my demons.

I begin reflecting on the last twenty-four hours, realizing how lucky I am to be alive. I expand my reflection to the last several days, weeks, months, and eventually the last several years of my life. Thinking about the messages in the book, *The Art of Happiness,* I realize the happiest years of my life have been while I was in Afghanistan. I take another bite of my Snickers. Frozen solid, it feels like chewing on a sticky rock. Eliminating the adrenaline, I have an epiphany. *I was happy because I was helping others.*

In Afghanistan, contrary to popular belief, I was helping villages keep the Taliban away. I was helping people who wanted to farm, live, and provide more for their family than what they had growing up. Over the last few years, I felt empty because, in my attempt to get my testosterone under check and to reintegrate, I had not done much of anything to help others.

Taking another bite of my Snickers, a half inch at a time, I mull. As fast as the first thought came, I had another realization. Many of the veterans, cops, first responders, and other individuals I know who have experienced trauma never take the time to revisit themselves after. Many of us return home from combat changed in one way or another.

In my case, I didn't feel like going camping. I didn't feel like hiking or going target shooting. I had spent the last year and a half with training and deployment living in tents, hiking, and shooting. What I didn't realize at the time was that any time my friends who knew me before deployment would ask to go do those things, I would decline. Eventually, they started inviting me to do things less and less, thinking I would say no. As a result, I isolated myself from them. I also discovered that I no longer had the desire to return to the same career.

Taking another bite, I continue to contemplate this. I begin to think of many of the other guys I knew who were returning home. Returning to marital problems, divorce, children, a job they may not like anymore but can't afford to change and may not have the resources or time to go back to school. Many of the guys, like me, drink copious amounts of alcohol, making many of our issues worse. We feel lost, depressed, and can't figure out why. We begin failing at our commitments, and eventually, many of us lose our marriage, children, and careers. We become engulfed in a downward spiral we can't get out of. Reflecting, I remember a quote from *The Art of War:*

"From time to time, the Warrior must recharge and replenish. Take a breath, go somewhere quiet. Get silent. Power up for the meetings, battles, treks, and wisdom circles. A warrior's heart is only as full as his spirit is quiet."

When I read that years ago, it didn't make much sense. However, that was the exact reason I couldn't explain why I wanted to go to the Himalayas. I couldn't verbalize it, but somehow, I knew I had to find the man I am and want to be after the dust settled. I somehow knew I had to go somewhere to take a step back and recharge. *Could it be? Maybe this is the problem with our service members coming back. Perhaps this is one of the major contributing factors that has led to an issue of suicide. Maybe this is one of the significant factors in the millions of veterans not tracked for substance abuse, alcoholism, womanizing, divorce, and abuse.*

We often aren't aware, but when we get home to our families after war, we're continuously reminded of the person we used to be. Even with as seemingly minor comments from loved ones like, "Why do you always sit facing the door now? You're being paranoid...Why do you always make me walk on your left side? Why do you get up in the night to make sure all the doors are locked or go check on normal creaks of the house?" Or worse, "You're so cold emotionally after the war, like a stone heart. I don't ever know how you feel about me. It's like I love a statue. You never used to be like this."

The thing most of us don't understand, and that our loved ones don't understand either, is that it is *okay* not to be the same person. It's okay to want them to be safe. It's okay to want to protect them, even if that means instinctively walking with them on our opposing gun hand side.

In many ways, we are a better, stronger person after war. We have gone out, discovered our limits, and found how much strength, courage, and grit we possess. We come back more confident, and often, as in my case, we no longer get into bar fights, altercations, or feel the need to boast, prove, or explain ourselves to a man who "rises and sleeps under the blanket of freedom we provide." We know what we're capable of; we have nothing to prove.

Hidden behind denial and fear of showing weakness, and contrary to many civilian beliefs, we can often *see* how we no longer have the ability to effectively communicate with the ones we love. The people who we used to communicate and express affection toward openly. At some point, usually after all of our loved ones walk away from us, we grasp the idea that we need to change something, but we don't know where to begin, and the ones we wanted to change and grow for are gone. Once they're gone, many of us write it off, continuing the vicious cycle of relationship failures.

Many people think the veteran or first responder rates of suicide, depression, substance abuse, and marriage failures are a direct result of combat exposure or high stress. My personal opinion is that combat isn't the problem—it's what happens when we come home and fail to fall back into the same routines we had before we left, forcing us to realize that we changed. To accept the fact that we can't go back to the person we used to be before war. For many of us in combat arms, when we leave for combat, we decide in our minds that we're already dead. Although morbid, we do this because we know that if we carry the fear of death, we will hesitate, and it will result in death. So, when we return home, we are at a loss for "what's next" and what our new purpose is, because we never thought we would make it home.

Maybe the answer for those of us returning is the idea that we have to take some time to recharge and decipher the "what's next." To figure out what our new purpose and life after war is going to be like. The solutions could possibly be as simple as answering the five Ws that we learned in elementary school—*Who, What, Where, When,* and *Why*. Who do I want to be now and who can help me become this person? What do I want to do with my life now, and what do I need to do to achieve this? Where do I want to live now? When can I put this plan in motion? And why is this going to change my outlook on life?

Taking another bite, a lecture from an undergraduate psychology course vividly pops into my thoughts. In the lecture, we had discussed grief and loss, and the theory proposed by Elisabeth Kübler-Ross and David Kessler in the *Five Stages of Grief*: Denial, Anger, Bargaining, Depression, and Acceptance.

Denial. In this stage, the individual refuses to accept the facts of their situation, or believes that it's a mistake and it can't possibly be true. Ultimately, they prefer to believe their own reality of what they wish the situation was.

Anger. In this stage, the individual can no longer believe their denial, and they become forced to accept the situation they're in. They often grow frustrated, lashing out at every individual around them. They begin to develop anger toward others, their religious beliefs, whatever God they believe in, or anybody else they can displace their anger toward. They frequently ask questions like, "Why me? This isn't fair! What did I do to deserve this?"

Bargaining. In this stage, the individual experiencing this looks to bargain with themselves, God, their loved one, and whatever else they believe in or can find to bargain with. They often look to compromise or negotiate an extended life or relationship in exchange for a reformed action and lifestyle.

Depression. In this stage, the individual suffers despair at the recognition of their mortality or situation. They don't see the point in changing or continuing on with their life, and they often grow silent, mournful, and reclusive.

Acceptance. In this stage, the individual accepts the facts of the situation. They recognize there's nothing they can do to change it. They stop resisting the inevitable and accept the fact that things cannot and will not change.

This theory was eventually expanded to personal loss such as a loss of job, death of a loved one, major rejection, the end of a relationship, drug addiction, incarceration, and terminal illness. These stages can occur out of sequence, at different times or simultaneously, and each stage can be repeated several times.

After thinking about my relationship with Peyton, family, friends, and all those I caused emotional pain or grief since my return, I have an epiphany. *This may be an idea that can be altered, refined, and applied to the reintegration from war. It seems to be the best explanation for all the conflicting emotions, frustrations, and issues that we have an extremely difficult time explaining to our loved ones, counselors, and friends.*

In this theory I modeled, similar to Kübler-Ross and David Kessler's, it would look like the following.

THE FIVE STAGES OF REINTEGRATION FROM COMBAT:

1. *Denial.* In this stage, the veteran returning is in denial that he has changed or that his life will be different. He refuses to believe the war or combat changed him, his relationship, and life. He attempts to phase right back into everyday life without any changes. Anecdotally, I have seen this last for the first six to twelve months home. He refuses to go to a doctor for sleep medication, anti-anxiety medication, or counseling/ Cognitive Behavioral Therapy (CBT), and over time, he self-medicates with alcohol and other risk-taking behaviors.

2. *Anger.* In this stage, the veteran grows angry at the civilian population who doesn't seem to understand what he went through. He becomes angry at his significant other, friends, and family for not understanding, not treating him the way they did before the war. He grows angry at everybody he feels doesn't see the best in him or who points out the changes caused by his time in combat. When the issues carried over by

the denial phase catch up, he lashes out angrily at everybody who points them out. In addition, when he realizes that he can't return to his unit, combat, or his previous life before combat, he grows angry with everything else in his life and lashes out at anything and everything he possibly can. For many of those, like me, when survivor's guilt begins, they grow angry at God, and many of them lose their religious and spiritual beliefs. For many, they say things like, "I don't believe in a God anymore. Because if there were a God, bad things wouldn't happen to so many good people. There wouldn't be so much suffering and evil in the world."

3. *Bargaining.* At this stage, it's a multifaceted dilemma. In the beginning, they start bargaining with anything and everything they can. Bargaining with those around them, saying things like, "If you just give me another chance, I'll change! I'll do whatever it takes to fix this and be the person I used to be!" Or, "God, I'll do whatever you tell me to if you'll fix my life and relationships!" Or, "God, I'll do whatever you want if you can just get me on another deployment back to combat!"

    In this phase, many of their relationships are falling apart. Lack of sleep, lack of happiness, the intense resentment toward the ones who don't see them the same builds, and quickly, the anger impacts every intimate relationship. In this phase, many of our significant others can't remain in a relationship due to the extremes of the denial and anger phase. The veteran attempts to bargain with the people who walked away from their relationships, promising to change their ways and outlook on life, stop their substance use, and become the happy, healthy person they used to be. They say anything and everything they can in an attempt to catch all of the "falling knives" in their lives.

Sometimes, those who walked away will give the relationship another chance. For a few days, weeks, or months, the veteran lives up to these bargains. He makes the changes, but because he hasn't made it to the fifth phase, he ends up dropping the falling knives. Often, catching these falling knives won't happen because we haven't worked through stage one and two. Finally, the last straw breaks, and our significant others leave. That was the final straw, and there won't ever be another chance, because there have already been so many "final chances." The changes our loved ones want—or catching the falling knives—can't occur until we get to the fifth phase and work through the core issues that contributed to the relationship failure.

4. *Depression.* In this stage, the veteran feels helpless and hopeless. He feels he's lost everything he once held dear. He feels he's lost the person he used to be and loved. He realizes there's no way to go back to the

person he desperately wants to be again. He begins retracting from society, cutting off communication with even other veterans in the community, consuming more alcohol than before, abusing substances, and looking for any sort of instant gratification or relief.

It becomes a downward spiral for months, even years. Unfortunately, he will remain in this stage with the occasional appearance of stages one through three, until there's a major event or catalyst for change.

5. *Acceptance.* In this version of five stages, the acceptance phase is the only phase that isn't truly achieved until moving forward from stage four. In previous stages, there might have been a hint of accepting their situation, but it's more like a denial form of acceptance. In this phase, it's the final fork in the road. There are only two directions to go, without going back to any of the previous stages, and we've seen it right in front of us, day after day.

Taking a left on this road is the darkness at the end of the tunnel—it's the end of the road and the final stop. It's the acceptance of the idea that things will never get better, things will never change, and all hope is lost. It is the feeling of being helpless or a victim of circumstances, and refusing to get help, medication, or make changes. At the end of this road, the veteran accepts the situation in a morbid, often close-minded view, making the irrevocable decision of suicide, ending their life.

Looking at the fork to the right, there's a light at the end of the tunnel. Taking the right turn, he heads down the path of recovery. He accepts that the previous stages led him to the situation he is in, and he accepts the fact that his life won't get better until he fully commits to and implements a change. Not a temporary change like the bargaining phase, but a real, tangible, permanent change. In this right-hand turn, the veteran seeks help. He is willing to get sleep medication, confront his depression, PTSD, shortcomings, and wrongdoings. He leaves behind the substances that he'd used to cope, gets back in the gym, and sees a counselor.

He understands he's at rock bottom, and the only way out is permanently changing and following the light at the end of the tunnel. He reaches out to those he wronged or emotionally hurt and offers an apology, knowing they may never accept it, understand, or forgive him. He does it for himself—to let go of guilt, anger, resentment, and other emotions holding his growth back. He perseveres months, even years, and eventually with enough commitment down this path, he secures a positive life, relationship, career, and family. He fights back and makes it through the depths of hell, back to a vibrant life.

In some cases, after enough time and work down

the right fork, he can finally catch the knives he felt were falling in the bargaining phase. In some cases, the relationships he felt were destroyed can be repaired and strengthened. In other cases, he gets remarried, starts over, has a family, and surrounds himself with healthy relationships. He is able to help other veterans out of the same dark tunnel toward *Fiddler's Green* that he was strong enough to pull himself out of.

I conclude my thoughts. I finish my Snickers, washing it down with a tiny sip of the now partially unthawed water. Tossing another Nifedipine and Dexamethasone pill down, I pick up my pack, stopping between gasps for air, and begin making my way off the glacier toward civilization.

After several hours of heading to the main trail, I run into my guide.

With shock and awe, he says, "Fuck! You're alive!"

Unable to speak, I give the man a huge hug, attempting through a hoarse voice, "Thank you."

Looking at me, confused, with a *why are you thanking me?* look, he turns around and walks toward the teahouses. As I walk into the teahouse where I had stayed three nights prior, I receive looks of shock. I must have looked like I just crawled out of a war zone. Without warning, the villagers and other guides begin swarming me asking, "Did you see *him*? Did you see *him*?"

Still dehydrated, confused, and extremely tired, I mumble out the words, "Who is he? Who did I see?"

The villagers grew even more excited, and I was unable to understand what they were saying as their English grew increasingly more broken. Interrupting them, a Sherpa who I didn't know said something in their language, and everybody dispersed. Pointing inside, the man motions for me to sit down. The local woman who owned the teahouse rushed out, grabbing water and fried rice and bringing it back to me.

"Get rest, we talk later," the Sherpa says.

Several hours later, the man came back in.

"Woke up at 4:00 a.m. when I saw your guide awake. Say you never come back. I try look but weather too bad."

"Thanks, man, you would have never found me though. I was deep into that glacier," I whisper between gasps for air after every word.

"Do you know who *he* is?" The man asks me.

The locals don't believe in one God, so who is it?

"I'm not sure. Will you tell me?"

"The Yeti."

"Like Bigfoot?" I say, even more confused.

"No, the abominable snowman," he says in all seriousness. In broken English, he continues, "Himalayan people used to work with the Yeti or abominable snowman. Many people think they bad or scary, but they not. One day, man harm Yetis who helping them, and all of them go back to mountains, glaciers, and crevasses. Now, only come out when man close to death."

"To help you live?"

"No, bring peace and comfort as you die or until you home. My father and grandfather both Sherpa, say they see Yeti same way as you. They didn't see the Yeti, but they knew in heart he there. They only hear his footsteps outside shelter, then feel warm and comfort knowing they weren't alone."

"Dude. I heard the Yeti."

* * *

THE NEXT FEW DAYS ARE A BLUR. I DIDN'T COMPRE-hend how severe my medical situation was. I wandered my way to Lobuche (I don't remember most of the hike in or making the decision to go there) and, quite honestly, was still under major delirium and in physical shock. However, this is very common with high-altitude complications and lack of oxygen, where you unknowingly make bad judgment calls and can't think clearly, similar to the climbers on Ever-est who pull their oxygen masks off above the death zone.

I run into some American climbers, whom I had met the first day in Lukla, who spot me outside of a teahouse.

"Hey, guys," I force out between gasps for air and a nearly silent, raspy voice.

"Holy fuck, man! What happened? You look bad!" they all say.

Taking several minutes, I tell them the story, and their reactions and disbelief at what happened kind of snaps me out of shock and cloudy reasoning.

"Holy shit, man! You bivouacked on your first climb and survived! You know what you went through often kills even the most experienced mountaineer, right?" one of the men exclaims.

"Dude, you're still symptomatic and you don't realize it. You are still in HAPE/HACE, and the meds are masking it. How many days of Dex do you have left?" one of the other men asks.

"Roughly four, plus one pill."

"Look, man, I've seen this before. You don't realize it now, but when you run out of those pills at this elevation, you have like a 90 percent chance of dying. You need to get back to Namche or Lukla for medical! Preferably Lukla, since it's a lower elevation!"

Another man from the group inserts more bad news: "Look, man, the weather is changing. Life flight isn't going to fly out of here. You need to get walking before those pills run out."

Not thinking clearly, still experiencing major effects, and low on cash at hand, I didn't even think about trying to pay somebody to take me to the hospital by yak or donkey.

I began the descent to Lukla over the next four days, and it took me twice the normal time, nearly twelve hours per day of walking, and carrying my gear. The weird thing about descending with HAPE/ HACE that I discovered is that your symptoms are masked, because you get more and more oxygen the farther you descend. You feel like you're getting better when, in fact, you aren't.

It was the night of the third day, and I was still coughing. However, the blood had stopped, and I felt much better. *Eh, those guys were wrong; you're getting better. Clearly, you're in the 10 percent—I mean, you've beaten the odds so far. Why would this time be different?* Pulling my phone out and connecting to the Wi-Fi, I send a text to my mom, "Hey, I made it to Namche, I'm feeling much better. I'll tell you what happened when I get home. I'm going to make it to Lukla tomorrow and try to get on the first flight out the day after. I love you."

The next morning, I wake up around 6:00 a.m. Eating breakfast, I pull my map out. *Alright, it should only take you like six hours from here. You descend almost an immediate 2,500 feet to 8,000 and some change. Should be easy—get to the hospital by 3:00 p.m.* Walking up to my room, I grab my pack, pulling out a pill of Nifedipine and my last tablet of Dexamethasone, taking one last swig to get them down.

As the day went on, the elevation decreased. However, my symptoms returned. I was once again coughing up bloody foam, and it was getting harder to breathe. By the time I got within three hours of Lukla, I was out of my emergency medications. I was coughing, vomiting bloody bile, out of breath when merely standing, and I had begun coughing green chunks out of my lungs.

I drop my bags at the teahouse, where I was going to rest and catch my breath until the morning. But things got worse. Standing next to some friends from the UK who are roughly my parents' age, I tell them what happened. Sharon, the man's girlfriend, interrupts me mid-sentence.

In a thick British accent, "Honey, are you okay? You sound and look bad—like really bad. With how heavy and labored your breathing is, I'm worried you won't make it to morning, sweetheart."

"Yes, yes, I'm fine. I think I'm gonna go get some rest," I say nonchalantly. *It isn't rest I need—it's a hospital.*

Exiting the teahouse, I begin to panic. *I am not okay. In fact, I am the opposite of okay. It's life and death opposite.* I can feel my throat closing as I wander down the street. Unable to maintain my calm demeanor, my airway is severely constricted, and I feel as if I'm breathing through a straw. *Hang in there. If you have a panic attack, you will die. You can't. Just hang on.*

"Help! Help! Hospital!" I silently gasp to a man on the corner.

He completely disregards me, so I continue begging every person I see to help me, with the same response. Getting toward the end of the town, I panic uncontrollably as black spots fill my vision and the tunnel of darkness tries overcoming me.

At the end of the seemingly pitch-black town, I see kids in a window of a house. *This is my last chance. If they don't help, I'm dead.* Hurling a small rock at the window, I say as loud as I can, barely speaking louder than an inside voice, "Please! Help me! Please! Hospital!" I say holding my throat.

Catching the kids' eyes, they come rushing out of the house. Two kids take off sprinting down the road. *You little fuckers; you guys are going to let me die too?* Suddenly, the other two grab an arm on each side, pulling me the last mile—uphill—to the hospital.

With every step, I struggle to get any oxygen at all. My muscles are burning, becoming weaker by the second from oxygen deprivation. With every ounce of willpower to fight and stay alive, I keep moving. *If you pass out, they can't carry you. You have to make it.* With every step, it becomes more and more difficult to move. When the gates of the hospital come into sight, closed. My heart sinks. *You made it all this way. And, it's, it's—it's over.* The darkness overcomes me and the gates, hospital steps, and rocky trail fade to black.

Coming back to, I have an oxygen mask on and I'm on a gurney. I have no idea how long I've been out because there are no windows in the room. Tubes are wrapped around my arm, and a nurse is coming at me about to stick me with a needle. Jumping up in panic, I start to fight the needle. Nepal has an HIV and Hepatitis C epidemic because hospitals tend to re-use needles. *Have I been stuck? Did I catch a dirty needle and make it all this way to contract Hep C or HIV?*

Noting my panic, a doctor rushes over to me.

Another doctor asks with a thick accent, "What you take get here? What you take keep you alive this shape?"

"40 mg Nifedipine, 20 mg Dexamethasone, 500 mg Diamox; and then 10 mg Nifedipine, 2 mg Dexamethasone every four hours, and 250 mg of Diamox twice daily since," I respond, lethargically, quietly, and exhausted.

"Are you an American doctor?"

"Yes, yes, I am," I lie, losing consciousness.

Shaking me awake, the doctor continues, "Four boys outside say are worried about you. They say they bring you here?"

"I have something for them. Will you get them, please?" I ask, still dazed.

The doctor nods, exiting the room. Coming back with the boys, I pull five American dollars out for each one of them. Handing it to them, as it was all I had on me: "You guys were the only ones who helped me. You saved my life. I would have never made it here. Thank you."

Looking at me perplexed, the doctor says, "You strong man. Never see any man so bad make so far, or survive night. You not pushed so hard get here, you been dead by morning."

I was told later that, as I fumbled in past the steps into the hospital, the two boys who took off running, ran to the doctor's house, woke him up, and got him out of bed. The reason I was getting less oxygen and having a harder time was because my throat and lungs had started to close off as the infection had become so severe once the Dex wore off. The local doctors told me that I had a double lung infection that went systemic, with a fever of 105 degrees and a blood oxygen percentage of 37 percent.

I ended up needing eight injections of corticosteroids and Dexamethasone, three IV bags of high-powered antibiotics, inhalation steroids, oxygen, and some medication that expels fluid from your lungs, which is an awful experience. When they did the x-ray on my lungs, they said they were over 70 percent full of fluid, pus, and blood.

At about 3:30 in the morning, the doctors decided I was stable enough to leave for the night. However, unlike American hospitals, when they left, I was alone and unattended to in the whole hospital. Pulling out my phone, I connect to the Wi-Fi and send a text to my family, Cash, and Jenny.

I'm okay now. I'm in the hospital. It will be a few days until I can fly internationally. I'm just lucky to be alive. I'm ready to come home.

Getting immediate frantic responses, I begin to break down, realizing how close this journey brought me to the brink of death. It was different than the fast and unexpected experiences. This one was slowly drowning, leaving me unable to prevent the inevitable.

Over the last two years since returning home from the war, I, as many veterans do, forgot how strong and bold we have had to be to survive the situations we have. Breaking down, I cry tears of joy. *I found exactly what I came for. The reason I was sent to the mountains was to be reminded that there are lots of lessons to be learned—and a few to teach. I know now that I haven't seen it all, and I am loved by many. I now understand what Mr. Marcus meant in his email.* I sigh with a sense of peace as everything suddenly makes sense.

Opening my phone to the slurry of messages, I read a response from my dad: *Son did you find what you were looking for?* Realizing how close I was to death, a tear falls onto the screen as I send my final response for the night: *I'm doing okay. Yeah Dad, I found what I was looking for. I realized the things I felt were lost or missing were never lost at all. My focus was simply too narrow. Once I widened my view, I could see that it's been there the whole time.*

"Sometimes we can't let go of memories because they are constant reminders of a great story that we never expected to end."

—JOFFREY LAGURA

CHAPTER 20

LETTING GO

———

SITTING ON THE PLANE, I FEEL THE THRUST OF THE
engines pushing us off the runway, hurling the giant hunk
of metal into the skies. With my headphones in, I scroll
through my podcasts, selecting an episode of the *Joe Rogan
Experience* I had listened to hundreds of times since Peyton
and I split up. For some reason, I feel as though I should
listen to it again. Habitually, I place a pinch of my lucky
Grizzly chew in my mouth and stare out the window as
the Chinese city below slowly disappears out of sight.

Soaring higher, the sounds of the passengers are muffled out as I close the window shade, reclining my chair
back. Closing my eyes, I allow the thoughts of reflection
to engulf my mind.

Feeling as if I'm listening to an old friend, "You know,
I have this friend who will remain nameless. But, we had
a conversation where he was getting dumped, and he was
super upset about it. He didn't know how to deal with it,

and he was asking for advice. And I said, 'Do you love this girl?' And he said, 'Yes.' So I said, 'Well, if you love her, you should want her to be happy. And if her being happy means her being with another man or another person, then you should respect that, and you should love her still. This is just another human being, and people break up.'"

As I listen, I contemplate the idea Mr. Rogan is explaining. *Did I only love Peyton because I wanted her to be with me? Am I being selfish for wanting her to end up with me?* The words continue to hit home as I think about all the hopes and dreams I had with Peyton.

Continuing: "I don't hate every woman I used to date. In fact, with time, I love all of them—even the ones that I didn't get along with, man. When I look back on every single girl that I ever dated, I swear to God, I will ONLY allow the positive things. Now I have some negative stories that are really funny, and I tell them. But in my mind, when I'm thinking about that person, I only think about them when I loved them. No matter what went wrong, you know. No matter what horrible thing was said that made the whole thing fall apart—I refuse to define them by that. Instead, I define them by their potential. By what they meant to me when they were at their best.

The harsh words begin to cut deep, and a cold pit of shame washes over my stomach. *I've been defining Peyton, my old platoon sergeant, and all those who hurt or wronged me in life for who they were at their worst moments and the mistakes they made. In the moments of controversy, I rumi-*

nated over their mistakes for weeks, even months at a time, sustaining the fights and silent treatment.

I never once truly forgave any of them and moved on. I always allowed the worst to dictate the future of my relationships. I couldn't see Peyton for what she meant to me when she was at her best, and at that phase of my life, it was impossible for me to define her by her potential. If it was impossible for me to define her by what she meant to me on her best days, why did I feel I could ask, even expect her to do it for me?

Sucked back into the show: "But one of the things is you can't be selfish. Because if you are selfish, you always want that person to be with you. And this is what I was saying to my friend. It's like, 'Dude, she does NOT want to be with you.' You have to accept that. You have to accept that this is a human being, and if you love that human being, you should want this human being to be happy."

Painfully, I see clearly that I'm Mr. Rogan's friend in this story. I had been holding on tight, wanting Peyton to love me. Over the last eight months, I prayed that God would lead my life and path back to her. I didn't want her to move on to other people, and I damn sure didn't want to move on either. I wanted her to "come to her senses" and reflect on our relationship, defining me by the man I was to her at my best, seeing the potential of the man I was going to become one day.

At that exact moment, I had a bittersweet revelation. *While dating, I thought I loved her unconditionally; the truth is, I didn't. I loved her, wanting her to be and have a life with me, and technically that's conditional.* Slowly, painfully, I begin to understand that the only way for me to truly love others unconditionally is to love and cherish the memories shared with them. However, I must let go and give them the freedom to choose their own happiness in life, even if that happiness doesn't involve me.

Now sitting straight up in my chair, I set my elbows down on the foldout tray, resting my forehead in my hands and continue listening. "There has to be a real connection, because if you don't have that, one of two things is happening: either you're not putting that out enough, or you're not a dynamic enough human—with your consciousness, objectivity, love, affection, or with your generosity. You are NOT putting out enough. And if you're not putting that out enough, people don't want to give it back to you. So this beautiful, attractive, healthy, vibrant, generous, loving human being won't be attracted to you, because you don't want to enhance them. You want to draw and take away from them."

With my eyes closed, for the first time in my life, I'm able to see myself and my coping mechanisms objectively. Suddenly, all of the fights Peyton and I had that pointed out my flaws, worldviews, and patterns of scorekeeping made sense.

Before all of the grief and experience, I had a bubbly personality. I could love without reservation and see the best in those around me. The reason I became cold, rigid, and expected the worst in everything was because it was the only survival mechanism I had. At first, death was extremely painful and consuming. I didn't have time to grieve the last death before having another death. There were times as a child when I attended four funerals of close relatives in a single year. The only survival tool I had was to become apathetic toward grief and life.

When I realized I wanted to marry Peyton, briefly—for a split second—I saw the positive and potential of our future together. However, looking into her eyes, holding her hand, even in the moments of intense love and intimacy, I could only see the inevitable end. I could only feel the loss I felt for everybody else I lost along the way. Looking at her and realizing how strong my love and affection was for her, I could see that she was one of the incredibly unique individuals who could penetrate my nonexistent grieving cycle.

Suddenly, I begin to see how I made every attempt to find something wrong, and I sabotaged our relationship. I sucked and drew energy away from her and our relationship. It was easier for me to hate and control when she left my life than to once again subject myself to the debilitating grief I knew I would feel if she, like the others I loved so deeply, were taken from me when I needed them most.

Continuing introspection, I think about my burning hatred for my old platoon sergeant and others who I felt hurt or wronged me. It dawned on me what the Dalai Lama explained about meditating, praying, and wishing good thoughts for people who have hurt, wronged, or made you angry. Wanting good things for them is the only way to let the past go and end the cycle of anger and resentment. Thinking back over my relationship with Peyton, clear as day, I could see it. *I wasn't the most dynamic with my objectivity, love, or consciousness. I was stuck in a world of pain, viewing the world as an evil place with lurking monsters. I thought I was ready for her, but like I knew the day I met her, I wasn't.*

I begin to see all the dreams I had with Peyton slowly disappearing, as I accept the fact that I needed to change my ways of thinking and love her still. The picture of proposing to her, her in a wedding dress, and us cooking dinner, walking the dogs, and having a family, all begin to fade and leave my mind as I watch as our paths veer into different directions. Replacing those desires, I picture her with a man who makes her giddy, happy, excited, and full of life. I can see the light he brings to her eyes with the same smile I brought her once upon a time. I watch as she walks down the aisle, holding his hand instead of mine, sitting at their kids' graduation, and having a blissful life together. Now, for the first time in my life, I understand the meaning of unconditional love. I just took the long, painful route to discover it.

Accepting this fact in my heart, I began to truly want and pray that she would find somebody who fills her life with so much love, joy, and happiness that she wants to scream it to the world—knowing this man wasn't going to be me. Peyton is one of the smartest, most charismatic, kind, and beautiful women I know. We both deserve to be with people who enhance our greatest qualities. As Mr. Rogan said, I have decided only to see the positive aspects, to judge the relationship and her based on the potential they had, to think of all the positive ways she filled my life with happiness, laughter, and smiles. Instead of looking back, wanting it back, trying to analyze every area I went wrong, I accept the idea that we were both young and didn't know how to be supportive of the other person, and that she came along for one of the most difficult times in my life.

I choose to look at the glass as half full instead of viewing it as this sadness, regret, etc. I choose to consider myself fortunate to have been blessed to meet a woman, although not a permanent fixture in my life, who gave me the gift of discovering that even after war, it's possible to feel love again. It's possible to open up to people again. I consider myself to have won the lottery to have met a woman who was strong enough to tell me when I was wrong, who gave me the gift of realizing that I'm not always right, and showing me the aspects of my personality that need to be worked on. The biggest gift she gave me in life was the feeling of pervasive love and loving another person more than myself outside of family. It's a supremely rare gift and valuable beyond measure.

With these realizations, it is important to clarify that I am NOT referring to abusive or dangerous relationships. I am NOT implying that you should only look at your relationship through rose-colored glasses, ignoring toxic, abusive, manipulative, deceitful, or other unhealthy relationship dynamics with your significant other, friends, and family. I'm not implying you should see the state of your relationship as solely your fault and responsibility.

Until I was able to pull myself out of it in the mountains, I was bitter and blaming her, the support system, and everybody else for the biggest failures of our relationship. This was followed by a stage where I felt it was all my fault. While alone in the mountains, I finally understood the very cliché saying, "Every relationship takes two to succeed and two to fail." I realized the fault line in both success and failure lies an equal distance between two people.

After my experience, I realized we as combat veterans have created an emotional armor for ourselves. Although for easily understandable reasons, we become jaded, viewing society for the worst we've seen, and we often don't show our generosity, conscientiousness, objectivity, or love. We irritably snap at people, becoming salty, gruff, and emotionally indestructible. We have conditioned ourselves to only allow people in to a certain extent. When they cross that threshold, often, without recognizing it, we sabotage, create fights, and push them away. We do this because we're outside the garden and still in survival mode. We left the war, but the war didn't leave us.

We ask each other how we keep finding ourselves in relationship failures, only seeing destructive things in the world. We look to catch our neighbor or friends in lies, wondering if they're trying to get ahead or wrong us. The reality is, whether we want to acknowledge it or not, we are further conditioning our brains to ignore positivity and to see the worst in everything. We fill ourselves with alcohol, drugs, sex, pills, adrenaline, or anything else we can find, attempting to muffle the sounds of our self-imposed prison instead of facing our mistakes, our toxic ways of thinking, and ourselves, with courage.

I'm guilty of many things, and I had to find a way to accept these facts about my past. There are many different opinions on how to repair this. However, with many veterans like myself before the Himalayas, we ignore the solutions on how to fix these shortcomings, and we choose to deny them. We often feel it is better to ignore, blame others, and with enough alcohol, our problems will go away on their own. The truth is they won't.

Outside of the bravado and grit, I don't care how tough or badass you are. You want somebody who will love you and stick by your side. Although you may react to sadness with anger like me, you cannot convince me that, when it's your actions that cause the person you love to cry or leave you, it doesn't hurt you inside. You may push it away, be angry, party, and do other things, but when nobody is around, it bothers you. Take it from a man who embraced the silent ethos: suffering in silence will destroy everything you hold dear. I am not talking about going out and boasting in bars and parties about everything you've done. I still embrace that portion of the silent ethos. I'm talking about the silence from professional help and the loved ones who don't deserve your silent ethos—the ones who want to help, not hurt you.

Many of you will never seek out counseling. You will continue this trend of self-sabotage and destruction, perpetuating the stereotype to the men you lead, just like my former platoon sergeant perpetuated to the men who followed him. You will simply move on to the next relationship or job, never allowing yourself to find happiness or true love.

There is one question for you. When you're at a party, you see the leader or NCO at a party stumbling over himself intoxicated, starting fights, brawling in bars, and walking around angry with a chip on his shoulder. Then you see another one of your leaders who is calm, cool, collected, and always encouraging the young warriors to better themselves or get help. He talks openly about his marriage flaws as a husband or leader, and the actions he isn't proud of. Which one of their advice do you value more? Chances are, it's the second leader. If we are truly meant to never open ourselves up for improvement, why don't you idolize the first leader? If the silent ethos is so effective, why is our divorce rate so high? Why do two dozen veterans a day take their lives?

I see so many leaders of the first example, preaching about the rates of veteran suicide and divorce. They might even post Facebook statuses and wear T-shirts to "raise awareness." However, they're sitting there like the platoon sergeant I had, telling men under their leadership, "Don't be a pussy, you need to man the fuck up, have a drink, and forget about it. So what if you're on your fifth divorce? Fuck her; it isn't your fault. Go find another." Then, when a soldier looking up to them for guidance takes the advice and, less than six months later, shoots themselves, the leader pulls his platoon together, reiterating what a "strong man" is, disregarding that they are a root of the problem.

The only way to fix this problem isn't through becoming soft or touchy-feely all the time. In most cases, tough love and telling your soldier to pull it together is absolutely required, and I encourage those moments. However, as a good leader, you must be in tune with your soldiers. You must recognize behaviors such as DUI, anger outbursts, seclusion, defiance, and total disregard for rules and regulations, ending of relationships, loss of humor if they're the platoon comedian, and other legal violations. When you're in tune or giving platoon meetings at the end of a deployment, you must explain how the strong man seeks professional help, and that even the strongest of warriors do this. "A warrior is only as strong as his soul is quiet." You must explain that the ethos of silence is in regard to boasting about war in bars and becoming a fool of arrogance with incessant war stories. The ethos of silence is about not trying to convince everyone around you that you're a badass. The ethos of silence is *not* about refusing help, and you must ensure they understand the difference.

There's a saying, "If you can't save yourself, how are you supposed to save the ones you love?" If you love your relationship, and you know she makes your world go 'round and makes you feel at home every night as you lay down next to her, stop wasting time, my friends. Don't make the same mistakes I did. You can't save your relationship until you save yourself. Tomorrow never comes. Stop pushing it off. Pick up the phone today, or in the morning, call a counselor, and understand that it may take four or five to find one that fits your personality. It can feel embarrassing, weak, and uncomfortable the first time you walk into an appointment. However, after two sessions per week for a couple of months, and a counselor who meshes with your personality, the anger, tension, and stress gradually begin to dissipate. In the beginning, cutting the wounds back open is very emotional and even difficult to continue. But it's always painful to lance an infected wound. And when it heals and you begin saving yourself, your marriage and relationships will heal too.

If you are the significant other during the time period your loved one is getting help or struggling, there are several things that are crucial for you to understand. During that time, your relationship and the emotional volatility of your loved one will *almost always* get worse before it gets better. This is often caused by the bottling of emotions over the years. When it's bottled up, you don't need to have a coping mechanism to get through it, because it's stuffed away. When you open the pressurized bottle, it comes bursting out unexpectedly like a hot beer can, without a way to handle or process all of it, because we've never had to. Essentially, we have to re-learn healthy coping strategies. Similar to re-packing and organizing the disheveled closet of our past, we must sort through the piles of baggage and place them into organized boxes that we can orderly place back on a shelf—it isn't an immediate process. It takes time.

You *must* be prepared for days with post-session anger, tears, and breakdowns. This response is normal—even encouraged. It is part of the psychological processing that occurs when unpacking and bringing emotionally traumatic events to the surface. Understand that your loved one is working through issues that you can never fully understand or comprehend. It is imperative that you communicate and ask what they need, even if that's being left alone.

Although they may lash out at you with anger, know that this is part of their healing process, and often, it isn't something that you did. If they're like me and the way I treated Peyton, they will blame it on a little thing you did— like folding the towel wrong, not responding to a text or phone call fast enough, and criticizing things we normally wouldn't. This is normal in the beginning; it's a result of overwhelming emotions. Like I've said many times: in war, we forget how to process feelings with anything other than anger. If this becomes permanent after three to six months, however, it's a different scenario and must be addressed.

The best thing you can do as a significant other is

counter their anger with love. Even the small subtleties of you rubbing your fingernails on their neck, holding their hand, and cutting them slack will go much further than you think. Be supportive and encouraging, and don't throw the length of time the counseling and change is taking in his face. As the renowned philosopher Plato said, "Never discourage anyone who continually makes progress, no matter how slow."

It will be difficult in the beginning for both of you, but over time, and with patience, it will get better. It is paramount that you don't match their anger with hostility, disdain, or passive-aggressive comments; this will only make things worse. As I said before, those actions are things that most likely trigger him to be authoritative or confrontational. You love the man. Recognize that he is bettering himself for *you*.

If you find yourself thinking, *A person should never change who they are for their significant other or anybody else,* I want you to understand that there is a vast difference between changing yourself into a person somebody else wants you to be and changing the parts of you shaped by violence, death, and survival. Our recognition that we have become one of the major problems in the relationship should be one of the biggest compliments and acts of love.

To a civilian, it is impossible to understand how sacred the brotherhood of war, combat arms, and the ethos of silence is to us. Know that if he is willing to break the silence forged through fire, pain, and blood, and seek help—his actions say without saying that he holds you with more importance, love, and affection than words can describe. He isn't changing himself to who you want him to be. He's doing his best to bury his skeletons and improve himself into the man he feels you deserve him to be.

Ultimately, it is your decision to take my advice. You can save your relationship, or you can destroy it. You can get help and encourage your brothers to get help, or you can keep telling yourself that *you're fine and it's them not you*, drinking yourself to numbness daily when she leaves and the issues from your past close in around you. Just like I did.

"It only takes one...
One tree can start a forest.
One smile can begin a friendship.
One touch can show compassion.
One hope can give strength.
One laugh can conquer gloom.
One day can make a difference.
One thought can change your world."

—UNKNOWN

CHAPTER 21

ESCAPING PRISON

———

I'VE SPENT LOTS OF TIME OVER THE YEARS WISHING
I could go back in time and kick my younger self's ass. It
wasn't until the Himalayas that I truly understood, "Mistakes are just another word for experience. You figure out
what you can and learn from them." The cliché, "some
things just aren't meant to be" carries a lot of weight,
and there is goodness in failing to meet a goal, losing a
relationship, and letting go of the past. The things that
"should have been" either come back to us or lead us down
the road we were destined for all along. If it doesn't come
back, it simply wasn't ever ours to have. All the difficult
experiences make us better or worse versions of ourselves.
Fortunately, it's up to us to decide which fork to take, and
lucky for us, these roads allow U-turns.

One of the things I accepted while escaping the prison
I made for myself was to forgive myself and let go. The
ironic part is the things I had to forgive myself for had

nothing to do with the war. They had to do with what I did to those I loved when I came home. I had said and done some extremely hurtful things to the woman I loved, my parents, little sister, and just about anybody else who had come into contact with me over the last few years. The truth was, I wasn't happy with myself. I had no idea who I was anymore, and I felt broken because I couldn't be the person I used to be. As a result, I lashed out at anybody who came across my path.

Since returning from the Himalayas, as if it were a modified twelve-step program, I made the attempt to make amends with many of the relationships I destroyed in an attempt to repair the feelings I hurt. I found that many of them, including Peyton, did not want to hear an apology. They had moved on without ever wanting to repair the relationship. I have seen this with many of my veteran friends as well. In all honesty, it pained me to know that I acted badly enough for them to not even want an apology—that what I did hurt them so badly they disconnected, never looking back, and found it on their own.

This bothered me for a very long time, and it wasn't until I spoke to a mentor of mine who helped me understand that I was able to move past it. He told me a story from the biblical book of James and the context behind it. "You see, man. You can make yourself crazy putting yourself on trial. Whether it's self-reflection or pleading your case to the ones you wronged. The fact of the matter is, you may never get the chance to justify your actions, tell your side of the story, or explain what you did and why you acted the way you did. However, if you did get the chance to justify your actions or apologize, that doesn't mean it will feel justified to them. You reached out, apologized, and did your best to make amends. At this point, if they don't want to accept it or even discuss it, that is their choice. As long as you made a genuine attempt, you must let it go."

What he explained is that, sometimes, we won't ever be able to fix the damage we caused, and we often won't repair that failed friendship, marriage, or relationship with *the one who got away*. Sometimes, even if we did get a chance to sit down, apologize, and explain our case, they may not forgive us or be in a place to be able to forgive us. If we don't find a way to accept that we're human, make mistakes, and realize the only way to happiness is forgiveness and letting go, then we can't expect others to move on and forgive us if we can't do it for ourselves.

Not enough people feed their soul with positivity, kindness, and love, or even know how to follow their heart and disregard what others may think. That is insufferable.

Life is too short for judging everybody else's flaws instead of fixing our own. Instead of gossiping and spewing hate, vitriol, or negativity at the local coffee shop, try realizing everybody has their own issues and heartaches. Instead of drama and petty trash talk, why not engage in intellectually stimulating conversation that breeds growth and positivity? Why not breed enlightenment and inspiration instead of hate and negativity?

The clock is ticking, second by second, with the time we will never get back. We can *choose* to spend it with those we love. We can *choose* to give second chances to those who are actively seeking to improve their flaws. We can *choose* every single day to love the special person in our life, even when they're angry, out of money, hungry, or nitpicking. We can *choose*—during all the times when they feel or act as if they're unlovable and broken—to love them anyway. And in those times when we feel they don't deserve our love, kindness, or affection, we can *choose* to give it anyway.

We can *choose* to view and define them by their potential and the person they're working toward, while understanding that they, just like ourselves, will always be a work in progress. Ultimately, it is *our choice* whether we act as another critic tearing them down, or as their North Star in the darkness, knowing that having them in our lives—even on the worst, most infuriating days—makes our lives better overall.

We can love—and love so ferociously—like it's our final days without fearing death. We can reflect within and work on our own issues and shortcomings to become better for those we love and ourselves. Or we can sit at home, play it safe, never give second chances, and never do the things that are scary. We can fear the inevitable end where we meet the reaper, regretting and wishing we could go back in time to swallow our pride, call *the one who got away*, apologize, and make all the areas we went wrong, right. Or, we can wish that we could go back to take those trips, talk to the stranger at the bar or restaurant, and wish that we hadn't gone through life viewing it for the worst it has to offer.

It's hard to get past things that hurt in life. It can be hard to see, at times, that our negative thinking is wrong. Sadly, once we're in it, that's all we see—the bad things happening to us and around us. In Nepal and Tibet, they call that the bonds of Maya, where we get wrapped into the illusory aspect of the universe, entrapping ourselves in a thought prison, only seeing the bad things happening around us. That's the thing, though—it's only an illusion.

Because we're the ones who entrapped ourselves into the bonds and prison, we're the only ones with the key to get ourselves out. To get out, we must seek out people, places, ideas, and experiences that will lead us to make a permanent change—whether that's finding our religious or spiritual beliefs in church, going to the wilderness, or whatever it is that forces us to do a very hard and critical self-evaluation. Use the evaluation to decipher which ways of thinking, experiences, toxic friends or acquaintances, and behaviors got you into prison in the first place.

In my opinion, the thought prison and its bonds—contrary to popular belief—isn't a bad thing. I believe it's quite the opposite. It's what makes every person's life, journey, wisdom, experience, and beliefs in this world unique. Each of us have different demons that we wrestle with and different keys and paths that will break us out of the bondage.

After my trip, I've only allowed the good memories and experiences of anybody I've run across to stay in my mind. If we choose to define and love a person, family, friend, or romantic partner by their potential, and we actively seek out the good things or acts of kindness in the world, we are able to eventually change our outlook to positivity on everything else in our lives and escape that negative prison.

I believe the reason so many people, especially veterans and first responders, are stuck in these negative views is because we're inundated with it on a regular basis. Frequently discussed in cognitive neuroscience, our brain has a function called "pruning." In pruning, our brain eliminates connections and pathways not commonly used to make room for new ones, making the machine more efficient. In my opinion, that is how the entire scheme of being jaded works. The longer the exposure to negativity, violence, hate, etc., the more efficient our brain becomes at spotting and reacting preemptively to violence.

Over time, the positive pathways are pruned back, until eventually, you can't see it. However, our brains and minds are very malleable and adaptive. It has been discussed by the Dalai Lama, Howard Cutler, and many others, that compassion, peace, and joy are learned behaviors. At first, it is very difficult to exercise these positive traits and behaviors. However, similar to working out at the gym over time, we can increase our endurance and remain more positive for more extended periods of time.

We can't make room for good things to happen in our life when we're stuck viewing the negative things from the past, whether that's war, family, friends, exes, or life. Because when we do, we attract more negativity from others into our life. When you find the key, you'll be amazed at how many great things happen and how many opportunities come your way. As I learned on the mountain that day, "Pain is temporary, quitting lasts *forever*. Forget yesterday, it has already forgotten you. Don't sweat tomorrow, you haven't even met. A negative mind will never give you a positive life."

The Dalai Lama offers a suggestion in *The Art of Happiness*: "Think of the most miserable people you know. Often, they have the most resources, time, money, etc. Many of these people do not give or help others because they believe if they give, they'll have less. You see, that's part of the problem. Why is the Dead Sea called the Dead Sea?

"The Dead Sea is the Dead Sea because it has all these inlets from different bodies of water giving to it. However, the Dead Sea doesn't have an outlet, and the water stays stagnant. This results in the most uninhabitable body of water. The same thing happens with people who are selfish and don't give anything. There are really only four pathways to happiness, and they all revolve around the same concept: helping and giving to others," the Dalai Lama says.

"You see, there are four ways to help somebody. The first is financially helping another person who may be down on their luck. The second is physically helping somebody, whether that's moving or lending a hand. The third is spiritually helping somebody work through their spiritual quest. And the fourth is helping somebody mentally by discussing their problems and helping them work through it as a mentor."

In hindsight, the times I felt most miserable toward myself after the war, while dating Peyton, were when I was focused on my own emotions, my own needs, and making myself happy. Right or wrong, I was acting very selfish, and the "water" of my life was stagnant and uninhabitable.

"A student says to his Master:
'You talk about peace, but you teach me fighting.
How do you reconcile the two?'
The Master replies:
'It is better to be a warrior in a garden,
than a gardener in a war.'"

—UNKNOWN ORIGIN

CHAPTER 22

THE GARDEN

——

AFTER RETURNING, I HAD THE PLEASURE OF MEET-
ing with a man I look up to a great deal—the owner of
Onnit and podcaster Aubrey Marcus. Before I went down
to Austin, I was excited and couldn't wait to pick his brain
on so many topics. What made me look up to the man and
his advice wasn't how well-known he is, but that it was
confirmed when we met that he is a genuinely kind and
loving man. He was incredibly humble, acknowledging
that, at the end of the day, we are all attempting to figure
out where happiness is for us. Nobody in this world is
immune from interpersonal conflict or struggle. No matter
how hard we try, everybody makes mistakes.

Before leaving Onnit, I asked Mr. Marcus how to deal
with the two-hat question of not telling your significant
other about things we've done in war or life that make
us the way we are. His advice hit home and replaced the
advice I received before dating Peyton.

"How much do you listen to the guy who told you that?" Mr. Marcus asked.

"Been years, but I can see both sides of the argument. After seeing what happened with Peyton, I think it's good to tell them. But at the same time, if you do tell them, they may treat you differently, and you can't even disagree."

"You know, man, if you're going to marry somebody and they're your person, they should be able to handle all the parts of you, the good and the bad, and they should love you for who you are. If they want to judge you based on what you did over there and not for the person they see in you now or why you became the way you did, then you probably shouldn't marry them."

A few weeks later, I spoke with Mr. Marcus again. "I have another question for you. Since returning, I have remorse and regret in a different way. I look back and see all these situations with my family, friends, and Peyton that I wish I had handled differently. I wasn't acting like myself then. I was a lost, broken man, grasping onto anything I could. Now that I'm back to my normal self, I wish I could go back and fix the damage or change things. How do you deal with that?"

"So, when you go back in time and think, *should have, would have, could have,* is it really helpful? Is that really productive? It never really is. It's just another way we punish ourselves under this false premise that we had more information and more availability then, with the information that we now have in our current time. You know, we did our best then, and maybe that is not our best now. Hopefully it's not, because hopefully we're better. We have hindsight and the ability to look back. We're the person that grew from those mistakes.

"We can't go back with the information we have now and say, 'I should have applied that to the criteria I had then.' It's just another way for our own internal critic to punish us based on a standard that's impossible to live up to. Know that whatever happened made you the man you are now, and be grateful for that.

"When you look back and say 'I regret something,' you have to be cautious about that, because like the saying goes, 'If we were the chef of our life, everything would be chocolate and caramel flavor,' you know? But we would get sick because there would be nothing salty and bitter that really sustains our health and makes us healthy and hearty. So be grateful for the salty and bitter things; that's what makes you a man; that's what makes you who you are. You don't regret that stuff—you learn from it and enjoy the process. Enjoy the mistakes; enjoy the victories. It's all the same. There's no pursuit of happiness. There's only pursuit *in* happiness."

In a way, Mr. Marcus was telling me something I already knew. As with the lesson from the silent treatment, I simply couldn't verbalize or make sense of it until it was said to me. Leaving, I still couldn't fully comprehend or process it. It seemed like good advice on a practical level. However, implementation seemed impossible and unreasonable.

It wasn't until a few days later when I got a phone call from my parents that I fully understood what Mr. Marcus told me.

"Steele, you need to come home. Kevin is dying. He's in the hospital, and he's been asking for you for the last four days. The hospital is going to send him home tomorrow for Hospice care."

Packing up and driving twelve hours, I finally made it to the hospital the following evening. Walking in, I saw a man I hardly recognized. I knew him my whole life, yet his eyes and cheekbones had sunken in, and he had the same gurgling sounds in his lungs that I had in the Himalayas. I knew it wouldn't be long before the congestive heart failure took him. Looking at him after seventy years of life had taken its toll, I couldn't help but wonder, *Out of everybody in the world, why is he asking for me?*

Sitting on a chair at the end of his bed, waiting for him to gain consciousness from high levels of morphine, I contemplate all the reasons he might have asked for me.

Coming to, I hear his voice between gurgles for air, "Steele, is that you?"

"Yeah, Kev, it's me. You sound like shit! Why don't I kick that oxygen machine off so we get you out of here a little faster?" I say with gallows humor, a long-standing tradition for us.

"I need to ask you something," he says with gasps for air between every word.

"Go for it. I'll try to answer whatever questions you have. You may not like my answers, but I'll do my best."

"How do you live knowing it's your judgment calls and actions that killed another human being? And you're the one to blame for it."

Taking a big sigh, I look at his wife, "Hey, will you go grab me a beer for this conversation?"

She leaves and returns with a six-pack of beer, and I dive into the question. We sit in silence for a few minutes as I attempt to figure out how exactly to answer his question. I was trying to piece together what exactly he meant and why he would ask such a question. It turns out, he had been in a car accident, his friend that was driving killed everybody in the car, including his little brother. Kevin was the only survivor and had been in a wheelchair since he was eighteen.

After a few minutes of silence: "Kev, I'm not sure exactly what you're talking about. To my knowledge, you've never killed anybody. My experience was indirect from aircraft coordinates and strikes with a few other guys. And all the times I fired my weapon, BDA wasn't able to be conducted because the area was too hot with gunfire. I'm fairly positive I shot them, but I'll never know for certain."

Sitting in silence for a few minutes, he says, "That day, my brother asked if he could go to the drive-in with us. My parents said they didn't care and it was up to me. I said I didn't mind and allowed him to come..."

He was unable to finish his sentence before breaking

down and sobbing. There's always something particularly heart-wrenching about watching a grown man cry excruciating tears filled with years of suppressed pain. It's tough to watch, and because I'm a bit rough around the edges when it comes to feelings, I often don't know how to console them besides silence.

Piercing through his sobs, "I killed my sixteen-year-old brother. And by the time I woke up from my coma, he had been buried for six months."

I take a long pull from my beer, wondering, *Why am I the person he feels the need to ask—to confess all these skeletons to? I'm twenty-four. I can't even answer these survivor's guilt questions for myself. I don't know how to answer them for you.*

Softly, his tears slow down as the morphine once again carries him out of consciousness. Silently, I'm left with my thoughts as to how to answer his question when I can't fully answer it for myself.

Thinking about what Mr. Marcus said to me just days ago, thinking about Afghanistan, and the years prior, I begin to slowly understand. Finishing my beer, popping the top on another, I continue to reflect over the guilt I felt in my own life. I glance over at him asleep from the drugs. *Poor Kev, I would have never known that he's suffered with this pain and held onto it for almost fifty years now.* Thinking back over every psychology textbook, video, and theory I could possibly remember, it dawned on me as he woke up again.

"Steele, are you still here?" he says quietly.

"Yeah, Kev, I'm not going anywhere."

Continuing, "Kev, I don't mean to disappoint you. I haven't fully answered this question for myself. I can empathize with where you're coming from. I know you see me in this positive light that can't do anything wrong, but I promise I do. Since I got back from overseas, I've said and done some really, really, hurtful things to my family and Peyton. You may not know the reason, but I went to the Himalayas because I was at the end of my rope. I figured I would find what I was looking for or I would die, and I was fully content with either option. Before I went, I learned of this theory. I can't remember what psychologist theorized it. I just remember the message. He hypothesized that we have two deaths in this lifetime. One is the day we leave the flesh, and the other is called the 'ego death.'"

Pausing to collect my thoughts, I take another sip of beer. "The ego death, Kev, is something that I believe spiritually and religiously is one of the critical lessons we must learn before we die. The ego death is often known as 'the Hero's Journey,' and it's explained that the ego death is what creates the final step in us having a life of happiness or accepting death without regret. There are several ideas of what the ego death is, but the one that stuck with me most is the idea that we are a slave to ourselves, society, and the global expectations for a good portion of our lives. We allow society and our friends to decide what is right or wrong for us—what we should feel guilty for and what we shouldn't. However, after a journey, trek, or a long period of misfortunes, we come to several epiphanies. Once we have an ego death, we have the ability to cut the strings of our societal subcultures, ideas, and reward system. Instead of working eighty hours a week to buy that next best thing, we decide to spend that time with the ones we love, and we dedicate our time for the greater good.

Once our ego death commences, it's hypothesized that we are able to transcend our personal ideologies to the existential natural self and live the true purpose of life. In my opinion, the true purpose of life is to bring happiness and love to yourself and everyone else around you. Because when we die, Kev, nobody remembers us for what car we drove or how much money we had. They remember us for the things we stood for. The good AND the bad."

Sitting in silence, tears stream down Kevin's face as he takes in every word I've said. Looking at the ground, I concentrate on everything I could remember about the ego death, unpacking every box of memories I had stowed away to never re-open.

I look back up at him and take another swig of beer, "You know, Kev, for a while, I thought the idea of an ego death was some hippy bullshit. I thought it was bullshit until I explained it to you. However, now I see how many years I've spent trying to please others and live up to their and society's expectations of what 'good' is. The truth is that what is good or right isn't always easy or pleasurable. Most of the time it's hard and painful.

I used to feel like God was punishing me by putting me in the situations he did. I felt it was karma or my punishment, but now I see what Mr. Marcus meant. They made me the unique man I am today. I know you grew up a devout Catholic. You stopped going to church and became an atheist after the accident. I think it's because you were angry at God for being put in the wheelchair and for losing your brother. It was easier to blame Him than understand the large scope of things. I'm guilty of this; that's why I didn't go to church for ten years. I was furious—even hated the man upstairs."

Interrupting me with his anger: "There is no fucking God, Steele. I find it hard to believe there is one because of all the horrific things that happen to people every day—or for putting me in this in the first place! It *is* my fault! I'm the one who killed my little brother!"

Allowing him a few minutes to compose himself, I continue, "I get it—I completely understand, and I certainly don't judge you for your anger. I felt that way for a long time. Ultimately, it made me a toxic person in the lives of all the people I cared about. It was easier for me to cope with those things knowing there was a master plan or path that I was destined to take. It made all the painful experiences make sense. If you think about it, you and your little brother—had that not happened, he would have been legal age and most likely drafted to Vietnam. It's highly probable that you or your brother could have died a much more painful death than what he did. I think everything happens for a reason, and in time, this will all make sense."

His tears continue for a few more minutes, when I quietly break the silence. "It isn't your fault your brother died, Kev. You can't hold yourself responsible. Maybe the lesson was that he had to die so you could learn how to forgive others and forgive yourself. Maybe that was what people like you and I were meant to learn all along."

I roll my chair over, putting my hand on his as he sobs. After a few minutes, he is able to get out a few final words. "I just don't understand why it's taking so long for me to die. I don't understand why I have to continue suffering."

I think back to a few months prior when I was lying in the rocks asking myself the same question. "Kev, you aren't going to die until you forgive yourself. It's not your fault. You have to stop blaming yourself. You need to decide if you are an atheist because you don't believe in God, or if you're an atheist because you're angry at God. There's a whole lot of difference, and I don't think you'll pass until you decide those things for yourself."

Setting my empty bottle down: "I'll stop by tomorrow evening, Kev. If you beat me to heaven, put a good word in for me and have some whiskey waiting. I'm not sure if Big J. will let sinners like me and my buddies in."

I lean over, giving him a long hug, and then I walk toward the door, looking back one last time. His eyes are closed, shaking, as large tears of pain stream down his face. With one last comment, I say, "Kev, it's not your fault. I hope you can find a way to forgive yourself and make peace with the things that are bothering you. I'll see you on the other side," knocking on the doorjamb as I walk out.

I knew in my gut that this would be the last time I would see Kevin. I knew the reason he asked for me was that he knew I wasn't going to sugarcoat anything. He knew I would tell him the way it was. The following morning, I woke up, went to the gym, and worked the rest of the day. Around 4:00 p.m., my phone rang with a call from my mom.

"Hey, Mom. What's up?"

Through a sad voice, "Honey, the social worker at Kevin's got ahold of me. Kevin's blood pressure is now sixty over forty. He's unconscious but responsive. The social worker said that before he went unconscious, he asked for you again."

Knowing what's coming, I say quietly, "Yeah, I had a feeling when I left last night."

"The social worker said he doesn't have much time. So if you want to say goodbye, you should head over there," my mom's voice cracked.

I jumped in my truck, driving as fast as I could. When I got there, I knocked on the door, and his wife answered the door with tears streaming down her face. "He just passed away two or three minutes ago. He's gone."

I sit down in the kitchen for a few minutes before deciding to say goodbye. "Is it okay if I say goodbye before I leave?"

Pointing back to their bedroom, I walk through the door to his bedside. There he lay, with blood next to his pillow, lifeless, like an inanimate object. It's a sight with which I am all too familiar.

Rolling my chair next to him, reaching over gently, I close his eyelids and move his lifeless hand onto his chest.

Putting my hand on his, "You know, Kev. I think you gave me the biggest gift. Suddenly, it all makes sense. All the heartache, feeling at the end of my rope, and as if life wasn't worth living—if I had never gone through it all, I wouldn't have been able to help you last night. I'm glad you finally forgave yourself. I love you, buddy."

I give his lifeless leg two taps with my hand, walking out of the room. As I get to the threshold of the door, I turn back around. "See you on the other side, my friend. Whatever side that may be."

Walking out to my truck, I climb back in, thinking over our final conversation and everything that happened. Pushing it away, I head to the local watering hole—the bar I routinely found myself at over the years after those close to me passed.

Asking the bartender for a shot of whiskey and a beer, I take my memorial bracelet off, setting it over the shot of whiskey—half-in, half-out. I think about everybody I have lost over the years and how many of them I wish were still here. How many I wish I could pick up the phone and call, or that they were there for the best moments of my life.

Finishing my beer, I pull my bracelet off the shot, wipe

the liquor off it, and place it back on my wrist. Grabbing the shot, I slam it down and head home. Lying in bed that night, I think about my final conversation with Kevin, as Mr. Marcus' message and the Garden of Eden crossed my mind with an epiphany.

Maybe the Garden of Eden in the book of Genesis is more of a metaphor or parable. Without understanding good and evil, right and wrong, evil and hate, is it really possible to experience happiness and love? If we never know about evil or pain, is it ever possible to recognize the good times, or to love people and experiences in our lives? Maybe therein lies the answer. The tragic or painful experiences of our life aren't bad or horrible in retrospect; they are building blocks to lead us to the better version of ourselves and possibly to the ego death. They allow us to achieve true love and happiness, or at least peace before we die.

Maybe the reason I clashed so frequently with Peyton, my family, and society is that I, like so many other veterans, am standing on the outside of the Garden after eating from the Tree of Knowledge. Watching as a good portion of the world stands on the inside without eating from the proverbial tree, and they're unable to see what it is that we're so fearful or worried about.

All the things I had experienced that seemed painful or traumatic were things I was grateful for. Had they not happened, I would have never been able to have the conversation I did with Kevin. I would have never gone to the Himalayas, and I would have most likely been six feet under. I wouldn't be able to recognize how special the relationships I had with Peyton, my family, and other people were had the worst not happened. I wouldn't have ever been able to see the light if I never experienced darkness. In that moment, I understood exactly what Mr. Marcus had told me. I realized all the things we often feel guilt, remorse, and regret over are things we should be thankful for. Without them, we would never learn and grow as people. We wouldn't be able to build relationships and friendships because we wouldn't ever learn that our words and actions have consequences. Eventually, we learn and progress over the years to hopefully become the best version of ourselves for ourselves and the ones we love most.

With one last thought before I fall asleep, *Pure and lasting love isn't easy. It doesn't come without pain, darkness, or fights. Real, lasting love is working through pain, conflicts, and at times, the urges to give up on each other. It's about fighting through all of that to see the light on the other side of the tunnel, knowing you guys can make it through even the worst of storms.*

Falling asleep, I finally put the hallucinations from the Himalayas and every other un-settled event to sleep with me, finding peace in all of the turmoil.

"So live your life that the fear of death can never enter your heart. Trouble no one about their religion; respect others in their view, and demand that they respect yours. Love your life, perfect your life, beautify all things in your life. Seek to make your life long and its purpose in the service of your people. Prepare a noble death song for the day when you go over the great divide. Always give a word or a sign of salute when meeting or passing a friend, even a stranger, when in a lonely place. Show respect to all people and grovel to none. When you arise in the morning, give thanks for the food and for the joy of living. If you see no reason for giving thanks, the fault lies only in yourself. Abuse no one and no thing, for abuse turns the wise ones to fools and robs the spirit of its vision. When it comes your time to die, be not like those whose hearts are filled with the fear of death, so that when their time comes, they weep and pray for a little more time to live their lives over again in a different way. Sing your death song and die like a hero going home."

—CHIEF TECUMSEH

CHAPTER 23

SINNERS LIKE ME

———

AFTER MY LONG FLIGHT BACK TO THE UNITED
States, I feel like a new person in spite of the jet-lag.
Walking into my old room at my parents' house, turning
on the bedroom light, I set my pack and climbing gear
at the foot of the bed, flopping down backwards onto
the bed. Sighing with relief, I'm still winded from the
gurgling of fluid in my lungs. Running and jumping onto
my bed, licking my face, my lab, Lucy, greets me after
nearly forty days apart.

Following behind, my mom walks into the room. Leaning up, sitting at the foot of my bed, "Aw, Lucy missed you
while you were gone. I'm heading to bed, and you should
get some sleep too. I just wanted to give you another hug
and tell you how thankful I am you're back and can recover
here for the next few months."

Standing up, out of breath from that little amount of
movement, I give her a hug.

"Honey, I just have one more question for you," my mom says in a skeptical, don't-you-dare tone.

"Yes, Mom?"

"Please, for the love of God, tell me you aren't going back to climb Everest!"

"I don't know, Mom." Looking down at the climbing gear at the foot of the bed, I finish my sentence: "Maybe."

As I open my truck door the following morning, sliding in across the warm leather into the driver seat, I can't help but take notice—even admire—how blue the skies are for the first time in years. With the sun rays beaming against my face, I slide the key into the ignition, hearing the pins of the lock clink into the grooves of the key. Turning the ignition over, hearing the sound of my diesel engine surge to life, I close the door. I reach over in one motion, pulling the seatbelt across my lap and click it into place. Pulling my sunglasses out from the visor above, I slide them on. Slowly backing out of the driveway, I guide my sails toward the nearest coffee shop.

Driving through town, I notice the joggers and the couples who are holding hands while pushing a stroller. I can't help but recognize my optimism for once again finding that for myself.

Feeling euphoric and high on life, I take notice of how lucky I am to live in America. I can't help but drive with an enormous grin on my face, realizing how fortunate I am to be alive. With the windows down, cruising down the road, warm air washes over me. I reach over, turning the dial up on the radio. *"I was fifteen when my daddy's old man caught me halfway through my first beer. He laughed so hard when my face turned green. He said, 'You come from a long line of sinners like me.'"* I continue to smile and sing along.

Turning the car off mid-song, I head toward the entrance of the grocery store, carefree, taking a leisure stroll with nowhere to be. After pulling a bouquet of flowers out of the water pot and placing them into a plastic bag, I make my way toward the coffee stand. I feel so content and at peace in my soul that I can't help but enthusiastically ask the barista how her morning is going. When she asks, I respond, "I live in America, it's another day in paradise—I surely can't complain!"

I get back in my truck, gently setting my coffee in the center console. Delicately, I reach over placing the flowers on the passenger seat and shut the door behind me. Turning over the ignition, I make my way toward an old friend. The speakers roar back to life, and Eric Church sings across the radio right where he left off. As if Mr. Church is sitting next to me, I sing along, *"Now me and my brother go to see him sometimes. But he don't have much to say anymore. So we sit on his headstone with a fifth of Jack D. Here's to a long line of sinners like me."*

Waiting to turn the engine off, I think about my time in Afghanistan. I think about the glacier. I think about my friends who battled their demons and succumbed to suicide. I think about how I never felt alone in what appeared to be my final moments. I know those I lost were there with me in spirit. They were there so I wouldn't cross alone. They were there to let me know there was more, and it wasn't my time. I turn the ignition off, softly grabbing the flowers off the seat as to not bump and shear a flower. I get out of my truck and walk toward the flag. Elegantly, Old Glory glides through the summer breeze, allowing the subtle winds to stoically ripple across her stars and stripes.

Looking down at the memorial stone, "Killed In Action, Afghanistan," chills shoot up my spine. *He was killed just before I enlisted. I'm now older than he was when he made the ultimate sacrifice.* Standing there in the light summer breeze, the words, "Greater love hath no man than this, that he lay down his life for his friends," reverberate in my mind. I kneel down, carefully removing the plastic from the flowers, placing them in the flower stand.

Looking down at the stone: "Hey, bro. It's been a while. Thanks for never leaving me alone. I know you and my other loved ones up there helped me make it through those bullets and explosions while I was in Afghanistan, and all of the crazy stuff since then. I owe you a beer and a glass of whiskey when I get up there. We have a lot to catch up on. You wouldn't believe I'm saying this, but I want to have a family one day, man. I finally let go and forgave myself, and I'm happy again. I'm hoping when my time comes that Big J has a sense of humor and will welcome in sinners like me and the guys. Keep an eye on the gates, man. We might need you to open the back door." Taking a few minutes to admire the flag above his memorial, saying a silent prayer, I walk back to my truck.

Looking in my rearview mirror admiring the flag as it slowly slips out of view, I turn the radio up, re-adjusting the sunglasses on my face. Reaching down to the center console and picking up my coffee, I feel the perfect summer breeze and fresh air blowing through the windows and onto my face. I slowly take a sip of the fresh iced coffee, and I begin to smile uncontrollably, taking joy in the little moments of the morning.

Go back for Everest? Maybe I will.

With perfect timing, the song continues through the stereo, *"On the day I die, I know where I'm gonna go—me and Jesus got that part worked out. I'll wait at the gates 'til his face I see. And stand in a long line of sinners like me."*

*"Every new beginning comes from
some other beginning's end."*

—LUCIUS ANNAEUS SENECA

About the Author

___

STEELE KELLY served in the US Army as a Forward Observer, earning the Combat Action Badge with more than 334 hours of dismounted combat patrols during Operation Enduring Freedom. In Afghanistan, Steele regularly took part in combat operations that ranged from an air assault mission in southwest Afghanistan to base security in Kabul. After an honorable discharge, he moved to a small mountain town with his truck and his dog, continuing his education in psychology and premedicine at Montana State University. He plans to attend medical school and further serve the veteran community.